C0-BFW-600

THE CONTEMPORARY WORLD

FROM 1945 TO THE 21st CENTURY

WITNESS TO HISTORY: A VISUAL CHRONICLE OF THE WORLD

THE CONTEMPORARY WORLD

FROM 1945 TO THE 21ST CENTURY

MARKUS HATTSTEIN AND KLAUS BERNDL

ROSEN PUBLISHING
New York

This edition first published in 2013 by:

The Rosen Publishing Group, Inc.
29 East 21st Street
New York, NY 10010

Library of Congress Cataloging-in-Publication Data

Berndl, Klaus.
The contemporary world: from 1945 to the 21st century/Klaus Berndl and Markus Hattstein.
p. cm.—(Witness to history—a visual chronicle of the world)
Includes bibliographical references and index.
ISBN 978-1-4488-7225-1 (library binding)
1. World history—Juvenile literature. 2. History, Modern—1945-1989—Juvenile literature.
3. History, Modern—1989—Juvenile literature. I. Hattstein, Markus. II. Title.
D840.B436 2012
909.82'5—dc23

2012011333

Manufactured in the United States of America

CPSIA Compliance Information: Batch #S12YA: For further information, contact Rosen Publishing, New York, New York, at 1-800-237-9932.

Publisher: Peter Delius

Contents

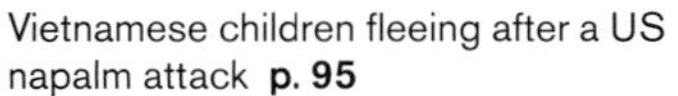

Vietnamese children fleeing after a US napalm attack **p. 95**

Denunciation during the Chinese "Culture Revolution" **p. 97**

The people of Berlin celebrate the opening of the Wall **p. 22**

Minutes of terror: A second plane flies into the World Trade Center **p. 121**

The Contemporary World

1945 to the present

After World War II, a new world order came into being in which two superpowers, the United States and the Soviet Union, played the leading roles. Their ideological differences led to the arms race of the Cold War and fears of a global nuclear conflict. The rest of the world was also drawn into the bipolar bloc system, and very few nations were able to remain truly non-aligned. The East-West conflict came to an end in 1990 with the collapse of the Soviet Union and the consequent downfall of the Eastern Bloc. Since that time, the world has been driven by the globalization of worldwide economic and political systems. The world has, however, remained divided: The rich nations of Europe, North America, and East Asia stand in contrast to the developing nations of the Third World.

The first moon landing made science-fiction dreams reality in the year 1969. Space technology has made considerable progress as the search for new possibilities of using space continues.

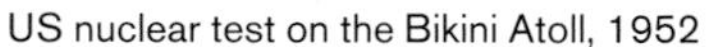

1 US nuclear test on the Bikini Atoll, 1952

2 Disarmament negotiations in Moscow, 1991

3 The Love Parade music festival, Berlin,1997

Contemporary History Since 1945

The outcome of World War II in 1945 was devastating: Approximately 55 million deaths worldwide, some 20 million refugees, and wide swaths of Europe and Asia destroyed. The mass murder of the European Jews by the Nazi regime and its collaborators meant an upheaval in modern civilization to an extent previously unknown. Many efforts of international politics in the immediate postwar period were aimed at preventing future catastrophes of this kind.

Between the East-West Conflict and Globalization

The world political situation between 1945 and 1989 was definitively shaped by the East-West conflict. The new leading powers—the United States and the Soviet Union—each attempted to leave their stamp on the postwar order. Due to their opposing views of government and economics, a fault line quickly became visible, and soon the world powers stood opposite one another in a "Cold War." An increasing number of nations became involved in the face-off and aligned themselves with one of the two power blocs. The competition expressed itself in an accelerating arms race that meant a growing danger of global ❶ nuclear annihilation. To avoid being subsumed by the bloc system, many former colonies, the majority of which gained independence after World War II, became part of the Nonaligned Movement.

4 West German border guards at the Berlin Wall, 1978

The end of the Cold War came with the opening of the western Hungarian border and the fall of the ❹ Berlin Wall in 1989 and was ❷ cemented in 1991 with the dissolution of the Soviet Union. Though the world did find peace, the number of wars and conflicts between individual states—often ethnically or religiously motivated—has increased and nuclear, biological, and chemical weapons have come into even more hands.

In the meantime, world politics is now strongly defined by the process of globalization. Europe, East Asia, and North America are the centers of this development, but through the integration of the whole world into an overarching economic and communication network, political and economic decisions often have cross-border effects. Since 1945, as in no other time period before, humankind has made progress in almost all areas of knowledge. However, the fruits of this progress are unequally distributed. It is mainly the Western industrialized nations that have benefited from the wealth globalization has brought. The world political conflict lines no longer run between East and West but between North and South, between rich and poor. Another new source of conflict is international terrorism. Combating it and its causes effectively is a major challenge of the 21st century.

Lifestyle and Values

In the affluent countries of the world, lifestyle and general values concepts have changed enormously in the last 50 years. As the length of education has increased, ❸ youth, which was previously only a short preliminary stage before adulthood, has lengthened to become a stage of life in itself. Tied to wealth and beauty, youth has become an ideal that shapes economics, advertising, and everyday life. Since the 1960s, a new leisure culture has emerged; vacations and travel have become important elements of modern life and a booming industrial sector. Since the 1970s, automation in almost all fields has meant that much of the heavy physical labor of working life has been taken away. This has opened up new jobs, particularly for women. These new jobs are often found in the service sector, which has a high standing everywhere.

5 Yin and yang: Taoist symbol showing the balance between opposites

A development that has taken place very recently in the Western world is a turn away

1945 | Potsdam Conference
1948 | Soviet blockade of West Berlin
1962 | Cuban Missle Crisis
1968 | Student movement in industrial nations
1969 | First human on the moon
1973 | First oil crisis
1985 | Gorbachev comes to power

Demonstration against "un-Islamic" clothing, Iran, 2004

Buddhist monks surf the Internet, 2005

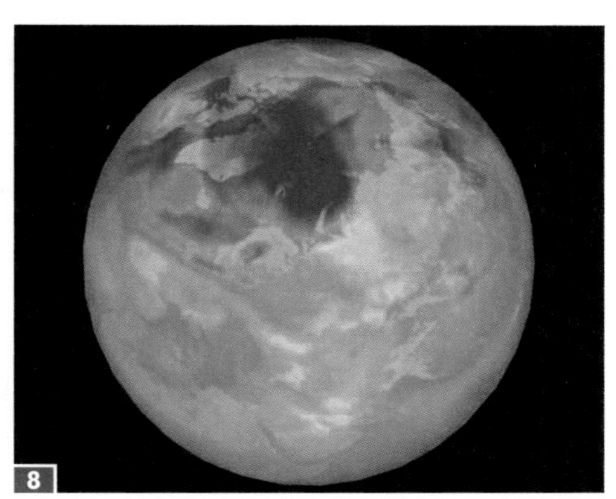

Ozone hole (dark blue) over the Antarctic, 2000

from traditional Christianity combined with an intensified search for the meaning of life. The orientation toward esoteric or ❺ East Asian lifestyles has increased, yet the search for happiness has been subordinated to constantly changing fashions. On the other hand, at the turn of the millennium, religious fundamentalism, particularly in Islam and Christianity, has strengthened in ❻ opposition, sometimes violently expressed, to the new Western lifestyle characterized by unchecked worldliness and secularism that has spread throughout the world as a standard.

The Mass Market of Culture and Knowledge

Cultural trends today circulate ever faster and wider and are increasingly subordinated to the laws of the marketplace. While, for example, music in the 1940s was limited to recreational and free-time entertainment, since the 1970s it has accompanied people wherever they go. Thus popular music has gained significance in comparison to classical music. Pop music exceeds itself in the rapid development and displacement of separate fashions and styles to satisfy the demand for easily consumed entertainment.

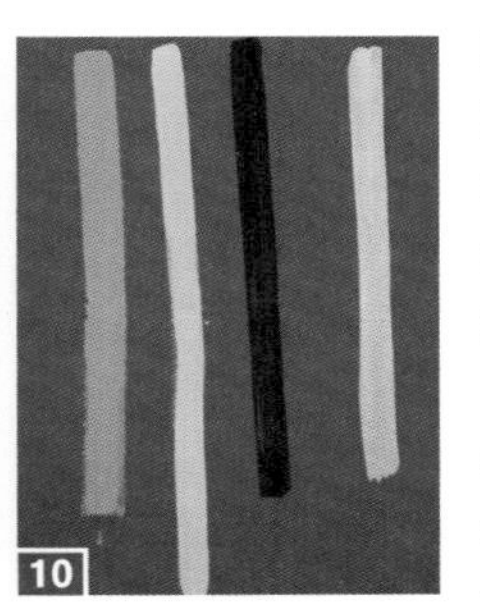

Streifenbild IV by Sigmar Polke, 1968

"High culture" has become more diverse and complex. New styles and trends, such as ❿ abstract painting, have established themselves worldwide. By the 1970s at the latest, talk of phases and movements was almost impossible, and one can now talk at most of schools. Distinctions between different art forms are no longer as clear-cut as they once were.

The developmental acceleration since 1945 also characterizes science. Never before have there been so many scientists, never before has research advanced so rapidly, and never before was there such a strong differentiation between research areas. English has asserted itself as the universal language of science. Newspapers present research findings quicker than books can, but the fastest and simplest form of knowledge communication today is the ❼ Internet, to which an increasing number of people have access.

Successes and Dangers of Progress

The scientific and technological successes of the last 60 years have been astounding. Cars, airplanes, radio, television, mainframe and personal computers, and the Internet have made the world smaller. In 1969 the first humans stood on the ❾ moon, and after 1987, the space station Mir made prolonged life in space possible. Medicine has made such progress that fear of epidemics such as cholera and polio no longer defines life, although new epidemics such as AIDS continue to emerge. At the turn of the millennium, telecommunication became mobile. Almost all the knowledge of humankind is available and can be accessed anytime, anywhere.

First moon landing by the United States, July 20, 1969

Even at the pinnacle of the belief in progress, however, the downside to the "always more, always further" motto became obvious. With the 1970s oil crisis, an end to the oil supply became conceivable, and the consequences this could have worldwide became foreseeable. Global damage to the environment and the advanced destruction of the ❽ Earth's atmosphere have emerged as the downside of industrial progress. Even the supposedly clean nuclear energy has, after the nuclear reactor catastrophe of ⓫ Chernobyl, left damage that will continue to have an effect for centuries. In a globalized world, the protection of the environment can, like the struggle against poverty and the containment of violence, perhaps only be achieved through agreements on a global scale, between states. These are the challenges with which the world is faced in the 21st century.

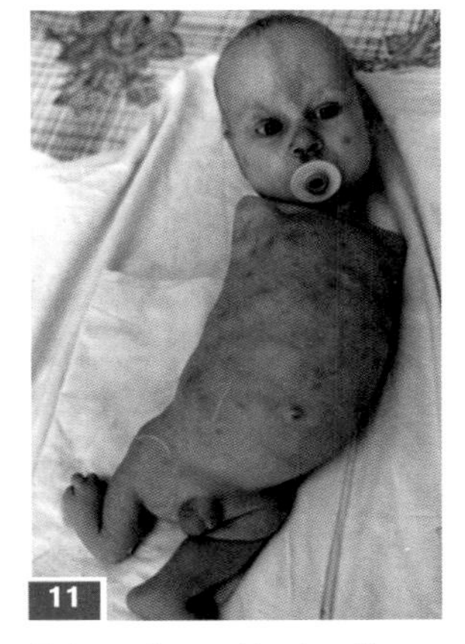

Baby malformed by the effects of the Chernobyl disaster, 1986

1987 | AIDS becomes a public concern
1991 | Dissolution of the Soviet Union

1986 | Nuclear accident in Chernobyl
Nov 9 1989 | Fall of the Berlin Wall
Sep 11 2001 | Terror attack in New York, Virginia, and Pennsylvania

Trends in World Politics since 1945

After the dissolution of the anti-Hitler coalition in 1945, the Cold War between the superpower nations—the United States and the Soviet Union—defined international relations until 1989. Conflicts between the ideological and military systems of the superpowers split the world into hostile blocs of countries and hindered the functioning of the United Nations as an instrument of global peace. The collapse of the Soviet empire in 1989 ended the ❶ Cold War, but fundamentalist terror and the uncontrolled proliferation of weapons of mass destruction created new problems and fields of conflict.

View of a painted wall on the Eastern side of the former Berlin Wall, 1990

The Cold War

After 1945, the European continent and virtually the entire world divided into the spheres of influence of the new superpowers, the United States and the Soviet Union.

Millions of refugees, deportees, ❷ prisoners of war, and concentration camp prisoners, referred to collectively as "displaced persons," presented postwar society with an integration problem.

Churchill, Roosevelt, and Stalin had already defined their claims in Europe in 1944. Following the war's end, the victors installed

Vietnam War: A civilian shows the body of his child to soldiers from the South

their political systems in the territories they controlled.

The division of Germany into four occupation zones prepared the way for the national partition into the Federal Republic of Germany (FRG) and the ❸ German Democratic Republic (GDR) in 1949. Parliamentarian democracy in the West opposed the dictatorial "peoples' democracies" in the East. In 1946 Churchill coined the term "Iron Curtain" to describe the unyielding separation between the Eastern and the Western Blocs. Europe was also economically divided. Reconstruction in the West was supported by the ❺ Marshall Plan; its counterpart in the eastern Bloc was the Soviet sponsored Council for Mutual Economic Assistance (Comecon).

The division into two hostile blocs affected the whole world. With the victory of the Communist party in China, the most populous country in the world became a member of the socialist camp. The first "proxy war" between the East and the West broke out in ❻ Korea in 1950, followed by later wars in ❹ Vietnam and Afghanistan. The Cuban Missile Crisis in 1962 almost resulted in nuclear war. During the period of détente in the 1970s, several control agreements were meant to curb armament on both sides. The Conference on Security and Cooperation in Europe (CSCE) attempted to introduce a process of détente beginning in 1974 by addressing economic and human rights issues.

The Cuban Missile Crisis

The stationing of Soviet nuclear missiles in Cuba led to the Cuban Missile Crisis, a confrontation between the United States and the Soviet Union in October 1962. President Kennedy demanded the removal of the weapons. When First Secretary Khrushchev refused, the US imposed a naval blockade,in the direction of which Soviet ships carrying missile components continued, having already set sail from Russia. At the last minute Khrushchev ordered the fleet to turn around and the missiles to be dismantled.

Khrushchev and the Cuban President Fidel Castro in New York, September 24, 1960

Posters with photos of missing German soldiers in the camp for those returning home, Friedland, 1955

Marx, Engels, Lenin: poster for a march in East Berlin, 1988

Train cars are delivered to the German State Railway as part of the Marshall Plan, November 1948

During the Korean War, US Marines keep a watch on North Korean prisoners, 1950

1944 | Declaration of the "United Nations" in Washington

4-11 Feb 1945 | Yalta Conference

1945 | Founding of the International Bank for Reconstruction and Development

24 Oct 1945 | Founding of the UN

The United Nations

The world community created the United Nations after World War II as an instrument to secure global peace. To this day, however, it remains dependent on the interests of the superpowers.

The United Nations organization emerged directly out of the military alliance against Germany. Initially, only countries that had declared war on the Third Reich by March 1, 1945, were eligible for membership, which allowed the admission of a large number of South American and Middle Eastern nations which had declared war on the Axis powers at the last moment. East and West Germany were not allowed to join until 1973. The aims of the ❼ United Nations since its founding on October 24, 1945, have been to secure world peace and to promote international cooperation. The UN's major organs are the General Assembly; the ❽ Security Council, with permanent and changing members; the Secretariat; and the International Court of Justice.

The East-West conflict, however, impeded the creation of a global system of peace. Unanimous decisions in the Security Council were repeatedly thwarted by use of the veto by one superpower or the other. The policy of détente at last led to joint treaties between the world powers, for example over the nonproliferation of nuclear weapons.

The nature of the United Nations was altered by the decolonization process after World War II. The number of members tripled, and the issues to be dealt with included the question of how to integrate the new members into the UN and the global order. Many former colonies joined, reducing the dominance of the industrial countries. The superpowers therefore tried to enlist the support of the nonaligned states. The UN guidelines were adjusted to new political requirements. Besides the protection of children (UNICEF), ❿, ⓬ world cultural heritage (UNESCO), and health (WHO), since the 1970s it has also been the United Nations' goal to reduce disparities between the North and South and to halt the overexploitation of natural resources.

The instruments for securing peace have changed since the 1960s. Initially, the organization was limited to diplomatic means, but now it can also deploy armed ⓫ UN peacekeeping troops, which are recognizable by their blue helmets. Despite some successes, the conflicts of interests of the member states that supply these troops have repeatedly hampered the ability of the United Nations to serve as "world police"—even after the end of the Cold War. Whether the United Nations can be made capable of meeting the new demands of the 21st century has been a subject of intense discussion within the world community.

Meeting of the UN Security Council in New York to discuss the uprising in Hungary, November 1956

United Nations Building, New York, lit up for the 50th anniversary of the founding of the UN, 1995

Blood test results are examined as part of the campaign by the World Health Organization against glandular fever, Angola, 1959

Stonehenge, England, given world cultural heritage status by UNESCO in 1986

British peacekeeping troops from the United Nations in former Yugoslavia, 1995

UNESCO helping illiterate people in Mexico, 1980

after 1945 | Beginning decolonization

1946 | Dissolving of the League of Nations

Sep 1949 | Founding of the People's Republic of China

1950-53 | Korean War

Oct 1962 | The Cuban Missile Crisis

Decolonization and the Dissolution of the Blocs

A period of decolonization began during the 1950s. Some of the states that emerged fell into neither the Western nor Eastern camps. Soviet reform policies starting in 1985 induced the implosion of the Eastern Bloc and ended the Cold War.

2 Standing in front of a statue of Lenin, Gorbachev addresses the Congress of People's Deputies, 1989

1 GDR citizens demonstrate for free elections, Leipzig, 1989

With India's release from British guardianship in 1947, after a long political struggle and the partition of the subcontinent into two mutually suspicious nations, India and Pakistan, a period of global decolonization began. In 1949, Southeast Asian countries such as Indonesia became independent, and in the 1950s and 1960s almost all of the colonies in ❸ Africa gained autonomy. The number of sovereign states rose from around 50 in 1900 to 180 in 1990.

The process of decolonization took place either violently, as was the case in Algeria, or through agreement, as in the case of India. Some of the colonial rulers—in both blocs—were replaced by dictatorial regimes. Dictatorship and the resultant corruption have been characteristic of many African independent countries. To avoid becoming pawns of the major powers, Third World countries in 1955 formed the Nonaligned Movement.

The end of the rigid bloc confrontation began in 1985, when ❷ Mikhail Gorbachev assumed office as the general secretary of the Communist Party of the Soviet Union. Increased armament, inefficient state structures, and rigid dogmatism had brought the USSR to an economic and social crisis during the preceding Brezhnev era. Gorbachev began a radical reform policy, with the bywords *glasnost* ("openness") and *perestroika* ("economic and political reform"). The claim to Soviet supremacy over the Eastern Bloc states was relinquished. Whereas the Soviet Union had sent ❹ tanks in response to the 1968 Czech uprising demanding reform, the suppressed societies in the satellite states now used their new freedom of movement for revolutionary change. ❶ Demonstrations, strikes, and mass exoduses in 1989 brought the communist regimes to the point of collapse. With the disappearance of the Eastern Bloc, the Cold War ended after nearly four decades almost without violence.

3 Nigeria: Celebrations on the occasion of the fifth anniversary of independence, 1965

4 Soviet tanks in Prague, 1968

The Nonaligned Movement

In April 1955, 29 countries, primarily from Asia and Africa, prepared the way for the nonaligned states movement. Nations such as China, India, Indonesia, and Yugoslavia condemned the confrontation of the blocs. The term "Third World" was coined there to differentiate the movement's members from countries aligned with the superpowers.

Nonaligned states conference in Bandung, Indonesia, April 1955

"Life punishes those who come too late!"

This famous statement by Mikhail Gorbachev was never actually made in public. When Gorbachev was met by East German general secretary Erich Honecker at the Berlin airport on October 5, 1989, Gorbachev said on East German state television: "I believe danger only awaits those who don't react to life."

Soviet General Secretary Mikhail Gorbachev greets Erich Honecker, 1987

The New World Order

The West's peaceful victory in the Cold War brought freedom and democracy to Eastern Europe. Wider access to weapons of mass destruction and the growth of international terrorism, however, presented the world with new challenges.

The ❽ fall of the Berlin Wall on November 9, 1989, symbolized the victory of the freedom-seeking movements in Eastern European nations and the rapid collapse of the Soviet empire. In effect, it initiated German reunification along Western lines. East Germany became a part of the Federal Republic of Germany and a year later a member of NATO.

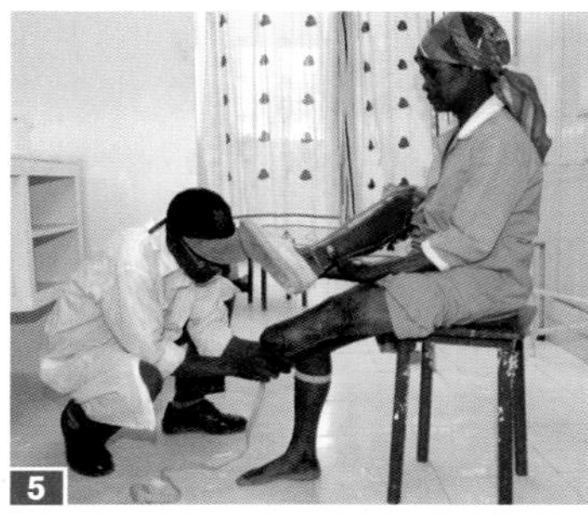

Angolan woman maimed by a land mine is fitted with an artificial limb in a local hospital, 2003

The European Union Parliament meets in Brussels, 2005

Debris in New York after the World Trade Center attacks, September 11, 2001

The Warsaw Pact, the Soviet bloc's defense alliance, fell apart, and its Eastern European member states joined the Western alliance after the United States made security reassurances to the Soviet Union and its successor Russia. At the turn of the millennium, a group of Eastern and Central European states, including Poland and the Baltic States, joined the ❻ European Union. The Commonwealth of Independent States (CIS) replaced the collapsed Soviet Union.

The collapse of communism brought democracy and Western civil rights to all of Europe. The decline and fall of the heavily armed Soviet Union, however, bore new dangers. The few that have prospered have become the new international super-rich, while the removal of basic social services previously provided by the state has left the poor, the sick, and the old in a much worse condition. As central control waned, weapons of mass destruction and nuclear know-how came into the hands of smaller and often unstable states, increasing the potential for a nuclear war. In addition, conventional weapons such as rifles and ❺ land mines were sold without controls and in enormous amounts on the black market. They were used in many brutal ❿ civil wars, for example, in the former ❾ Yugoslavia at the beginning of the 1990s and in Somalia in 1995.

A new threat for the world community was created by the use of ⓫ terror as a political means by non-state interest groups working through globally organized networks. After the ❼ terrorist attacks on New York and Washington, DC, on September 11, 2001, by fundamentalist Islamists the United States and its allies called for a political, economical, and military "war on terror." The sociopolitical consequences of this for democracy remain unforeseeable.

The Berlin Wall is demolished by Berlin citizens,1989

Civil war in former Yugoslavia in 1992: a sign in Sarajevo tells people to beware of snipers

Child soldier of the Union of Congolese Patriots

Reconstruction of a British bank in Istanbul, Turkey, after having been destroyed by a bomb attack, 2003

9 Nov 1989 | Fall of the Berlin Wall

1 Jul 1991 | Dissolution of the Warsaw Pact

8 Nov 1991 | Founding of the CIS

11 Sep 1991 | Terror attacks in New York and Virginia

THE PATH TO EUROPEAN UNITY

Immediately after the war, Europe had to be rebuilt. In the western half of the continent, the United States ❶ fostered the establishment of market economies, while in the east the Soviet Union saw to the installation of centrally planned economies. The political structures also developed in divergent ways, and two political and economic blocs became established. Until the end of the confrontation between these two blocs, European interest in integration was confined to the West. After 1989, the expansion of the union eastward made it possible to overcome the division of the continent.

1 German poster promoting the Marshall Plan, 1948

Between Division and Rapprochement in Europe

The different economic policies of the Allies divided Europe into two opposing camps and resulted in cohesion within the blocs.

George Marshall, the US secretary of state, announced a reconstruction program for Europe on June 5, 1947. The ❷ "Marshall Plan" was formally offered to all European states, but the Soviet Union refused to participate and prevented the acceptance of the plan within its sphere of influence. The distribution of Marshall Plan aid in Western Europe was taken over by the OEEC, a supranational board that was succeeded by the Organization for Economic Cooperation and Development (OECD) in 1961. In Eastern Europe, the Council for Mutual Economic Assistance (Comecon) oversaw the development of centrally planned economies.

3 "What's behind it?" Booklet about the Schuman Plan: Robert Schuman (left) and Konrad Adenauer, 1951

Plans for European unity in Western Europe emerged as soon as World War II was over. These were implemented initially on an economic and military level. French foreign minister ❸ Robert Schuman, for example, encourged the joint management of coal and steel production, which was intended to benefit economic development and also to contribute to the prevention of war in Europe. France, Germany, the Benelux states, and Italy became members of the Monetary Union in 1951. The ❺ Treaties of Rome followed in 1957, containing a protocol to found a European Economic Community (EEC) with the aim of establishing a Common Market and a unifying economic policy. Further elements were the founding of the European Atomic Energy Community (Euratom) for peaceful nuclear energy research and development.

The Western European countries moved closer together militarily as well. In 1948 France, Great Britain, and the Benelux states signed the Brussels Defense Community treaty. This was superceded by the North Atlantic Treaty, signed in 1949 by ten states of Western Europe as well as the United States and Canada, which led to the foundation of the military and defense alliance of the ❹ NATO (the North Atlantic Treaty Organization). In response, the military-backed ❻ Warsaw Pact was founded in Eastern Europe, and the division of the continent had become fact.

2 Marshall Plan aid for France: tractors from the United States arrive in Le Havre; ca. 1948

4 NATO conference in Paris, 1959

5 Signing of the Treaties of Rome on March 25,1957, in Rome

6 The GDR becomes a member of the Warsaw Pact in 1956

5. Jun 1947 | Signing of the Marshall plan
1948 | Brussels defense treaty
1949 | NATO Treaty
1955 | Founding of the Warsaw Pact
1957 | Treaties of Rome

From the European Community to the European Union

In 1965 the European Community was founded. Later restructured as the European Union, in the course of its existence it has taken up numerous new members and expanded geographically. Simultaneously its economic and political challenges have grown.

The development of Europe as a political union was initially slow. France refused political involvement in a supranational framework. Instead it intensified cooperation with Germany: On January 22, 1963, French president Charles de Gaulle and German chancellor Konrad Adenauer signed the ❼ Élysée Treaty, which called for mutual consultation on all important decisions concerning foreign policy and in cultural areas. However, the process of European economic integration could not be forestalled. In 1965 the European Coal and Steel Community, the European Economic Community (EEC), and Euratom formed the European Community (EC). A European Council was founded, in which individual governments were represented, along with a joint ⓫ commission that guards the interests of the EC on an international basis. Further governmental organs include the ❿ European Parliament, which is elected directly by the people of the member states, and the European Court of Justice.

7 The treaty concerning the cooperation between Germany and France is signed in Paris at the Elysée Palace on January 22, 1963, by Konrad Adenauer and Charles de Gaulle

A further milestone on the path to a united Europe was the Maastricht Treaty, signed on February 7, 1992. It forms the basis for a joint European foreign and security policy, closer cooperation in the areas of justice and home affairs, and the creation of an economic and currency union. The European Community became the European Union (EU) on November 1, 1993. In 1999 the ❽ euro replaced the local currencies of twelve EU countries. From that point on, the ⓬ European Central Bank became responsible for EU monetary policy.

8 The euro: the currency of the European Union

Several additional European states strove to take part in the strengthening European Union. Whereas before the disintegration of the Eastern Bloc in 1989 only Western European states had joined, since then many countries in Eastern and Central Europe have applied for membership; ten of them were accepted into the union in 2004 and 2007.

EU laws now noticeably affect the work of national governments, which has led to criticism of the lack of transparency in the decision-making structures of the ❾ Brussels bureaucracy. Each country has different future goals; whether the EU should be oriented more along political or economic lines is debated. The 2007 Treaty of Lisbon has created the basis for a stronger political union.

Members of the EC / European Union

with their dates of accession:

1958: Belgium, France, Italy, Luxembourg, the Netherlands, West Germany
1973: Denmark, Ireland, the United Kingdom
1981: Greece
1986: Portugal, Spain
1995: Austria, Finland, Sweden
2004: Cyprus, Czech Republic, Estonia, Hungary, Latvia, Lithuania, Malta, Poland, Slovakia, Slovenia
2007: Bulgaria, Romania

Poland becomes a member of the EU on May 1, 2004; a Polish and a German border official open the border crossing

9 Farmers demonstrating against the agrarian reform of the EU "Agenda 2000" in Schwerin, Germany, 1999

10 House of the European Council and the European Parliament in Strasbourg, France

11 View of the European commission building in Brussels, Belgium

12 The European Central Bank building in Frankfurt

22 Jan 1963 | German-French Treaty
1965 | Combination of the ECSC, the EEC, and Euratom to form the EC
7 Feb 1992 | Treaty of Maastricht
1999 | Introduction of the euro
2007 | Treaty of Lisbon

1

GERMANY SINCE 1945

Even after the defeat of the Nazi regime, Germany was seen as the "key to Europe." Due to its economic potential and strategic position, it became hotly contested between West and East. This brought with it the ❶ partition of the country. The symbolic focus of the Cold War was the city of Berlin, a city partially controlled by Western forces in the middle of the Soviet occupation zone. In 1989 the fall of the Berlin Wall at the Brandenburg Gate became the symbol of the demise of the Communist state system.

Brandenburg Gate in Berlin is blocked off with barbed wire on August 14-15, 1961

2

Refugees from the East on their way to Berlin, 1945

The "Zero Hour"

With the surrender of the German armed forces, fascist rule came to an end. The aftermath of the Nazi destruction policies, as well as hunger and displacement, shaped the first postwar years.

The political reconstitution of Germany lay in the hands of the ❺ Allies. They had already agreed on the division of the country and its capital into four zones of occupation, the creation of an Allied Control Council, and the demilitarization and denazification of the country. Austria was reestablished as a separate republic, though it was granted sovereignty only after ten years under Allied administration. Saarland came under French control, and the land east of the Oder and Neisse rivers was transferred to Poland, which fell under Soviet control. In the Sudetenland region annexed to Czechoslovakia, the German population that had not yet fled was ❷ displaced.

3

Trial against prisoners of war in Nuremberg; in the first row from the left: Göring, Hess, Ribbentrop, Keitel

Important components of the demilitarization of Germany included the dissolution of the army and the Prussian state. Denazification culminated in the ❸ Nuremberg trials of Nazis concerning the crimes committed under Hitler.

Criticism of the dissimilar practices of the Allies quickly began. In the Soviet zone, denazification was linked with political reform. After 1946, every German in the Western zones had to complete a form for political inspection. Numerous perpetrators were able, through ❹ attestations of discharge or so-called "Persil certificates" (named after a German laundry detergent), to "wash themselves clean."

Der öffentliche Kläger
beim Entnazifizierungshauptausschuß
für den Kreis Plön

Plön, den 25. Febr.1949
Ge.

Entlastungszeugnis

Hiermit wird bestätigt, daß Herr
Vor- und Zuname Leo de Laforgue, geb. 9.2.02
Anschrift Laboe, Krs. Plön
auf Grund der Vorschriften des Gesetzes zur Fortführung und zum Abschluß der Entnazifizierung § 11 als entlastet in die Gruppe V eingestuft worden ist.

Öffentlicher Kläger Vorsitzender

4

Attestation of discharge, 1949

The democratic reconstitution of West Germany began on a regional level. The federal states were created, and in the fall of 1946 the first elections took place. In the East, the Soviet occupation army had called for the formation of political parties in June 1945 but heavily supported the German Communist Party, which was led by Soviet immigrants of the "Ulbricht Group."

The Allied Control Council

The four commanders in chief of the Allied forces took over the government responsibility for "Germany as a whole" with the Berlin Declaration of June 5, 1945. The Control Council had no executive power and so was reliant on the cooperation of the respective military governors in each region. The diverse interests of the Allies prevented agreement on almost every issue related to demilitarization and denazification. In March of 1948, the Soviet representatives withdrew from the Control Council, and it never convened again.

Onlookers outside a Control Council meeting

5

Americans and Russians shake hands on a destroyed bridge near Torgau, April 25, 1945

5 Jun 1945 | Berlin Declaration of the Allied Control Council

1945–46 | Energy crisis and food shortage

Apr 1946 | Founding of the SED

1 Jan 1947 | Unification of the American and British occupation zones

3 Mar 1948 | Dissolution of the Allied Control council

The Founding of the Federal Republic of Germany and the GDR

In Germany, cooperation between the centrally planned economy of the Soviet occupation zone and the market economy of the other zones did not take place even in the most extreme situations.

During the ❻ harsh winter of 1945–1946, energy and food supplies in Germany were exhausted. The immediate hardship was eased somewhat by the ❽ CARE (Cooperation for American Remittances to Europe) packages that were sent to individuals in Germany beginning in August 1946. After the failure of the Soviets to provide sufficient food supplies, the Western allies blocked the payment of German reparations to the Soviet Union. The July 1946 suggestion from the United States for the economic unification of the occupied zones was refused by the Soviet Union, as it suspected economic imperialism was behind the suggestion. As early as 1945, land reforms and expropriations had paved the way for a centrally planned economy in the Soviet zone. In April 1946, the Social Democratic party and the Communist party in the Soviet zone merged as the Socialist Unity party; other political parties were then forcibly integrated into this single party.

The Americans and British unified their occupied zones on January 1, 1947. A currency reform was implemented in the combined zone as part of the newly created ❾ Marshall Plan to help a destroyed Europe recover; the new ❿ German mark was introduced on June 21, 1948. When the Western powers introduced the German mark in their sectors of Berlin, the Soviets responded with a blockade of the city. For eleven months, Berlin was supplied by an ❼ air bridge: some 277,000 flights brought 2.3 million tons of goods into the city before the Soviets lifted their blockade in May 1949.

Thus, currency reforms were followed by the founding of two German states. In July 1948 the Western allies asked the prime minister of the federal states to call for an election of a constituent National Assembly. The ministers instead worked out a Basic Constitutional Law. Signed on May 8, 1948, by the Parliamentary Council, which was made up of the federal state parliaments, it was approved by the Western allies and proclaimed on May 23, 1949. In the Soviet zone, a People's Chamber that was dominated by the Socialist Unity party signed a draft constitution in May 1949, which it claimed applied to all of Germany; on October 7, 1949, the ⓫ German Democratic Republic was officially founded. With the establishment of the competing states, the division of Germany for the next 40 years was sealed—even as both sides claimed to speak for Germany.

6 Women warm their hands after clearing up the rubble, 1945–1946

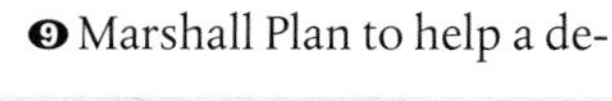

7 Arrival of a "raisin bomber" bringing food to Berlin, 1948

8 Distribution of CARE packages, 1946

10 Temporary money, 1948

Ernst Reuter

Born in 1889, Ernst Reuter was a Social Democrat from 1912 and briefly a member of the German Communist party. After his 1933 internment in a concentration camp, he went to Turkey as an adviser in 1935. In 1947 he was elected mayor of Berlin but was prevented from taking office until 1948. As mayor from 1950 until his death in 1953, he led the resistance against the Berlin Blockade in 1948–1949: "Peoples of the world, look to this city."

Rally in front of the Reichstag: Ernst Reuter asks for help against the Berlin Blockade, September 9, 1948

9 Houses are built for refugees to replace emergency accomodations

11 Founding of the German Democratic Republic (GDR) on Oct 7, 1949; Wilhelm Pieck at the microphone

21 Jun 1948 | Introduction of the German Mark
24 Jun 1948 | Beginning of the Berlin Blockade
May 1949 | Signing of the Basic Law
May 1949 | End of the Blockade
Oct 1949 | East Berlin becomes the capital of the GDR
7 Oct 1949 | Signing of the proposed constitution

East Germany: The Ulbricht Era 1948–1971

The Stalinist government of East Germany had to struggle against popular resistance to it among the people. Consolidation was only possible through coercion.

❶ Walter Ulbricht (1893-1973), a founder of the German Communist Party, was the first secretary of the Socialist Unity party of Germany from July 1953, the same year the German Democratic Republic was accepted into the Council for Mutual Economic Assistance, the Soviet counterpart to the Marshall Plan. The Socialist Unity party had presented the first five-year plan in 1951.

In 1952 the Western allies rejected Stalin's suggestion for a neutral Germany, so the aim of Soviets became the integration of East Germany into the Eastern Bloc. The establishment of an army posed economic difficulties for the young republic, which were to be solved by overtime and the reduction of wages. Resistance in the party and society was broken through "cleansings" and repression. When the party increased the work requirements for industrial factories in May 1953, uprisings took place in Berlin and almost all other large cities on ❷ June 16 and 17—the first people's rebellion in an Eastern Bloc country. ❹ Soviet tanks suppressed the uprising, and in its wake, the state government bolstered the secret police of the Ministry of State Security—a force referred to as the "Stasi"—headed by ❻ Erich Mielke. Under massive pressure, the ❺ nationalization of agriculture into production cooperatives and of businesses into people-owned enterprises was carried out. The level of production, however, did not improve, which fanned opposition to the government among many parts of the population. The short political "thaw" after 1956 did not alter the inadequate situation. The most visible form of resistance was citizens "voting with their feet"—leaving the country. It was determined that ❸ sealing of the borders was necessary to save East Germany from economic collapse, and on August 13, 1961, construction of the Berlin Wall was started. Many citizens lost their lives trying to cross the wall.

In the following years, the import of food from the Soviet Union to East Germany provided some relief. The political system opened itself slowly and economic reforms led briefly to a mood of new beginnings.

1 Walter Ulbricht

2 Uprising in East Berlin; a burning police station, June 17, 1953,

3 Sign at the border between East and West Germany, 1988

4 Uprising in East Berlin; Soviet tanks at Potsdamer Platz, June 17, 1953

"Voting with the Feet"

In the first year of the German Democratic Republic, 130,000 of its citizens fled to the West; in the year of the 1953 uprising, it was 330,000. In total, some 2.5 million people—a seventh of the population, of which 60 percent were employed—had left East Germany by the time the wall was built.

GDR border officials arrest a citizen who was trying to flee through the sewage system, 1962

5 A former manor is divided into lots and given to industrial workers, 1945

6 Erich Mielke, minister of state security in the GDR from 1957-1989, in 1980

1951 | First five-year plan
Jul 1953 | Walter Ulbricht becomes general secretary of the SED
1953 | Death of Stalin
16–17 Jun 1953 | East Berlin uprising
1954 | Recognition of GDR sovereignty by the USSR

East Germany: The Honecker Era 1971–1989

The supply situation improved, yet due to its high debts, East Germany was dependent on the West. The refusal to reform led to the demise of the state.

East German general secretary ⓫ Erich Honecker, who took office in 1976 after the death of Walter Ulbricht, proclaimed "real existing socialism"—meaning that one should no longer hold off for a coming communist paradise but should attempt to improve contemporary living conditions. In fact, the national income of the country rose steadily until it reached its highest level in 1975, giving East Germany the highest ⓬ standard of living in the Eastern bloc. ⓾ Housing reform was implemented; while West Germans spent 20 percent of their income on rent, an East German spent only five percent. Medical care was free, and family support led to an increase in the birth rate.

In 1974, East and West Germany were welcomed into the United Nations together, and the equal participation of both states in the Conference for Security and Cooperation in Europe (CSCE) was a successful step on the way to international recognition. In September 1987, when Honecker was received in Bonn by West German chancellor Helmut Kohl with all the honors of a state leader, de facto recognition had been acknowledged.

The country could not finance the desired increase in social spending, however. Due to inadequate modernization, productivity stagnated. The finance gaps were bridged by credits from the West. In 1983 Bavarian prime minister Franz Josef Strauss provided a billion-mark loan, which gave the East Germans some breathing space. Wages once again rose, yet there was less and less to buy. The average citizen had to wait ten years for a car, and the only choice was the locally manufactured and poor quality Trabant, known as the ❾ Trabbi. Television sets were present in 90 percent of the households, however, and most of them could receive broadcasts from the West. In response to the growing discontent, the state government increased ❼ propaganda and the development of the Stasi.

The expatriation of the politically critical singer Wolf Biermann in 1976 pushed the East German cultural elite into the opposition. Under the protection of the church, the environmentalist and ❽ peace movements gathered. In 1984, 32,000 citizens applied for permission to leave the country; by 1988, this figure had risen to 110,000. Honecker's refusal to implement the reforms recommended by Mikhail Gorbachev proved disastrous and within a few months would bring the East German regime crashing down in ruins.

7 Honecker portrait on display, 1986

8 Members of the peace movement demonstrate in Dresden, 1987

9 A "Trabbi," ca. 1970

10 View from within the ruins of the newly constructed buildings for the social housing program in Berlin, ca. 1955

11 Erich Honecker, front, at the eighth party meeting of the SED, June 15, 1971: In front of the committee, from left to right: Stoph, Brezhnev, Ebert, Sindermann

12 Uniforms of the GDR youth organizations Young Pioneers and Free German Youth Organization (FDJ), 1972

Commercial Coordination

Since the 1960s the Stasi officer Alexander Schalck-Golodkovski had built up a shadow economy empire to supply foreign currency for the servicing of foreign government debt. Rubbish was imported, and expropriated antiques, weapons, and the blood of East German citizens were exported. Political hostages whose freedom was purchased by the Western powers were also a source of income.

13 Aug 1961 | Building of the Berlin Wall
1962 | Dissolution of the Soviet command in East Berlin
1974 | Entry of the GDR in the UN
1976 | Erich Honecker becomes General Secretary
1983 | Taking-on of the "billion-mark loan"

West Germany: From Adenauer to Brandt 1949–1974

Konrad Adenauer tied the Federal Republic into the Western alliance. Willy Brandt's primary foreign policy achievement was the easing of tensions with countries from the Eastern Bloc.

While the Socialist Unity Party ruled as the single party in East Germany, the Federal Republic built up a multiparty system, dominated by the Christian Democratic Union and the Social Democratic Party. On August 14, 1949, the first election for the Bundestag took place. ❶ Konrad Adenauer of the Christian Democrats was elected federal chancellor with a one-seat majority.

1 Konrad Adenauer

2 Prof. Dr. Walter Hallstein

Adenauer's policies were aimed at tying the country into the Western alliance system. He pushed through West Germany's entry into the ❺ European Coal and Steel Community, Euratom, and the European Economic Community. In 1951, the Treaty of Paris paved the way for the Federal Republic to become a sovereign state and join NATO in 1955. Adenauer sought reconciliation with France, which led to the Élysée Treaty in 1963. It called for close cooperation in foreign, defense, and education policies. In 1952 Adenauer signed the Luxembourg agreements with Israeli Foreign Minister Sharett, which became the basis of reparations (*Wiedergutmachung*) legislation. Adenauer insisted that the Federal Republic represented all German citizens. This attitude was mirrored in the ❷ Hallstein doctrine of 1955: Bonn broke off diplomatic relations with any state—except for the USSR—that recognized East Germany.

3 Demonstration against the war in Vietnam, Berlin, February 18, 1968

4 Television: an example of the new prosperity, 1952

Adenauer's successor was the former minister of economics, Ludwig Erhard, who went down in history as the father of the ❹ economic "miracle." When Erhard's government coalition broke in 1966, he resigned. A coalition of the Christian Democrats and the Social Democrats took over government. The next chancellor, Kurt Georg Kiesinger, was heavily criticized for his earlier Nazi party membership.

In the face of a lack of opposition in the Bundestag, an ❸ extraparliamentary opposition formed as a protest against solidified structures, the Vietnam War, and the Emergency Acts of 1968. This movement molded the societal climate into the 1970s.

In 1969 a social-liberal coalition of the Social Democrats and the Free Democratic Party took power under Willy Brandt, promising to modernize the country. Brandt's principal foreign policy achievement was the policy of détente with the East, culminating in the completion of the Eastern Treaties (1970–1973). His recognition of the Oder–Neisse line as the border between Poland and East Germany was opposed by the Christian Democrats.

Compensation

Adenauer sought reconciliation with the young state of Israel. In the reparations treaty signed with Israel on September 10, 1952, West Germany pledged to pay three billion marks in material value to Israel. The agreement was approved on March 18, 1953, only after the third reading; numerous delegates refused their consent, on the basis that the Federal Democratic Republic was a state unrelated to the Third Reich. The votes of Social Democrats secured the acceptance of the draft.

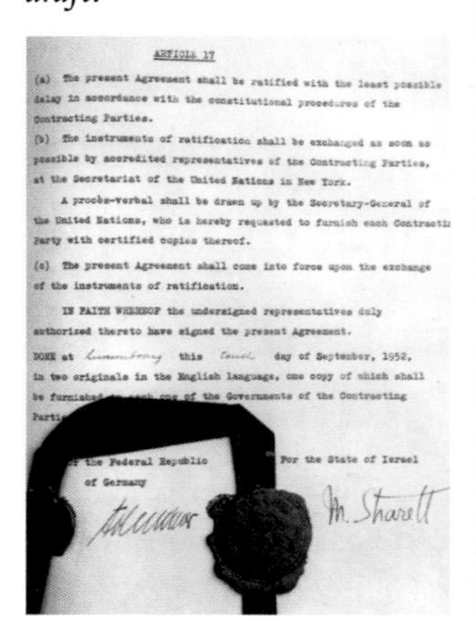

ARTICLE 17

(a) The present Agreement shall be ratified with the least possible delay in accordance with the constitutional procedures of the Contracting Parties.

(b) The instruments of ratification shall be exchanged as soon as possible by accredited representatives of the Contracting Parties, at the Secretariat of the United Nations in New York.

A procès-verbal shall be drawn up by the Secretary-General of the United Nations, who is hereby requested to furnish each Contracting Party with certified copies thereof.

(c) The present Agreement shall come into force upon the exchange of the instruments of ratification.

IN FAITH WHEREOF the undersigned representatives duly authorized thereto have signed the present Agreement.

DONE at [illegible] this [illegible] day of September, 1952, in two originals in the English language, one copy of which shall be furnished to each one of the Governments of the Contracting Parties.

For the Federal Republic of Germany — For the State of Israel

M. Sharett

German–Israeli treaty, 1952

5 Talks prior to forming the European Coal and Steel Community; including Robert Schuman and German Chancellor Adenauer, 1951

14 Aug 1949	First Bundestag election
Sep 1949	Konrad Adenauer becomes Federal Chancellor
18 Mar 1953	Reparations treaty with Israel
1955	Soveignty of the GDR; Entry into NATO
1955	Hallstein doctrine
1963	Signing of the Élysée Treaty

West Germany: From Schmidt to Kohl 1974–1989

In the mid-1970s West Germany suffered an economic crisis, but the European integration process and the opening to the East continued.

When it emerged that one of Chancellor Brandt's personal assistants, ❿ Günter Guillaume, was an East German agent, Brandt resigned in 1974. His successor in office was Helmut Schmidt. During Schmidt's time in government, the first harsh economic crisis hit the Federal Republic.

The domestic climate was shaped by the terrorist acts of the Red Army Faction and the countermeasures of the state. In foreign policy, Schmidt set out on the course of compromise: He visited ❼ East Germany and took part in meetings of the Organization for Security and Cooperation in Europe (OSCE). Closer European unity was achieved together with French President Valéry Giscard d'Estaing; in 1975, the two government leaders initiated the ❾ economic and political cooperation of the then G-6 states (today the G-8).

Around 1980, politics once again became dominated by world political tensions. Schmidt advocated the stationing of intermediate-range nuclear missiles in Europe, which was opposed by the burgeoning ❽ peace movement and parts of his own party. This, and worries about the environment, became the impetus for the founding of the ❻ "Greens" movement, which was soon able to enter parliament as the fourth political party.

In 1982 the social-liberal era ended when the Free Democratic Party withdrew from the government coalition and instead formed an alliance with the Christian Democrats. ⓫ Helmut Kohl became the new chancellor and Hans-Dietrich Genscher the new foreign minister. Kohl's government was able to stabilize state finances, lower tax burdens for businesses and private households, and curb inflation. It was unable to manage the unemployment situation and many necessary reforms were not made. Among the people, disenchantment with politics took hold and electoral participation dropped. Externally, Kohl's government continued the policies of its predecessors: Contacts to the East were built up and European unity was promoted in partnership with the French.

7 Helmut Schmidt, left, on his visit to East Germany; Erich Honecker, right, 1981

9 Economic summit on July 16, 1978 in Bonn; from left to right: Carter, the Japanese Prime Minister Fukuda, Schmidt, and the French Giscard d'Estaing

11 After the general elections: Helmut Kohl is sworn in as chancellor, 1982

8 Pins with the symbol of the peace movement

10 Chancellor Willy Brandt (left), together with his personal assistant Günter Guillaume

6 Election poster of the "Greens": "We have only borrowed the Earth from our children," 1983

The Red Army Faction

In the 1970s the left-wing terrorism of the Red Army Faction shaped the political climate in West Germany. The group's methods included attacks, kidnappings, murders, and blackmail, which they used to destabilize the state. More than 45 people fell victim to their attacks, including the president of the German Employers' Association, Hanns-Martin Schleyer. Most of the terrorists were arrested. The Red Army Faction stopped fighting in 1992 and dissolved in 1998.

Red Army Faction on a "wanted" poster put up by the Federal Criminal Police Office, 1972

since 1968 | Creation of the APO
1969 | Willy Brandt becomes chancellor
1970–73 | Conclusion of the Eastern Treaties
1970 | Kidnapping of Schleyer by the RAF
1980 | Founding of the "Greens" party
1982 | Helmut Kohl becomes chancellor

German Reunification 1989–1990

The rapid collapse of the East German government accelerated the unification process. The Kohl-Genscher Government won the support of the four Allies for the reunification of Germany.

After the opening of Hungary's western border in the furtherance of *perestroika* on September 11, 1989, tens of thousands of East German citizens left their country for the West. Others fled through the West German embassies in Warsaw and Prague. That month, peaceful protests began against the East German government's unwillingness to reform, and the number of participants in the ❷"Monday demonstrations" increased steadily. On October 23, 300,000 people marched through central Leipzig under the slogan "We are the people." On ❹ November 4, 1989, a million citizens gathered at Alexanderplatz in Berlin to demand freedom of opinion, freedom to travel, and free elections. The Socialist Unity Party finally opened the ❺ border to the Federal Republic on November 9, 1989, but by then the aim had gone beyond simply reforming the German Democratic Republic. Instead, demands for unification of the two German states became louder.

The first ❻ free elections to the *Volkskammer* in East Germany took place on March 18, 1990, and the Socialist Unity Party's successor—the Party of Democratic Socialism—won only 16 percent of the votes. The conservative Alliance for Germany, under Minister-President Lothar de Maizière, took power and began negotiating a reunification treaty with the West German government.

The rapidly worsening economic situation in East Germany and the continuing wave of departures led to the ratification of an ❶ economic, currency, and social union between the two states. It came into effect on July 1, 1990, as an important first step to reunification. The actual merger of East and West into a single Germany could only be achieved with the acquiescence of the victorious powers of World War II, however, and so the ❸ "Two Plus Four Agreement" was negotiated among both German governments and the foreign ministers of the Allied forces, giving back full sovereignty to a unified Germany 45 years after the end of the war. The reunification was sealed on October 3, 1990.

2 One of the demonstrations that were held every Monday, Leipzig, October 1989

Willy Brandt on German Reunification, November 1990

"Now what belongs together will grow together."

Willy Brandt during a rally of the Social Democratic Party in Leipzig, February 25, 1990

1 The unification treaty between the FRG and the GDR is signed, 1990

The Accession

On July 22, 1990, within the territory of East Germany, the East German states of Brandenburg, Mecklenburg–Western Pomerania, Saxony-Anhalt and the Free States of Saxony, and Thuringia were refounded. These five new states joined the Federal Republic on October 3, 1990, and the German Democratic Republic ceased to exist. A day later the Bundestag had its first session in Berlin. Five former East German politicians were sworn in as new state ministers.

3 Meeting prior to the "Two Plus Four Agreement," Genscher (third from left) and Meckel (second from right)

4 West and East Berliners atop the Berlin Wall after the opening of the East German border on November 9, 1989

5 Berlin, after the border at the Glienicke Bridge was opened, November 10, 1989

6 Election posters for the Volkskammer in East Germany on March, 18, 1990

11 Sep 1989 | Opening of the Hungarian border
18 Mar 1990 | First elections to the Volkskammer
9 Nov 1989 | Opening of the East-West German border
23 Oct 1989 | March of 300,000 people through central Leipzig

Germany in the Present

The unified Germany had to fight economic and domestic difficulties even as it actively participated in the project of European integration.

The protest movement in East Germany gave birth to numerous opposition parties and organizations which were so large that the state's repressive apparatus could not contain them. In 1990, East German civil rights groups joined together with the West German Greens to form "Alliance 90–The Greens." The representatives of these civil rights movements played a decisive role in the ⓫ dissolution of the GDR's Ministry for State Security and the public release of secret service documents.

The first German Bundestag elections brought a clear victory for the governing coalition under Chancellor Helmut Kohl, showing broad public support for the unification process. Still, the implementation of the unification proved to be an immense economic and political challenge. The ❽ ailing industries in the East almost entirely collapsed, in the context of the competitive West German industrial structures and the ensuing loss of jobs and social welfare cuts led to mass protests in many eastern German towns.

7 German UN peacekeeping soldiers

8 The Wildau Company, starting in 1951 an East German state-owned mechanical engineering company, in 1994

9 The new Federal Chancellery in Berlin, built between 1997 and 2001

About a year after unification, numerous attacks by right-wing radicals on foreigners and asylum seekers shook the country. The excesses were watched with worry both inside and outside the country, particularly given Germany's historical record of fascism and xenophobia. At the end of 1992, however, 100,000 people staged a demonstration against racism and intolerance.

Today Germany is the most populous nation in Europe and is still ❿ economically strong. After the successful reunification, it has actively campaigned for the unification of Europe: the currency union and enlargement of the European Union to the east have been shaped by German initiatives. The country has taken on increasing global responsibilities. An important expression of this was the participation of German soldiers in the ❼ UN peacekeeping operation in Kosovo in 1999, agreed to by the Red-Green coalition under ❾ Gerhard Schröder, who won the Bundestag elections in 1998 and 2002. As the first female chancellor, Angela Merkel of the Christian Democrats has continued this foreign policy since 2005.

10 The modern architecture of Potsdamer Platz, all built since 1989 on the site of the former no-man's-land around the Berlin Wall, 2000

11 The former GDR Ministry of State Security in Berlin-Lichtenberg

1990 Treaty on the Final Settlement with Respect to Germany, Article 1.1

The united Germany shall comprise the territory of the Federal Republic of Germany, the German Democratic Republic, and the whole of Berlin. Its external borders shall be the borders of the Federal Republic of Germany and the German Democratic Republic and shall be definitive from the date on which the present Treaty comes into force. The confirmation of the definitive nature of the borders of the united Germany is an essential element of the peaceful order in Europe.

1 Jun 1990 | Economic, currency, and social union
3 Oct 1990 | Reunification
1990 | Formation of the Alliance 90–The Greens
2 Dec 1990 | First German Bundestag elections
2005 | Angela Merkel becomes chancellor

Austria SINCE 1945

Austria's independence was restored after the end of ❶World War II. In 1955 it achieved total sovereignty through the Austrian State Treaty with the Allies, on the condition of its perpetual neutrality. This later helped Austria to maintain relations with both Western countries and the nations of the Eastern bloc. Since the end of the Cold War and Austria's entry into the European Union, the neutrality policy has again become a topic of discussion. Domestically, the republic was characterized over the decades by the major political parties that formed a coalition government for a stable balance of interests.

1 British soldiers before Schönbrunn Castle in Vienna, April 1945

Independence and Neutrality

Following the end of the war, Austria once again became independent and obligated itself to strict neutrality. The Republic became the seat of many international organizations.

With the approval of a broad section of the populace, Austria annexed itself to the German Reich in 1938. The restoration of an independent Austria after the war was envisioned in 1943 by the Allies, who agreed to divide the country following the same model used in Germany; Austria and its ❻ capital Vienna was divided into four ❸ occupation zones and a common control council was set up. The Social Democratic Party, the Communist Party, and the mainstream Austrian People's Party were able in 1945 to settle on a declaration of independence and a provisional government headed by the Social Democrat Party leader, Karl Renner. A modified form of the constitution of 1929 came back into force, and all the National Socialist laws added during the period of annexation were annulled. The first election on November 25, 1945, resulted in a majority for the People's party, which formed a coalition government with the Social Democrats and Communists.

2 The Allies withdraw after the signing of the state treaty, 1955

5 OPEC headquarters in Vienna

After prolonged negotiations between the Austrian government and the Allies, a ❹ state treaty was concluded in 1955 and was signed on May 15 in Vienna, restoring the ❷ sovereignty of the nation. A condition insisted upon by the Allies was the assurance of "everlasting" neutrality, which was established in the Federal Constitutional Law on the Neutrality of Austria on October 26. This day has been celebrated as a national holiday since 1965.

In 1960, Austria, like all neutral European states, joined the European Free Trade Association. Austria developed close economic ties especially with its neighboring Eastern bloc states. Austria has been a member of the United Nations since 1955, and Vienna became one of the four official ❼ UN sites in 1979. Furthermore, thanks to its neutral status, Austria has become home to numerous significant international organizations, among them the International Atomic Energy Agency (IAEA), the Organization for Security and Cooperation in Europe (OSCE), and the ❺ Organization of Petroleum Exporting Countries (OPEC).

3 The Allies shake hands; (from left) American, British, French, and Soviet military police show their support and cooperation in Vienna

4 The signatories of the state treaty on the balcony of the Belvedere Castle, May 15, 1955

6 Destroyed houses on the banks of the Danube, Vienna, 1945

7 UN complex in Vienna

1938 | Austria annexes itself to the German Reich

1943 | Allies agree on Austria's independence

25 Nov 1945 | First elections

15 May 1955 | Austria's sovereignty

26 Oct 1955 | Constitutional Law on the Neutrality of Austri

Economic Development and the Neutrality Crisis

Austria became a service industry nation with a strong tourism sector. Since the 1990s, alongside the major parties, the right-wing populist Liberal Party has been gaining popularity.

The Marshall Plan provided Austria with the economic means with which to develop a new economy in the first postwar years. Heavy industry and banks were nationalized in 1946. Also facilitating recovery was the "social partnership," a close cooperation of the major economic interests with the government, which is still in practice today. The intervention by the Soviets in their occupation zone in Lower Austria led to an industrial flight to the traditionally purely agrarian west, which permanently altered the economic and social structure of the country. Since the 1970s, the service sector has surpassed all others. To this day, Austria owes its supranational importance primarily to ❽, ❾,❿ tourism—particularly in the Alpine regions—and Vienna's status as center for headquarters and congresses.

The People's Party and the Social Democrat Party have been forming predominantly coalition governments since 1947, although occasionally the People's Party has governed alone. For a long time, only the Liberal Party stood in opposition to the major parties. Founded in 1949, the Liberal Party emerged out of the electoral alliance of independents, a sort of catch-all for less incriminated ex-National Socialists. Beginning in the 1990s, the party rapidly gained popularity under its right-wing populist chairman, Jörg Haider (died 2008). In 1999 it became the second strongest party after the People's Party and formed the government with them in 2000. The Greens have established themselves since 1986 as a second opposition party. Since 2007 the People's Party and Social Democrats have formed the government.

9 Skiers in the Karwendel range, 2003

12 Bruno Kreisky, 1973

13 The Austrian Chancellor and chairman of the SPÖ, Franz Vranitzky, 1992

Austria has used its neutrality as an active peace policy since Chancellor ⓬ Bruno Kreisky's term of office (1970–1983). Among other things, the country has provided military contingents for the peacekeeping activities of the United Nations in the Golan Heights, Cyprus, as well as in Bosnia-Herzegovina and Kosovo. In addition, Austria participates in the NATO Partnership for Peace program.

Austria's neutral status, however, has been an issue of discussion domestically since the 1980s, when membership in the European Community was proposed in order to be a part of the European Common Market. In 1989, the government of ⓭ Franz Vranitzky made a formal application, resulting in ⓫ EU membership in 1995 and the Euro monetary system in 1999. Austria, however, has never officially given up its neutrality.

8 View over Salzburg; the Fortress Hohensalzburg in Salzburg, (front right) Kollegien Church, 2002

10 "Fiaker," an Austrian coach, Salzburg

11 Celebrations on the Heldenplatz in Vienna following Austria's assumption of the European Union presidency in1998

The Waldheim Affair

Kurt Waldheim, ca. 1985

The election of Kurt Waldheim as Austrian federal president in June 1986 provoked controversy at home and abroad because he had been an officer in the Nazi German army. Waldheim had been UN general secretary from 1972 to 1981 and entered the elections as a People's Party candidate. He commented on his past in the following way: "I did nothing different in the war than hundreds of thousands of other Austrians, namely, fulfilled my duty as a soldier." Although it could not be proven that he was guilty of any war crimes, Waldheim remained internationally isolated.

1955 | Austria joins UN
1960 | Austria joins EFTA
1970–83 | Federal Chancellor Bruno Kreisky
June 1986 | Waldheim Affair
1989 | Government of Franz Vranitzky makes formal application to EU
1995 | Austria joins the EU

"No" ballot papers from the referendum on EU membership, December 6, 1992

Switzerland since 1945

The traditionally stable Swiss governmental system rests on consensus, direct democracy, and federalism. Switzerland is one of the wealthiest countries in the world as a result of its finance industry. The service sector has also come to play a significant economic role. Relations with the European Union are close, but Switzerland continues to ❶ reject membership, as it does not want to compromise its traditional policy of neutrality.

Economic Boom and Criticism after World War II

Switzerland experienced a rapid rise in its economy after World War II. The conduct of the banks cooperating with the Nazis during the war became the subject of sharp criticism.

As a neutral state, Switzerland dissolved its extremist left- and right-wing political parties and was not an active participant in World War II although it was obliged to have commercial relations with the Axis Powers. Its production facilities remained to a great extent undamaged. This facilitated the country's swift ❷,❹ economic resurgence after the war. Switzerland has achieved one of the highest per capita incomes in the world, with low unemployment and a low budget deficit. The service sector has grown to play an increasingly large role; its main business sectors are banking and insurance as well as ❺,❻ tourism. Switzerland preserved its strict neutrality, remaining outside the United Nations (until 2002) and the North Atlantic Treaty Organization, although it did decide to join the European Organization for Co-operation and Development.

Headquarters of the Swiss UBS bank in Zurich, 2001

As a ❸ financial center, Switzerland—which owes its leading position to the combination of strict banking confidentiality, the neutrality of the country, and the security of its "Swiss numbered accounts"—came under criticism after the end of the war. The Nazis had moved a major part of the valuables they had stolen during their time in power to Switzerland, and Swiss banks profited greatly from their crimes. In 1946, the remaining German assets were transferred to the Allies for reparations. Treaties with Poland and Hungary in 1949 resulted in the return of assets to the heirs of victims there. In 1962, a law was passed to force the banks to provide information on and pay out the remaining fortunes of those persecuted by the Nazi regime. In 1995 Switzerland was once again accused of having profited from the smuggling of stolen goods. In response, the Swiss government set up an international commission of experts to investigate, but foreign pressure increased to the point that a payment was agreed upon before the investigation was completed. Despite this process, the conduct of the banks had damaged Switzerland's reputation to some extent. Switzerland's refugee policies during the war also came under fire. Around 25,000 Jewish refugees were turned back at the Swiss border. In 1996, the president of the confederation, Ruth Dreyfuss, made a formal Swiss apology for this.

An economically profitable Swiss tradition: chocolate by Lindt and Sprüngli

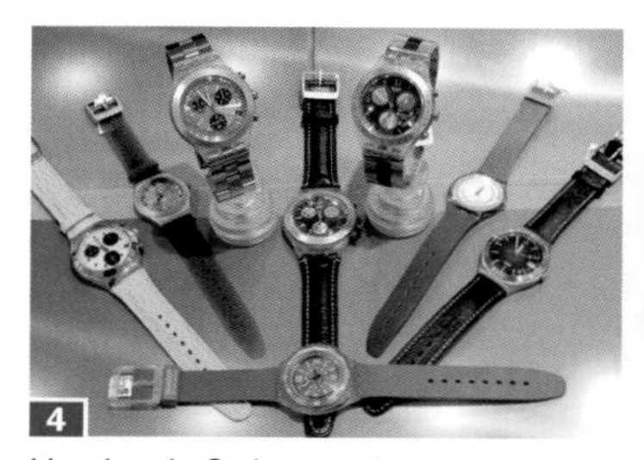

Handmade Swiss watches have long been a desired quality item: modern Swatch watches, 2003

The Matterhorn mountain in the Swiss Alps

The Kapel bridge over the Reuss River, Lucerne, 2000

1848 | Signing of first constitution

1946 | German assets transferred to the Allies

1949 | Reparation treaties with Hungary and Poland

1953 | Introduction of the "Magic Formula"

1962 | Repayment law

The Political System and Neutrality

Switzerland remains a parliamentary federal state with 26 cantons committed to neutrality. Political decisions are made by consensus.

The federal constitution Switzerland adopted in 1848 remained in force through 1999, with only one revision in 1874; a new constitution came into force in 2000. Since 1959–1960, Switzerland has been a concordance or "consensus democracy," in which as many parties, associations, and social groups as possible are included in the political process and decisions are made by consensus. This principle is the basis of the ⓫ Federal Council. According to the so-called "magic formula," it is composed of representatives of four parties, who jointly seek political solutions. This system of government is very stable due to the lack of any opposition. The national government, however, only holds the authority mandated to it by 22 cantons, themselves in turn dependent on the "grass-roots" democracy of the 3000 municipalities, and decisions on the federal and canton levels can be contradictory. Women were granted suffrage on the federal level in 1971, for example, but the women in ❼ Appenzell have been able to vote in their canton only since 1990.

The Swiss people have a long tradition of sometimes voting directly on important issues in open-air assemblies, especially in some mountain cantons where in the spring the citizens vote by a show of hands. This is particularly true with respect to changes to the constitution. Consequently, the Swiss decided by referendum against joining the European currency system in 1992, against joining the European Union in 2001, and in favor of membership in the ❿ United Nations in 2002. Although Switzerland was a founding member of the European Free Trade Association in 1960, which does not conflict with the political principle of their neutrality, most Swiss citizens felt that EU membership would mean political ❾ integration into the community of European nations. Switzerland is already closely linked economically with the European Union through bilateral contracts, such as the agreement on ❽ Alpine transit for heavy traffic, but the abandonment of traditional neutrality is rejected by most of the citizens.

9 Swiss raw milk cheese does not conform to EU regulations

7 The electors of the community of Hundswill, Appenzell, return after meeting to vote on the issue of suffrage for women, 1989

8 Bridge of the North-South railway of the Gotthard Pass that runs through the Swiss Alps

10 Posters in favor of (right) and against (left) Swiss membership in the United Nations, during the second referendum in Switzerland on the United Nations membership February 2002

11 Federal Council meeting room

The Magic Formula

The "magic formula," introduced in 1953, describes the longtime composition of the Swiss Federal Council: two members each from the Liberal, Christian Democratic, and Social Democratic Parties and one from the Swiss People's Party. This splits the cabinet seats between the main four parties. The magic formula was altered in 2003 when, after successes at the polls, the People's Party claimed a second seat in the council and the Christian Democrats were forced to give up a seat.

above: The seven members of the Swiss government, 1999

1971 | Women's right to vote introduced

1990 | Women's suffrage established in Appenzell

2000 | New constitution passed

2001 | Referendum against joining EU

2002 | Joins UN

London, Trafalgar Square, ca. 1950

Great Britain: From Commonwealth to European Union since 1945

Despite the loss of its former position as a superpower, the ❶ United Kingdom was influential in the global reorganization after 1945. As a close ally of the United States, politically the country stood opposed to the Soviet Union in the division of Europe and the world. Great Britain was one of the founding members of the United Nations and is a permanent member of its Security Council. The process of decolonization contributed to fundamental changes in the country and its foreign policies. Since 1973, Great Britain has been a critical but active member of the European Community.

The Transformation of a Global Power

Great Britain's foreign policies after 1945 were determined by the confrontation of the Cold War and decolonization.

Winston Churchill, the British prime minister until July 1945, played a decisive role in the conferences of the Allied powers during the war and took a hard line toward his erstwhile partner Joseph Stalin. In the ❷ postwar Potsdam Conference, the Allies reached relatively consensual agreements on the division of zones of occupation, but the conflicting policies of the Cold War began soon afterward. The British had little room to maneuver in the shadow of the new superpowers, the United States and the USSR. The debt caused by the war tied the country to the United States, to which it already had a sense of connection through their historically and culturally determined "special relationship." As founding member of the ❸ United Nations and a former Ally, Great Britain was granted a permanent seat on the UN Security Council.

Signing of the UN charter, 1946

In 1945, British possessions still spanned a quarter of the Earth. However, by 1947, ❺ India, the centerpiece of the empire, had been granted independence, and almost all of the British colonies cut ties with their former motherland within the next 20 years. They stayed united as the British Commonwealth of Nations, later renamed the Commonwealth of Nations. To this day the British monarch is the head of the Commonwealth, although this position holds no political authority.

Just how limited London's international influence had become was demonstrated particularly in the ❹ Suez Crisis of 1956. Together with France, Britain occupied the Suez Canal after it was nationalized by Egyptian President Nasser. The operation failed because of the opposition of the Soviets and the Americans. Politics were no longer possible without both superpowers.

Elizabeth II

Born in 1926, Princess Elizabeth married Philip Mountbatten, who was given the title the Duke of Edinburgh, in 1947. She succeeded her father, George VI, to the throne in 1952. Queen Elizabeth II has been the head of state of the monarchy of Great Britain for half a century and thus also the head of the 54 member states composing the Commonwealth of Nations. She embodies continuity in a time when Britain has fundamentally altered.

Elizabeth II, queen of the United Kingdom and Northern Ireland, head of the Commonwealth, ca. 1953

Potsdam Conference, July 17–August 2, 1945; Churchill, Truman, and Stalin in front of Cecilienhof Palace

Warships on the Suez Canal, November 1956

Lord Mountbatten, General Governor of India, with his wife during a celebration in the seat of the governor, New Delhi, 1948

1945 | Labor government under Clement Attlee
17 Jul–2 Aug 1945 | Potsdam Conference
1946 | Bank of England nationalized
1947 | India's independence
4 Sep 1949 | NATO founded
1949 | Iron and steel industries nationalized

Postwar Economic Development

Extensive social and economic reforms were carried out in Britain after the war in order to alleviate the postwar problems. Economic and political involvement and cooperation with the Continent increased.

After ❻ World War II, in the United Kingdom, a national consensus calling for better living conditions emerged, which allowed a fundamental political and social restructuring of the state. In 1945, the newly elected Labor government of Prime Minister ❼ Clement Attlee instituted an extensive program of state welfare reform, featuring the introduction of a free national health service and unemployment insurance. The ❽ Bank of England was nationalized in 1946, followed by telecommunications, civil aviation, major sections of the energy and transport sectors, and in 1949 the iron and steel industries. The pendulum swung back in 1951 when Churchill returned to office for a second term, and he and his Conservative successors steered again toward economic liberalism. This meant a temporary break from further development of the welfare state and ushered in the beginning of reprivatization.

7 Clement Attlee, photograph, ca. 1935

Due to its very close economic links to the nations of the Commonwealth and its international interests that transcended Europe, Great Britain initially remained outside the newly founded European Community. Nevertheless, to intensify its economic contacts and trade with the Continent, Great Britain cofounded the European Free Trade Association in 1960. However, this contract group could not compete with the economic success of the larger European body, and in 1973 Britain chose to join the European Community after a first attempt in 1963 was vetoed by the French President de Gaulle. Military and political ties to the Continent and the United States were guaranteed through its ❾ NATO membership.

6 Damage in London after an air raid; the cupola of St. Paul's Cathedral in the background, photograph, 1941

The European Free Trade Association

The European Free Trade Association (EFTA) was founded in Stockholm on January 4, 1960, with the aim of promoting growth and prosperity in the member countries and trade relations and economic cooperation in Western Europe and the world. Its founding members were Austria, Denmark, Great Britain, Norway, Portugal, Sweden, and Switzerland, later joined by Finland, Iceland, and Liechtenstein. Because Austria, Denmark, Finland, Great Britain, Portugal, and Sweden have since joined the European Union, EFTA now has only four member states. With the exception of Switzerland, these EFTA states formed the European Economic Area in 1994 to participate in the Single Market with the EU member states.

above: Conference of the EFTA Council of Ministers in Bern, October 11, 1960

8 Bank of England, built from 1788 to 1833, photograph, 2000

9 The British foreign secretary Anthony Eden (middle) at a NATO Conference in Paris, 1952

1951	Churchill reelected
1952	Elizabeth II crowned
1952	NATO Conference in Paris
1956	Suez Crisis
1973	Britain joins EU
4 Jan 1960	EFTA founded

British Domestic Politics from the 1960s to the Present

Relative economic prosperity reigned in Great Britain through the 1960s. Thereafter, the country was gripped by a long-lasting economic crisis.

Britain, the birthplace of industrialization, had already lost its industrial and technical lead to European and American competition as far back as 1900, but as London was then the flourishing ❶ hub of world trade, the British did not tailor their economic policies to this development. When the pound continually weakened during the 1960s, however, the roots of the economic crisis were laid bare: The British economy threatened to collapse as a result of outdated production facilities, loss of production through numerous strikes, and the overstretching of the budget through steadily rising social expenditures. Conservative and Labor governments replaced each other, neither able to control the financial crisis.

Beginning in 1979, the newly elected Conservative prime minister, Margaret Thatcher, followed strict liberal economic policies. These included the state's withdrawal from the economy, extensive privatization, and tax relief, but also a ❸ reduction in workers's rights and state social benefits. As a result, inflation slowed and investment rates increased, but large numbers of companies also went bankrupt. The number of unemployed reached a record three million in August 1982, and the disparity in incomes widened even more. With decreasing popularity in the electorate, the Conservative Party rebelled at the beginning of the 1990s, when a further recession was begun and Thatcher wanted to introduce a ❹ poll tax despite nationwide resistance. The party elected ❷ John Major her successor as prime minister in 1990, but the privatization of railways, postal services, and coal mining that he implemented was no more popular. In 1992 the value of the ❺ pound fell dramatically again, forcing Britain to pull out of the European Monetary System, which controls monetary stability in Europe.

The parliamentary elections of 1997 brought a landslide victory for the Labor party under the leadership of Tony Blair. Under the motto "New Labor," Blair attempted to find a "third way"— one that would equally consider free enterprise and social demands—in which to lead the country. In 1999, separate parliaments were established in Scotland, Wales, and Northern Ireland. Gordon Brown succeeded Tony Blair in 2007. The Conservative David Cameron took office in 2010.

2 John Major, British prime minister, 1992

1 Royal Exchange in London, 2000

3 Miners on strike in Nottinghamshire, 1984

4 Demonstrators against the poll tax, 1991

5 Hustle and bustle at the stock exchange in London

Margaret Thatcher

The chemist and lawyer Margaret Thatcher was a Conservative member of Parliament in the House of Commons from 1959 to 1992. She became leader of the opposition in 1975, then prime minister from 1979 to 1990; since 1992, she has sat in the House of Lords as Baroness Thatcher of Kesteven. As a result of her inflexible determination, she was dubbed the "Iron Lady." The term "Thatcherism" was coined for the reduction of state economic and social involvement and giving the "powers of free enterprise" free reign in the battle against inflation.

Margaret Thatcher, 1983

from 1949 | Pound devalued
1960 | Great Britain applies to join EEC
1973 | Great Britain joins EEC
from May 1979 | Margaret Thatcher elected Prime Minister
1982 | War over the Falkland Islands
1982 | Record unemployment

British Foreign Policy from the 1960s to the Present

Skepticism of the European Community in Great Britain remained even after the country joined it. The relationship to the United States has characterized foreign policies.

As early as 1960 and shortly after the founding of the European Free Trade Association, Great Britain applied for membership in the European Economic Community. The application was denied twice due to the veto of France, but in 1973 Great Britain became a member. By that point, though, the growth spurt that the EEC members had experienced as a result of the introduction of the free market had already slackened. Instead, the explosion in the price of oil in 1973 and the resulting economic crisis put the brakes on economic development. Consequently, EEC membership hardly had a noticeable positive effect in Britain. In 1984, Prime Minister Thatcher was able to gain a considerable reduction in Britain's membership contributions to the community.

Great Britain's relationship to the European Community remained inconsistent also in the ensuing period. The criticism reached a high point when the European Union imposed a ban on British beef imports in 1996 in the face of massive outbreaks of the cattle disease BSE on the island. Anxiety about being dictated to by the EU leadership in Brussels is generally behind the British skepticism of the Union. Nevertheless, the establishment of closer ties to the Continent continues. An illustration and important contribution to this is the ❾ railway tunnel under the English Channel, which connects Great Britain and France and was completed in 1994. The British government pulled out of financing the project, but an international consortium guaranteed the completion of the project.

British Prime Minister Tony Blair (left) and US President George W. Bush, 2004

Alongside European involvement, the historical relationship with the United States characterizes British foreign policy. American satellite information helped the British win victory over Argentina in the ❽ war over the Falkland Islands, a British crown colony, in 1982. As its most significant ❼ ally, Great Britain has assisted the United States in its ❻ military actions against Iraq.

British aircraft carrier on its way to the Gulf region, January 2003

War over the British crown colony Falkland Islands: British paratroopers search Argentinian prisoners of war for weapons, 1982

Irish construction workers celebrate the breakthrough of the first tube of the railway tunnel under the English Channel, 1990

BSE

Bovine spongiform encephalopathy (BSE), commonly called "mad cow disease," is a disorder that causes changes in the brain. The processing of infected sheep carcasses into animal feed enabled the transmission of the disease to cattle and eventually even to humans. The disease first appeared in Great Britain in 1986. The European Union's 1996 import ban on British beef led to a severe crisis in livestock farming. So far, only control on the production of feed meal or the banning of the use of sheep carcasses in feed production in 2000 has proven effective in the fight against BSE.

Early diagnosis of BSE is still problematic

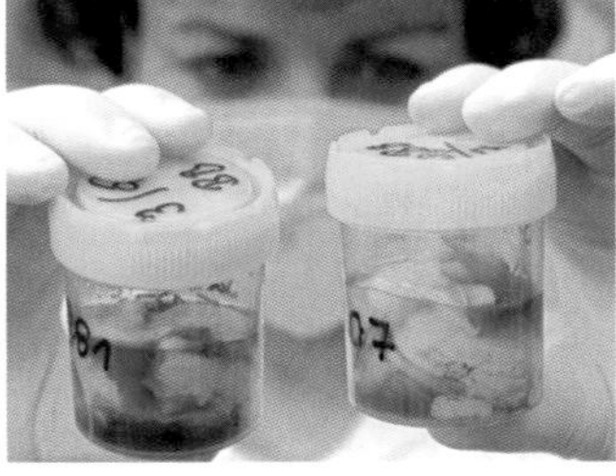
The brain of a cow is examined in a laboratory with safety precautions

1990 | Prime Minister John Major elected

1992 | Pound devalued again

1994 | Euro Tunnel opened

1996 | BSE crisis

1997 | Tony Blair wins elections

IRELAND SINCE 1945

The Republic of Ireland *(Eire)* left the British Commonwealth in 1949. Despite this, economic relations with the United Kingdom remained close, due to historical ties and geographic proximity. Ireland, more than Britain, benefited from joining the European Union in 1973. The country rose to become a prosperous EU nation. This independent flourishing growth facilitated the achievement of an agreement in the ❶ Northern Ireland conflict.

Scene from the civil war in Belfast, mother with child passes while a British soldier holds a machine gun, 1996

Anglo–Irish Ulster agreement is signed; British Prime Minister Thatcher (right) and her Irish counterpart Fitzgerald, November 15, 1985

Economic Development

The Irish economy has been growing steadily since the 1960s. It was also given a boost by Ireland's EU membership, as a result of which capital was invested in the national economy.

Ireland remained neutral during World War II. Nonetheless, the country suffered under the postwar recession, which was alleviated by monies allocated through the Marshall Plan. In the 1950s, Ireland again went through an economic depression. The balance of payments was negative, inflation high, and the number of emigrants grew steadily. Some improvement was seen at the end of the decade. The ruling Fianna Fáil party, under Seán F. Lemass, who served as prime minister from 1959 to 1966, used the ensuing economic boom to push through liberal economic policies.

Heads of state and government of the European Community in front of the state department of the Irish capital in Dublin, 1990

Great Britain was and remains Ireland's most important trading partner. In rapid succession, the two island nations concluded numerous trade agreements, and the tense ❷ relationship between them relaxed through the granting of mutual advantages in the economic exchange. Irish economic policies, however, also aimed to conquer other markets, specifically the ❹, ❺ tourism industry. The economic situation improved, if not without interruptions; inflation rates and the ❻ number of unemployed repeatedly shot up. ❸ Membership in the European Community in 1973 had long-term positive effects on the Irish economy; financial aid allocated by the community was invested, with an eye on the future, in the transport and education systems. As the economy grew, unemployment and emigration were reduced. The population soared from 2.9 million in 1970 to 4.2 million in 2006. After its dynamic growth, Ireland has severely suffered under the global financial crisis of 2008/2009.

House on the scenic Ring of Kerry with a 99-mile (159 km) coastline, one of the finest in Europe

Pub in Dublin, 2002

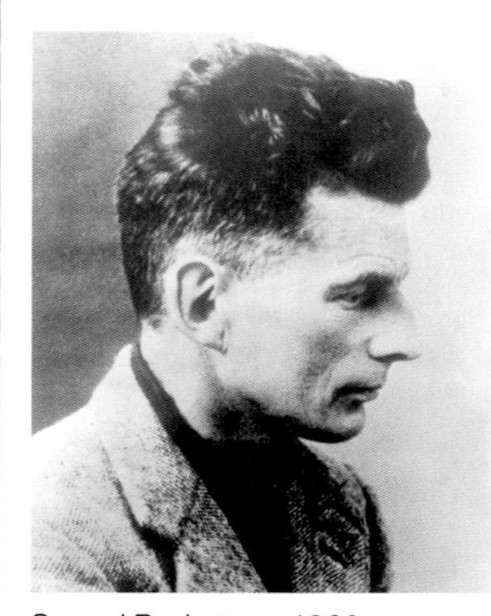

Samuel Beckett, ca. 1960

Modern Irish Literature

Irish literature experienced a phase of renewal and flowering in the 20th century, in English as well as Gaelic. After independence, there was a decline in the heroic mood and a spread in the tone of disenchantment. P. O'Leary and P. H. Pearse wrote short stories in Gaelic. Internationally renowned novelists included Liam O'Flaherty, Flann O'Brien, and Brendan Behan, who wrote in both Gaelic and English. James Joyce gained world fame with his novel Ulysses, *as did his friend, the dramatist and poet Samuel Beckett, who won the Nobel Prize for Literature in 1969. His drama of the absurd,* Waiting for Godot, *was one of the seminal pieces of modern theater. Ireland produced yet another important dramatist in Sean O'Casey.*

Old man begs in the streets of Dublin, 2003

1921 | Division of Ireland
1949 | Ireland leaves Commonwealth
1955 | Ireland joins UN
1959-66 | Prime Minister Seán F. Lemass
1967 | Northern Ireland Civil Rights Association founded

The Northern Ireland Conflict

After seceding from the Commonwealth, the young republic became a member of several international organizations. Its domestic politics were overshadowed by the Northern Ireland conflict.

The separation from the British Commonwealth and the proclamation of the Republic of Ireland in 1949 dissolved the last constitutional ties to the United Kingdom. Citizens of Ireland nevertheless continued to enjoy free entry to England and voting rights there. New links were soon created within international organizations; Ireland joined the United Nations in 1955. However, the country that was divided in 1921 was shaken in the 1950s by renewed eruptions of the conflict over Northern Ireland. The banned Irish Republican Army (IRA) made its presence felt once more with attacks on posts on the ❽, ⓬ border with the British province of Northern Ireland. The ❾ Irish government tried to master these attacks through common action with authorities in the north, which resulted in a government crisis in the Irish republic.

In 1967, the Northern Ireland Civil Rights Association was founded in Northern Ireland as a civil rights movement intended to fight for equality for the Catholics in the north. However, the protests that were peaceful at first were answered with violence. A bloody civil war—the "Troubles"—developed in Northern Ireland in the late 1960s in which close to 4,000 people had died by the end of the 1990s. Two antagonists faced each other in the North: the ⓫ Protestant unionists, who wanted to retain the union with Great Britain, and the Catholic ❼ nationalists or republicans, who sought to merge with Ireland. A climax of the confrontations was reached on January 30, 1972, ⓭ Bloody Sunday, when 13 Catholics were shot by the British military. The British government dissolved the Northern Irish parliament in March, to which the IRA responded with numerous bombings. Negotiations between Dublin, Belfast, and London failed.

A breakthrough was achieved with the ❿ Good Friday Agreement, concluded on April 10, 1998, and signed by the governments of the United Kingdom and Ireland and the political party leaders of Northern Ireland. Ireland agreed to abstain from its constitutional goal of reunification, cooperation between all the governments was resolved, and the paramilitary units, in particular the IRA, agreed to a decommissioning of weapons. Britain promised a significant troop reduction and police reform, as well as allowing the greater participation by the Catholic Sinn Féin party in the government of Northern Ireland. Separate referendums in both countries helped achieve the success of the agreement. Despite attacks by the Real IRA in 2009, life in Northern Ireland has gradually become less marred by violence.

7 Exterior of a house in a Catholic district of Derry, painted in memory of a schoolgirl who was killed by a rubber bullet fired by a British soldier

10 Prime Minister Tony Blair (center) with the Protestant Ulster Unionist (UUP) David Trimble and the Catholic Social Democrat (SDLP) John Hume in Belfast, 1998

12 British army watchtower, barred as a protection against stone throwers in Derry

8 Road in a Catholic and Protestant area closed off by a steel gate, Belfast, 2004

9 Stormont Castle in Belfast, seat of the parliament and cabinet of Northern Ireland, 2004

11 Painted exterior of a house with a Protestant UFF (Ulster Freedom Fighters) mural, Belfast

13 Bloody Sunday 1972: A member of a British paratrooper unit beats a demonstrator

Beginning of the German-French friendship: President de Gaulle (right) meets the German chancellor Adenauer

France since 1945

France had suffered greatly through World War II. General ❶ de Gaulle's provisional government took action against the collaborators and tackled reconstruction. The Fourth Republic did not last long, however. A revolt in the colony of Algiers led to a crisis in the government and finally to the founding of the Fifth Republic. As president, de Gaulle followed a policy of independence from the power blocs of the Cold War. His successors returned to a stronger engagement within Europe.

From the Fourth to the Fifth Republic 1946–58

In the first postwar decades, France became an industrialized nation. The unstable Fourth Republic collapsed in 1958 and was replaced by a presidential system.

By the end of the war, France was in many regions a ❸ destroyed country. Though Paris was largely intact, other cities, especially ports such as Le Havre and Brest, lay in ruins. After the "cleansing" of society of perhaps thirty or forty thousand actual and supposed collaborators, the ❷ provisional government under Charles de Gaulle began reconstruction. Banks, insurance companies, and large enterprises such as Renault and Air France were nationalized, and welfare reforms were carried out. The state used economic planning to steer development beyond the reconstruction phase, transforming France from a predominantly ❺ agrarian country to an ❻ industrial nation in the second half of the century.

Allied advance towards a damaged city in Normandy, 1944

After de Gaulle resigned, the constitution of the Fourth Republic was adopted on October 13, 1946. The National Assembly gained authority; the president and the government were subordinated to it. Women's suffrage and proportional representation were adopted from the provisional republic, but the latter led to a political division. The government changed almost every six months, which inhibited the functioning of the executive.

Oxen transporting hay in a French village in the 1950s

Citroën DS, the flagship model of the French carmaker, 1960

The Fourth Republic eventually broke down in 1958 over the issue of the ❹ Algerian War of Independence. In order to prevent a military dictatorship and civil war, the National Assembly decided to recall ❼ de Gaulle to power. His government worked out the details of the constitution of the Fifth Republic. It was presented to the public in a referendum and was passed with an overwhelming 79 percent in favor. The Fifth Republic remains in force to this day.

The Fifth French Republic

According to the constitution of the Fifth Republic, adopted in 1958, France is a presidential democracy. The head of state and the head of government both share the running of the country. The president, who is elected directly by the people, however, has had special powers since 1962. He chooses the head of government and the cabinet, is commander in chief of the armed forces, has the right of veto over laws passed by parliament, and has the power to dissolve the National Assembly.

Opening meeting of the National Assembly which decided on the constitution in a liberated Paris, 1944

State crisis after an army putsch in Algiers: demonstration, Paris, May 1958

Charles de Gaulle (right) with President René Coty, 1958

13 Oct 1946 | Constitution of the Fourth Republic

1946–54 | War of liberation in French Indochina

1954 | War of independence begins in Algeria

1956 | Morocco granted independence

1957 | Tunisia granted independence

From Colonial Power to Development Aid

Decolonization was a crisis-ridden process for France, particularly in the case of Algeria, but later new forms of cooperation with former colonies were found.

8 The Viet Minh on top of a shot-down French B26, 1954

A ❽ war of liberation took place in the colony of French Indochina in 1946–1954, involving heavy losses on both sides, after which France declared its withdrawal from the region. The protectorates of Morocco and Tunisia were given independence in 1956 and 1957, respectively, but the colony of Algiers, home to about a million European settlers, was retained as part of France. A law entitled Algerian Muslims to be elected as deputies to the National Assembly in Paris and set up an Algerian legislative assembly with equal representation of French and natives, though the latter outnumbered the former by six to one.The Arab population demanded their freedom and waged a bitter war of ❾ independence after a revolt in 1954. The French military stationed in Algiers acted on its own, taking advantage of the weakness of the Paris government, which was ready to recognize the right of the Algerians to self-determination. Radical French Algerians founded a terror group, the *Organization Armée Secrête* (OAS). Because Egypt was supporting the Algerian freedom movement, France, together with Great Britain, occupied the Suez Canal, but they were forced to withdraw by the United States, the Soviet Union, and the ⓫ United Nations. Against the embittered resistance of several generals, ❿ de Gaulle initiated political negotiations with the Algerian government in exile. The Treaty of Evian of April 8, 1962, brought Algeria independence from France.

The plebiscite to introduce the constitution of the Fifth Republic in 1958 was held not only in the motherland but also in the overseas territories. A rallying point for the colonies was the provision in the constitution for the founding of a "Communauté française;" acceptance of the constitution meant admission into this community. Only Guinea rejected membership. With the amendments to the constitution in 1960, former colonies that had already gained independence could also join, and most of the former French African territories did so.

France sought thereafter to develop equal partnerships with its former colonies. French development aid focused to a great extent on these countries, and cooperation in foreign, security, cultural, and economic policies was regulated by treaties.

9 The Algerian War of Independence 1954–1962: French propaganda postcard with laughing French soldier and Algerian children

10 Charles de Gaulle during his visit to Algiers, June 1958

France's Overseas Possessions

Iles de Saintes, Guadeloupe

The four overseas départements of French Guyana, Guadeloupe, Martinique, and La Réunion are legally almost completely equal in status to the French départements or counties. The French overseas territories of French Polynesia, New Caledonia, and Wallis and Futuna in addition have their own executive and an advisory parliament. French laws are valid there only if expressly so designated, although Paris can intervene in the governing of the land by decree.

11 Suez conflict 1956–1957: A United Nations peacekeeping force watches the retreat of the warring troops

Economic and Domestic Policies of the Fifth Republic since 1958

The constitution of the Fifth Republic concentrated power in the office of president.

After the end of the colonial wars, de Gaulle was able to improve the state finances. ❷ Economic growth soon picked up as trade barriers across Europe fell. However, as French society changed along with the economy, the paternalism and conservatism of de Gaulle and of public life in general seemed to many to be increasingly outdated. In 1968, this frustration among the younger generation erupted into protests after a dispute between students and university authorities. It broadened when unionized workers joined the radical students and intellectuals in challenging the government. ❻ Demonstrations, factory sit-ins, and ❹ street fighting took place, culminating in a general strike. Although de Gaulle survived the immediate state crisis, he was weakened and resigned in 1969.

His successor, ❶ Georges Pompidou (1969–1974), introduced reforms, but the energy crisis of 1973 proved a setback. The government of ❺ Valéry Giscard d'Estaing (1974–1981) was particularly successful in foreign affairs; together with German chancellor Helmut Schmidt, he instituted an annual summit meeting of the heads of state of the leading industrialized nations, then known as the Group of Six or G-6, which was meant to fight the economic crisis. In France, however, unemployment continued to rise.

A left-wing government came to power with the election of ❸ François Mitterrand (1981–1995) as president and the victory of his Socialist party in the parliamentary elections of 1981. Mitterrand sought more state planning and a redistribution of income, but the budget deficit and a double-digit rise in prices forced him to change course by 1983. His room to maneuver was further reduced by the establishment of the European Common Market in 1984.

Mitterrand lost his absolute majority in parliament in 1986, and the Gaullist ❼ Jacques Chirac became prime minister, marking the beginning of the phase of "cohabitation." To avoid such forced coalitions, France introduced the majority vote. However, the 1997 elections also led to a cohabitation government in which President Chirac had to share his power with Lionel Jospin, the socialist prime minister. Chirac was followed by the Gaullist Nicolas Sarkozy in 2007.

1 Inauguration ceremony of the French President Georges Pompidou (front) in Paris, June 20,1969

2 Baker's shop in France, ca. 1960

3 François Mitterrand, 1991

4 Students in street fights with the police, Paris, 1968

5 French President Valéry Giscard d'Estaing (left) meeting the German Chancellor Helmut Schmidt in Bonn, capital of West Germany (FRG), 1975

6 Student demonstrations, Paris, 1968

Cohabitation

In France's semipresidential system of government, both the president and the prime minister have important powers. "Cohabitation" is the name given to the situation in which the two offices are held by different parties. The two leaders must continue to conduct affairs of state despite their political rivalry. In 1984, Mitterrand made a tacit agreement with Chirac over the division of responsibilities: the president took the lead in foreign policy while the prime minister concentrated on domestic policy.

7 President Jaques Chirac, 2003

24 Jan 1960 | Revolt breaks out in Algeria
21-22 Apr 1961 | French army coup in Algeria
1963 | Franco-German Treaty
May 1968 | Unrest and general strike
28 Apr 1969 | Resignation of de Gaulle

France in Europe

De Gaulle's policy of a "Europe of Nation States" stressed the autonomy of France. The "grande nation" has nonetheless been central to the European integration project since the 1950s.

France and Germany have long been considered the ❽ engines of the European Union. Both nations have played key roles in shaping the evolution of postwar Europe. France's role has undergone significant changes over the last 50 years. After the bitter experience of defeat on the part of the German Reich during World War II, its first concern was to establish safeguards against its neighbor, in cooperation with Great Britain and the Benelux countries. The first European treaties—agreements on atomic energy and the joint management of coal and steel—were signed with the intention of making a future war between the two nations impossible.

The new Airbus A380 jumbo jet, a collaborative industrial venture of France, Germany, the UK, and Spain, 2004

As France's colonial empire dissolved, the country's leaders increasingly looked to ❾ Europe. However, France was still concerned with further securing and building up its own independent position of power within and outside the community. The ❿ Franco-German treaty of 1963 tied the onetime adversaries tightly together. London's application to join the European Community was twice vetoed by de Gaulle because he feared that Great Britain's entry would endanger France's leading role in Europe. France's withdrawal from the military part of NATO also served primarily to demonstrate France's independence.

After de Gaulle's resignation, France's European policies changed. Under Pompidou, France finally agreed to Britain's EC membership; under Giscard d'Estaing and Mitterrand, France reengaged with the process of integration. As president of the European Commission, Frenchman Jacques Delors was also a key architect in the launch of the European single market in the 1980s. The historic 2004 enlargement, which saw eight former communist countries join the EU, was the culmination of a ⓫ long political process supported by France. However, in recent years there have been signs that the French people have become increasingly anxious about the direction of the European project. The French rejected the European Constitution in a referendum in 2005. The Lisbon Treaty was ratified in 2008 without a popular vote.

70th German-French conference; in the center Jaques Chirac, directly to his left the German Chancellor Helmut Kohl; Weimar, Germany, 1997

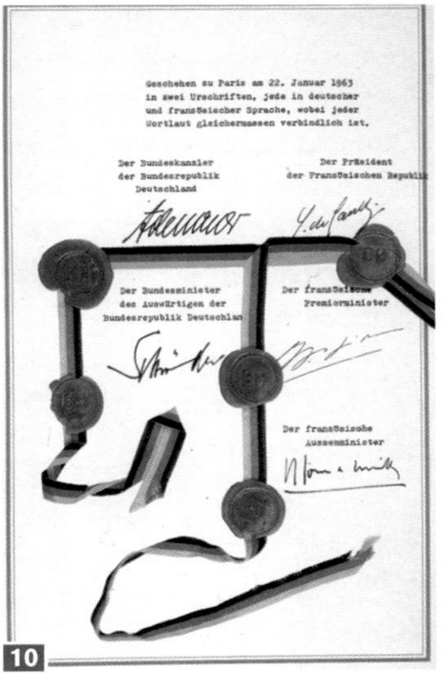
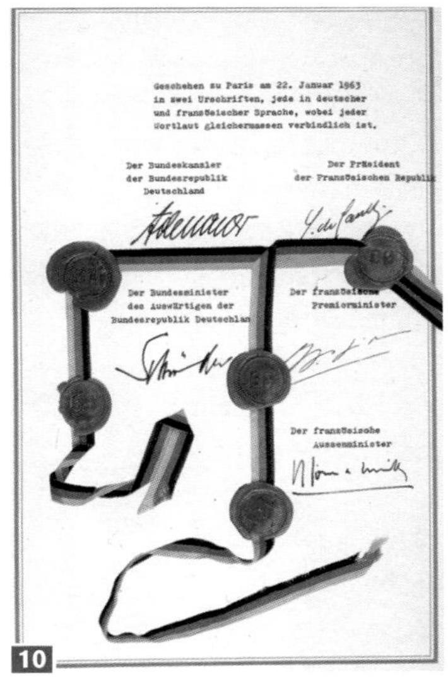

Geschehen zu Paris am 22. Januar 1963
in zwei Urschriften, jede in deutscher
und französischer Sprache, wobei jeder
Wortlaut gleichermassen verbindlich ist.

Der Bundeskanzler
der Bundesrepublik
Deutschland

Der Präsident
der Französischen Republik

Der Bundesminister
des Auswärtigen der
Bundesrepublik Deutschland

Der französische
Premierminister

Der französische
Aussenminister

The Franco-German treaty, signed by Charles de Gaulle and Chancellor Konrad Adenauer, in Paris, 1963

Heads of states and governments after finalizing plans for the admission of new members to the European Union, Amsterdam summit, 1997

François Mitterrand

François Mitterrand joined the French resistance in World War II and in 1944 became a minister in de Gaulle's provisional government. He was a member of parliament and a minister in the Fourth Republic. In the Fifth Republic, he united the splintered left in the Parti Socialiste, of which he served as chairman until 1980. In 1981 Mitterrand became France's first Socialist president and served until 1995. After initial setbacks in economic policy, he withdrew to a more statesman-like role. Mitterrand smoothed the way to German reunification and gave impetus to the European integration project.

President Mitterrand throws flowers into the River Seine, where right-wing extremists murdered a Moroccan, Paris, 1995

1969–74 | Pompidou presidency

1974–81 | Giscard d'Estaing presidency

1981 | Mitterrand elected president

1986 | Chirac becomes prime minister

1 May 2004 | Enlargement of the EU to 25 members

Belgium, the Netherlands, and Luxembourg since 1945

After the end of World War II, Belgium, the Netherlands, and ❶ Luxembourg decided to cooperate economically, culturally, and politically under the collective name Benelux. They integrated themselves into the emerging Western security structures, giving up their traditional neutrality by joining NATO. The Benelux states were also founding members of the European Economic Community in 1957. Within this framework, all three countries rapidly recovered from the war and became prosperous and stable liberal democracies. The course of development of each state differed in some important respects, however.

Street decoration marks the marriage of the Luxembourgian grand duke, 1953

Flags of the member states in front of the NATO headquarters in Brussels

The Benelux Idea

During the war, Belgium, the Netherlands, and Luxembourg were all occupied by the Nazis. Out of this common experience the Benelux Union was created. All three countries became respected bastions of liberal democracy and provided many leaders for international organizations.

Belgium, the Netherlands, and Luxembourg were among the first victims of the Nazi war of conquest. These traumas left a particularly strong mark on Luxembourg, where in the postwar period French language and culture were privileged over German. In order to be able to demonstrate more strength in the future, the governments in exile of the three nations decided upon a customs and economic union in September 1944, introducing the collective name "Benelux;" the customs union came into force on January 1, 1948.

NATO Secretary General Willy Claes, 1995

In 1949 the three countries agreed on a "pre-union," which was meant to coordinate their economic structures and dismantle trade restrictions. In 1958, a full economic union was established in the Treaty of Benelux Economic Union. Internal borders were abolished in 1970. From then on, the three countries spoke with one voice, gaining added weight through their common actions, and this became a model for the process of European unification.

With a total population of 27 million at the beginning of the 21st century, the Benelux states are jointly the fourth largest economic player in the world. Even if the Benelux Union in recent times has been eclipsed by the steadily expanding ❺ European Union, the continuing close cooperation ensures the three countries power to achieve their aims that is many times greater than other, solitary EU member states.

The seat of the Council of Europe in Brussels, 2003

Another political change took place in the postwar era. By taking part in the Marshall Plan, the Benelux states firmly aligned with the US during the Cold War period, ending their traditional neutrality. They joined the United Nations as founding members in 1945, and in 1948 they signed the Brussels Treaty with Britian and France, seeking to establish collective defense arrangements. They also became founding members of ❷, ❻ NATO in 1949. Of the ten NATO secretaries general, four have come from the Benelux countries: Paul-Henri Spaak and ❸ Willy Claes from Belgium, and Dirk Stikker and ❹ Joseph Luns from the Netherlands.

NATO Secretary General Joseph Luns, 1976

Meeting of the NATO Security Council in Mons, Belgium, 1949

1945 | Benelux states join the United Nations
1 Jan 1948 | Benelux customs union
1948 | Brussels Treaty concerning defense
1949 | Benelux entry into NATO
1951 | Baudouin I accedes to the throne

Belgium from Centralized to Federal State

After the war, the center of ❼ Belgium's economy shifted to the Flemish part of the country. The conflict between the Flemish and the Walloons led to the establishment of a federal state.

Belgian heavy industry, which had emerged almost unscathed by World War II, provided the country with a strong economic base in the late 1940s. Once the importance of industry diminished, however, Belgium fell into an economic crisis. This was offset by the positive effects of the Benelux Union and membership in the European Economic Community that was founded in 1957. Whereas the Francophone Walloon part of the country had dominated the economy in the preceding decades, new investment flowed primarily into the Flemish areas, especially the ❿ port of Antwerp. The Flemish region now took over the lead role, which stirred up conflict between the two ethnic groups and repeatedly led to domestic crises. Several constitutional reforms were made, and Belgium became a federally organized parliamentary democracy in 1993, composed of the regions of ❽ Flanders, Wallonia, and the capital region of ❾ Brussels. The economy and administration have been decentralized, and the regions were granted cultural autonomy.

8 Flemish coat of arms

The early postwar years were overshadowed by a dispute concerning King Leopold III, who stood accused of treason and collaboration with the Nazis. Leopold returned to the Belgian throne in 1950, but unrest forced him to abdicate in favor of his son Baudouin I in 1951. Baudouin was able to hold the country together through strict impartiality in the ethnic conflict. He was followed on the throne by his brother, Albert II, but Albert did not come into a trouble-free inheritance. A bribery scandal in which many ministers were involved led to the resignation of the government in 1994, and new elections brought a breakthrough for the right-wing parties.

Belgium was shaken between 1990 and 2000 by numerous corruption scandals and the botched investigation of child molester and murderer Marc Dutroux. In October of 1996, 325,000 citizens gathered for the ⓫ "White March" in Brussels—a silent demonstration against political intrigue, moral decay, and the laxity of the justice system in the trial of the pedophile serial killer and his associates.

10 Heavy cranes load ships on the docks of the Belgian port of Antwerp

7 The "Atomium", the main attraction at the 1958 world exhibition in Brussels

9 Town hall in the gothic quarter of the Belgian capital of Brussels

Baudouin I

Baudouin I, King of the Belgians from 1951

Baudouin (Boudewijn in Flemish), born in 1930, returned to Belgium in 1950 with his father Leopold III, who had been taken prisoner by the Nazis and transported to Germany. Baudouin succeeded to the throne in 1951. In 1960 he declared the Belgian Congo's independence. King Baudouin died in 1993 after a popular 42-year reign. The Belgian royal house serves as a unifying and stabilizing factor in a federal state threatened by cultural divisions.

11 Mass demonstrations in the wake of a pedophile scandal, 1996

1958 | Treaty of Benelux Economic Union
1960 | Independence of Belgian Congo
1970 | Abolition of internal borders
1993 | Death of Baudouin I
Oct 1996 | White March in Brussels

Luxembourg

Luxembourg's development has been determined by its relationship to its neighbors. The steel industry and financial sector are equally dependent on cooperation with the bordering nations.

As early as the 1920s, ❶ Luxembourg, an independent grand-duchy, bordered to the west and north by Belgium, was able to establish a customs, trade, and currency union through its economic association with Belgium. The iron and steel industries were of particular international significance because of the rich ore deposits in Lorraine. Furthermore, Luxembourg was of high strategic importance for armies attempting to move through Belgium into France. After the end of World War II, the Grand Duchy of Luxembourg began by joining the Benelux customs union and then became a champion of the ❷ European Coal and Steel Community (ECSC) and was thus involved in the process of European unification. Appropriately, the ECSC high authority chose Luxembourg as its seat in 1952; the treaty had a fixed term of 50 years, and the high authority was abolished in 2002. Other important European offices are also located in Luxembourg, including the ❺ European Court of Justice and the European Investment Bank.

Signing of the ECSC treaty, 18 April 1951

Jaques Santer, president of the EU commission, 1996

Luxembourg gave up its neutrality in 1949 and joined NATO. Its foreign policies are almost exclusively determined by EU policies. The long terms of office of Luxembourg politicians especially qualify them for the European stage. Among them are ❸ Jacques Santer, president of the European Commission from 1995 to 1999, and the current prime minister of Luxembourg, Jean-Claude Juncker, who has made a name for himself as a negotiator within the European Union. Being a small nation, Luxembourg is very intent on not being left out of European committees. Since 2003, the Benelux states have been demanding a commission that is smaller and therefore more capable of acting, whose seats would be equally allocated according to a rotation system. Luxembourg is one of the most important ❹ finance centers of the world. Financial management is of vital significance to the country. EU efforts to create an interest tax and the abolishment of bankers' confidentiality are therefore seen as an economic threat. A related EU law was prevented by Luxembourg's veto in 1989.

The old town of Luxembourg along the River Alzette, in the Grund Valley

Building of the DG Bank Luxembourg on the Kirchberg in Luxembourg, 1997

The original seat of the European Court of Justice in the Kirchberg area where many European institutions are clustered, Luxembourg

Charlemagne Prize to the People of Luxembourg

The people of Luxembourg were awarded the Charlemagne Prize by the city of Aachen in 1986. Since 1950, this award has been presented annually for services to European unity. The Luxembourgers were deemed worthy of the prize because, as founding members of the European Union, they were among the first committed Europeans, and Luxembourg politicians have made essential contributions to the unity of Europe. The medallion was given to Grand Duke Jean representing the citizens of Luxembourg.

Former Grand Duke Jean with his wife, 1953

1945 | Independence of the Dutch East Indies
1949 | Luxembourg joins NATO
1952–2002 | Seat of the European Coal and Steel Community in Luxembourg
1958 | Construction of the Europort begun

The Netherlands

After World War II, the Dutch economy was dominated by industry and services. The social structures also changed.

The Netherlands conducted massive "cleansings" and criminal prosecutions of collaborators after 1945. It was estimated that close to two per cent of the Dutch population had collaborated with the German occupiers. Over 90,000 people were arrested and the Dutch Nazi Anton Mussert was condemned to death. Unlike neighboring Belgium, the Netherlands had suffered great ❻ destruction in the war, but with assistance from the Marshall Plan, it achieved a rapid recovery. The Netherlands could no longer continue as an agricultural and colonial power. The Dutch East Indies (modern Indonesia) had been occupied by Japan and in 1945 proclaimed its independence, which was recognized by the Netherlands after difficult negotiations and fighting in 1949. In 1963 the territory of Western New Guinea was handed over to Indonesia, and in 1975 Surinam gained independence.

The process of decolonization contributed to the Netherlands' transformation to an ❾ industry- and service-oriented nation after the war. The Dutch iron processing, electrical appliance, and ❿ petrochemical industries are among the most successful economic sectors worldwide. The Dutch social structure also changed in the mid-1970s. Up until then, individual social groups had lived side by side as "pillars," culturally inclusive communities with their own social facilities who hardly ever came in contact with one other. There were Catholic, Protestant, Social Democrat, and Liberal pillars. As religions lost their significance, these firmly set worlds gradually dissolved. The student unrest of the 1960s also provided for a more porous social structure.

Juliana of the Netherlands

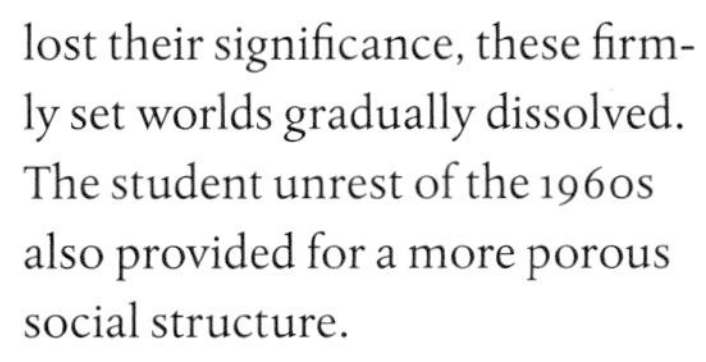

After 1945, a coalition government of Catholics and the social democratic Labor party was established; it lasted until 1958 when Labor withdrew. Thereafter, the Netherlands was governed by a shifting coalition of centrist parties; Labor has sat on the government benches only occasionally since then.

The Dutch Queen Beatrix, 2004

The monarchy suffered a crisis in the 1970s. The husband of ❼ Queen Juliana, Prince Bernhard, was involved in a bribery scandal and in 1976 resigned from his military offices. ❽ Princess Beatrix, the heir to the crown, had married a German diplomat in 1966, triggering heated domestic political debates. Nevertheless, after her mother's abdication in 1980, Beatrix was able to once again win over the people to the idea of monarchy.

Ruins of the Dutch city of Rotterdam following the bombardment,1940

The Europort

Between 1958 and 1981, an outer harbor for Rotterdam was constructed on a branch of the Rhine for large ships. The Europort is one of the most modern and, when measured by goods turnover, largest port complexes in the world. Grouped around it are the oil and chemical industries and warehouses for automobiles, grain, and iron ore.

above: Deap-sea container ships in the Europort

The Erasmus Bridge that spans the River Maas, Rotterdam

Oil tank of the Shell refinery in Rotterdam

1963 | Independence of West New Guinea
1975 | Independence of Surinam
1980 | Beatrix becomes Queen of the Netherlands
1986 | People of Luxembourg receive the Charlemagne Prize

ITALY since 1945

Although Italy suffered considerable ❷ destruction during World War II, the former ally of the German Reich was rapidly reconstructed with the help of American financial aid. The ❶ Italian economic miracle of the 1950s saw a boom in its film industry, tourism, and industrial production. The Italian political system is "stably unstable." A serious problem in the country was, and continues to be, organized crime and corruption, which in individual cases reaches all the way into state institutions and the economy. The economic policy system collapsed in the 1990s, though this did not result in structural changes.

"Fiat 1400, the progressive car," advertisement for Italy's leading car manufacturer, 1951

Italy's Political System since 1945

Italy founded a constitutional republic after World War II. The Christian Democratic party was a member of the subsequent governments in shifting ruling coalitions.

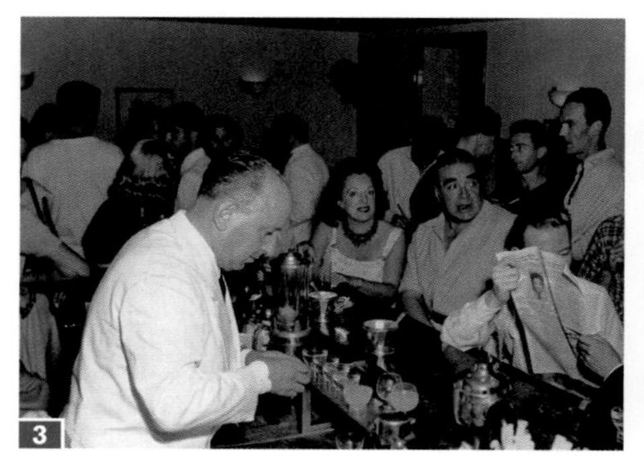

Guests in Harry's Bar in Venice, ca. 1950

Aldo Moro, ca. 1971

As the result of a plebiscite on June 2, 1946, Italy became a republic with a parliamentary democratic constitution. ❺ King Umberto II, who had taken over from Victor Emmanuel on May 9th, 1945, in the hope of preserving the monarchy which had been gravely compromised by its tolerance of Mussolini's unconstitutional regime, left the country. The Republican majority was two million from the 23, 400,000 votes cast. The centrist Christian Democratic party became the leading force in politics. It governed from 1947 to 1953 with an absolute majority in a Chamber of 556 seats and thereafter in changing coalitions where it regularly had more than a third of the votes. The Socialist party lost its number two position in the parliamentary landscape in the 1950s to the Communists, while the Neo-Fascists established themselves on the extreme right. Between 1945 and 1989, there were 48 changes of government. The causes for this were peculiarities in the Italian constitution as well as the attempt to keep the Communists permanently out of government coalitions.

In the second half of the 1970s, Christian Democratic president ❹ Aldo Moro was in favor of coming to grips with the economic crisis by means of a "historical compromise," that is, with the support of the Communists, but he was kidnapped and murdered in March 1978 by the leftist terrorist group the Red Brigade.

Government crises continued to shake Italy into the early 1990s. Diverse coalition governments were formed with three or four parties. There was practically no effective opposition left. The parties permeated Italian ❸ social and political life almost completely, creating a client or patronage system that was maintained through corruption.

The damaged monastery of Montecassino, 1944

King Umberto II at his wedding to Maria Jose, Rome

The Italian Constitution

Italy's constitution was a compromise, drafted in the postwar era by an amalgamation of anti-Fascist parties and came into force in 1948. Characteristic of it is the great opportunity given to the citizens for taking part in legislation as well as the composition of the two-chamber parliament. A vote of no confidence in the government from one chamber alone can bring it down. The president has little formal influence and no authority to set guidelines. In a coalition, this arrangement considerably weakens the executive powers of the government.

House of Representatives, Italian Parliament, Rome, 1999

1929 | The Vatican becomes a sovereign state

1946 | Departure of Umberto II, the last king

2 Jun 1946 | Parliamentary-democratic constitution

1947 | End of the coalition with the Communists

1949 | Founding member of NATO

Economic Development and Integration into the European Union

he Marshall Plan and European integration assisted Italy's economic development and stabilized conomic policy.

7 igning of the Treaty of Rome in 1957; on the right, e Italian President Antonio Segni

8 Alscide de Gasperi, ca. 1950

'he ❾ Partito Comunista Italiao (PCI) was one of the strongest Communist parties in postwar Vestern Europe. The US-funded Marshall Plan was designed to estrict its influence and prevent t from gaining further support mong the poverty-stricken postvar population. In 1947, President ❽ Alcide de Gasperi, a Christian Democrat, terminated the coalition with the Communists, who rom then on remained excluded rom government. The reconstruction of the ❿ economy and he implementation of social and grarian reforms began with the help of the money that flowed nto the country at the time. Despite the remarkable economic recovery, however, the number of emigrants continued to remain high.

Italy was among the founding members of NATO in 1949, the European Coal and Steel Community in 1951, and the European Economic Community, which was established by the ❼ Treaty of Rome in 1957. The Common Market had a very positive effect on the Italian economy. Northern Italy's industries in particular were able to link up with the rest of Western Europe, which remains a vital market today. The process of European integration also proved to be beneficial in other areas. In order to join the European Monetary System, it was necessary to reduce debt and lower the inflation rate, thus stabilizing the economy. Both chambers of parliament gave their approval for the implementation of the necessary measures. In 1999, Italy, along with ten other nations, entered the last stage of European economic and currency union and introduced the euro as the new common currency. The economically supportive and politically stabilizing effects of the European process of unification are directly noticeable in pro-Europe Italy, which has joined the ❻ Group of Seven, the organization of the leading industrialized states, which is now the Group of Eight (G-8). This integration gives Italy the opportunity to help shape supraregional economic issues and political processes, despite its comparative economic weakness.

9 The founder, general secretary, and leading theorist of the Commmunist Party of Italy (CPI), Antonio Gramsci, ca. 1920

6 G7 Conference concerning employment policy, 1996

10 Production line packaging cheese, Monza, 1950

The Vatican

The Vatican City, which is located in the middle of the Italian capital Rome and is the seat of the Roman Catholic Church, is a UNESCO World Heritage site. Although Italy sees itself as a laicized state, the significance of the Curia in an almost exclusively Catholic country is not only of a religious nature. The Vatican is also an economic factor and was able to exert political influence through the Christian Democratic party.

St. Peter's Square with St. Peter's Basilica, the center of the Vatican City, Rome

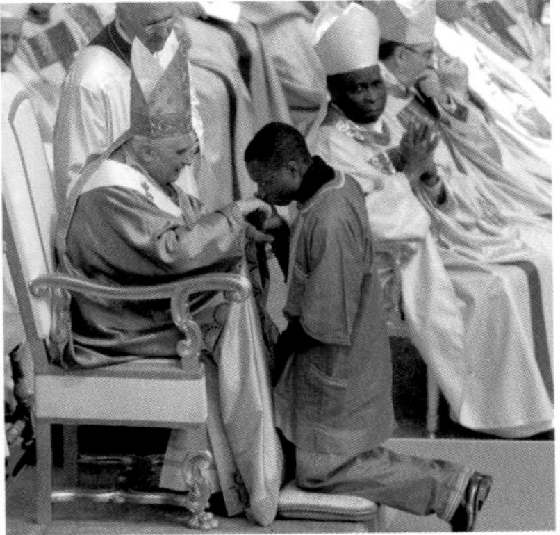

Inauguration of Pope Benedict XVI on St. Peter's Square in Rome, April 24, 2005

1951 | Founding of the European Coal and Steel Community
1955 | Italy becomes a member of the United Nations
1957 | Founding member of the EEC
1978 | Murder of Aldo Moro
1999 | Introduction of the euro

The Peculiarities of the Italian Economy

Since the late 1960s, the signs of an economic crisis in Italy had been multiplying, as industrial production stagnated. Organized crime played a role in this development.

1 Fiat factory in Turin, ca. 1965

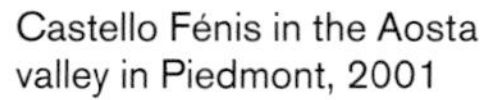

2 Castello Fénis in the Aosta valley in Piedmont, 2001

3 Turin in Piedmont with the cupola its architectural symbol, the Mole Antonelliana, 2001

Despite the successes of the postwar period, the Italian ❶ economy showed distinct symptoms of a crisis from the late 1960s on. Inflation was high and the lira was weak. The national debt in 1997 reached a high point of 120 percent of the gross national product, of which 42 percent was earned by state enterprises. This high percentage of state enterprises contributed to the origin of the crisis: Companies that came into difficulties could seek state support or sell company shares to the state. Once they regained economic health, these shares could be repurchased. In this way, unproductive sectors came under the responsibility of the government and restoring these companies to profitability was done at public expense.

Italy suffers a strong north–south disparity. The Northern Italian regions of Lombardy, ❷, ❸ Piedmont, and Veneto, along with Latium in the central region, are industrialized to a high degree and have well-developed service sectors. ❹ Northern Italy is among the wealthiest regions of Europe. The south of the country, the "Mezzogiorno," is primarily ❻ agrarian. Its population density is irregular, with heavy concentrations side by side with deserted areas. Structural aid from the state and the European Union has been unable to alleviate the economic weakness of this region. This seemingly insurmountable division of the country impairs social and political stability. Separatism is an oft-expressed political demand in the north; in the south, large sections of the population migrate north—or leave the country—because of high unemployment. Furthermore, Southern Italy remains a region plagued by ❺ organized crime, or the Mafia. The struggle against this is becoming increasingly difficult as much of the Mafia's capital has flowed into the legal economy and it has many and diverse international ties at its disposal.

4 The fashion capital Milan: Models pose in a shop window, 2002

5 The Neapolitan Mafia boss "Lucky" Luciano at home, 1958

The Mafia

Originally a secret society of major Sicilian landowners and their field guards, the Mafia today is a synonym for organized crime that has long since extended far beyond Sicily throughout Europe and into the United States. The main sources of income are drug trafficking, arms smuggling, prostitution, human trafficking, and the extortion of protection money. In addition, the Mafia engages in subsidy fraud and corruption in the allocation of public commissions in the building trade, for example, through blackmail of influential figures. Their code of conduct is characterized by the obligation of secrecy (omertà) and revenge (vendetta). The secret cooperation of state officials and the mafiosi has, over the course of time, made the Mafia a political player in Southern Italy.

A special unit of the police in the fight against the Mafia, on a mission, Naples, 2004

6 Picking of world-renowned Italian olives in the agrarian south, Sicily, 2004

1980 | Bomb attack on Bologna station

1990 | Strong devaluation of the lira

1992 | Corruption scandals lead to state crises

1992 | Scalfaro becomes president

The Italian "Revolution" of the 1990s

The Italian political system collapsed at the beginning of the 1990s. It was not reformed despite an unprecedented wave of trials against corrupt industrialists, public officials, and politicians.

7 Bettino Craxi, president 1983–1987

8 Antonio Di Pietro, former investigator of corruption

9 Massimo D'Alema, leader of the PDS party

The structural problems of ⓫ Italy's political system escalated in the 1990s. After the breakdown of the Eastern Bloc in 1989, the exclusion of the Communist party from government was no longer justifiable when it had widespread support. The intertwining of political parties with the economy and state also came under increasing criticism. Though the collapse of the lira at the beginning of the 1990s promoted Northern Italian exports, it wiped out huge amounts of savings. The call for separatism in the northern regions became louder; the Lega Nord party demanded the division of the country in order to detach itself from the backward South.

A few committed public prosecutors took action against organized crime, and the Mafia defended itself with ⓬ terror attacks. The Mafia's connection to the judiciary and politicians came into the open. Even previously respectable politicians such as Christian Democrat Giulio Andreotti and Socialist ❼ Bettino Craxi were charged. After the corruption of the parties in the allocation of public commissions became public, first the Christian Democrats, followed by almost every other party, disbanded. Whole government departments were brought to a standstill through the arrest of public officials. By 1994, 6,059 persons had been investigated, half of whom went to jail. This operation, called "Mani pulite" (Clean hands), was conducted by the Milan public prosecutor, ❽ Antonio di Pietro. Even new parties such as Lega Nord and Silvio Berlusconi's Forza Italia had to explain themselves to the Italian courts.

11 The Italian tricolor in Rome

New Christian Democratic parties emerged from the former Democrazia Cristiana party. The terms Socialist, Republican, Social Democrat, and Liberal became meaningless. The Communist party reestablished itself as the ❾ *Partito Democratico della Sin--istra* (Democratic Party of the Left). ❿ Forza Italia and Lega Nord gained in popularity, as did the successor of the Neo-Fascists, the Allianza Nazionale.

After the elections of 1994, more than 70 percent of the members of parliament were new. Despite this, neither chamber could agree upon a reform committee. The proposal to introduce the majority electoral system to concentrate political power was rejected in a referendum in 2000 after minor parties and the Forza Italia spoke against it. Therefore reforms to the political system did not take place.

12 Mafia-assassination of Judge Borsellino in Palermo, Sicily, in which five died and 17 were injured, 19 June 1992

10 Silvio Berlusconi campaigning, 2004

Silvio Berlusconi

Since he was first elected prime minister, as chairman of the right-wing Forza Italia party, which he founded in 1994, media tycoon Silvio Berlusconi has been the dominant figure in Italian politics. In 2008, he was elected prime minister for the fourth time. The powerful politician has had to defend himself several times in front of a court and is strongly criticized for his heavy influence on the media both domestically and internationally.

above: The Italian media tycoon and prime minister Silvio Berlusconi, 2000

1994 | Berlusconi becomes prime minister

1994 | Founding of the Forza Italia

1996 | Prodi becomes prime minister

2000 | Rejection of the majority voting system

2001 | Reelection of Berlusconi as prime minister

Spain: From Military Dictatorship to Constitutional Monarchy since 1945

Gen. Francisco Franco was Europe's last fascist dictator. After the end of World War II, the country was politically and economically isolated, and the situation improved only with the opening up of Spain to the world economy in the mid-1950s. Spain became industrialized and developed a tourism industry that attracted visitors from across Western Europe, but still remained a dictatorship until ❶ Franco's death in 1975. His successor, King Juan Carlos I, oversaw a smooth transition to democracy. This opened the way to membership in the European Economic Community and a rapid rise in living standards.

General Franco with his successor, Juan Carlos, 1970

Franco's Dictatorship 1945–1975

Fascist Spain was gradually able to free itself from its isolation after the war, but only limited political reforms were achieved.

❷ Francisco Franco, the dictator who had emerged victorious out of the Spanish Civil War, restored the Spanish monarchy in 1947 and named himself president *(Presidente del gobierno)*. Don Juan Carlos de Borbón refused to accept the crown from him, however, leaving Spain a kingdom without a king. A monarchical opposition sprang up, which Franco suppressed as brutally as he had the liberals. There existed strict censorship of the press, and the Catholic Church dominated the educational system.

Gen. Francisco Franco y Bahamonde

Prime Minister Luis Carrero Blanco

Politics of the Cold War facilitated the ending of Spain's international isolation in 1953 through an agreement granting the United States use of military bases. In the same year, a concordat was signed with the Vatican, and in 1955 Spain became a member of the United Nations.

During the 1960s, alongside economic reforms and cosmetic changes to the constitution, limited political reforms were made. Workers, supported by elements of the Church, were granted the option to form independent unions and to strike. ❹ Opposition movements in the Basque region and Catalonia vehemently demanded independence.

The aging dictator's regime lost its stability. He named Prince Juan Carlos heir apparent to the throne in 1969 and two years later made him his deputy. Franco also made ❸ Luis Carrero Blanco prime minister, though he himself remained head of state. In December 1973, Carrero Blanco was murdered by the Basque separatist movement ETA, and political repression was once again increased. Franquists and reformers were irreconcilable under Prime Minister Carlos Arias Navarro after 1974, but the old dictator Franco ❺ died on November 20, 1975.

Franco's Regime

General Franco supported his regime with a state party—the fascist nationalistic Movimiento Nacional—but also relied on the military and the Church. Their support increased the dictator's credibility significantly. But the Falange—the nucleus of the Movimiento Nacional—lost political power as soon as Spain held free elections in 1977.

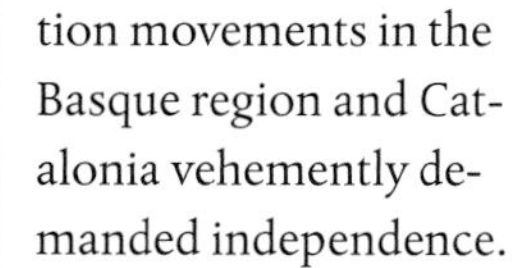

above: Insignia of the fascist Falange group

The six suspects put on trial for membership in an illegal Basque nationalist group

Tomb of Franco in the "Valley of the Fallen Soldiers" (*Valle de los Caidos*), a memorial to those who died during the civil war

1928 | Founding of the Opus Dei movement

1947 | Reintroduction of the monarchy under Franco

1953 | American-Spanish agreement over military bases

1955 | Spain joins the United Nations

Economic Development until 1975

Spain's transition from a backward agrarian economy country to an industrialized nation and tourist destination began slowly in the 1960s. The distribution of wealth remained unequal.

As Spain was excluded from the distribution of the Marshall Plan monies, the autarkic economic program of the state party, the Falange, continued in force after 1945. The focus of reconstruction after 1939 and the civil war was heavy industry, though not until 1950 did industry reach the production level of 1929. Spain was still an agrarian land— although it was unable to feed its population sufficiently in the 1940s and 1950s. Four-fifths of the population belonged to the impoverished ❻ lower class.

The crisis-ridden situation improved, after the 1953 military base agreement with the United States brought with it US economic aid. Radical economic reform was introduced with the announcement of a stabilization plan, which was a prerequisite for Spain's acceptance into the International Monetary Fund (IMF) in 1958. The economic opening of the country stimulated industry; by the end of the 1960s, 33 percent of the workforce was employed in that sector.

Under the influence of the new power elite—members of the right-wing conservative Opus Dei, among others—trade tariffs were liberalized and money was borrowed from foreign creditors. The decade of the 1960s was a time of privatization and acceptance of foreign investment. Economic plans and guidelines were introduced. The first four-year plan of 1964 focused on transport and energy; the second, through 1971, promoted public education and agriculture. In 1970, Spain signed a free trade agreement with the European Economic Community and became one of the largest ❼ industrial nations in Europe. Growth rates exceeded five percent by 1974.

7 Factory in Sant Adria del Besos

Tourism played a significant role, and Spain became Europe's number-one ❿ vacation destination. A generation of working-class Britons enjoyed their first foreign holidays on package tours to the south coast of Spain. Money sent home by Spanish "guest workers" from wealthier countries such as Germany and France also served to boost the country's living standards and provided the regime with vital foreign currency.

However, the benefits of this economic growth were not evenly distributed. Tourism was largely limited to the Mediterranean coast, and revenues went to a wealthy few or corrupt officials. Much of the country's interior was also bypassed by industry as new ventures were concentrated around Madrid, ❾ Barcelona, and the northern Basque region, resulting in large-scale ❽ migration from rural areas to the cities.

9 Tourists sitting in a street café in Barcelona, 2002

6 Slums in a suburb of Madrid, ca. 1950

10 Cala Bassa beach in the Spanish Mediterranean island Ibiza, 2000

8 An abandoned farm in Extremadura

Opus Dei

Opus Dei ("Work of God") is an influential right-wing conservative lay movement within the Catholic Church. It was founded by a Spanish priest, Josemaría Escrivá de Balaguer y Albas, in 1928 with the goal of establishing Catholic principles in private and professional life. Opus Dei has come under heavy criticism for its cooperation with Franco and its sect-like recruiting methods, as well as its heavy-handed treatment of opponents within the Church.

Josemaría Escrivá de Balaguer y Albas, canonized in 2002

1959 | Stabilization plan
1964 | First four-year plan
1969 | Nomination of Juan Carlos as the heir to the throne
1970 | Free trade agreement signed with the EEC
20 Nov 1975 | Death of Franco

The Development of the Constitutional Monarchy since 1975

King Juan Carlos I helped shape the transformation of the Franco dictatorship into a democracy. This system change took place largely peacefully.

Juan Carlos I ascended to the Spanish throne ❶ on November 22, 1975. Together with the premier he appointed in 1976, ❸ Adolfo Suárez, the king introduced the structure of a democratic system. Suárez's middle-of the-road Democratic Center Union won a victory in the election of the constituent National Assembly in 1977. A new constitution, approved by the people with a large majority in 1978, made Spain a constitutional monarchy. This and the dissolution of the former state party, the *Movimiento Nacional,* in 1977 brought an end to the fascist system shortly after Franco's death.

However, this change did not take place completely without resistance. On February 23, 1981, ❹ Lieutenant Colonel Antonio Tejero stormed parliament with members of the paramilitary *Guardia Civil* and took members of parliament hostage. The military took a wait-and-see stance, even approving in part. It was the king's staunch public declaration of his belief in democracy that thwarted the attempted coup.

The elections in 1982 brought a change in government. The winning party was the leftist Spanish Socialist Workers' party. Prime Minister ❺ Felipe González Márquez was confronted with a dissatisfied military and a rise in unemployment. At the same time, Spain was moving closer to Europe and the West. In 1982 Spain became a member of NATO and on January 1, 1986, joined the ❷ European Community. After losing the election in 1996, González relinquished the government to the conservative Popular Party. Thanks to Spain's economic growth under ❻ José María Aznar, the unemployment rate dropped significantly. However, he was heavily criticized for numerous scandals and his support of the US in the Iraq war.

The PSOE formed a minority government led by Zapatero in 2004. Since 2008, Spain has severely struggled against the world economic crisis which has caused a renewed increase in unemployment and ❼ poverty.

1 On November 22, 1975, two days after Franco's death, Juan Carlos takes his oath on the Bible and the constitution, becoming king of Spain

2 The Spanish national flag is raised in front of the headquarters of the EC in Brussels on December 25, 1985

3 Adolfo Suárez is sworn in as prime minister with the Spanish king

4 The rebel Antonio Tejero holding a raised gun in the Spanish parliament

5 Felipe González Márquez

6 The Spanish prime minister, José María Aznar (left), congratulates his successor José Luis Rodriguez Zapatero, who was elected in 2004

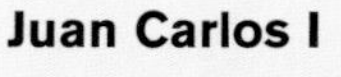

Juan Carlos I

Juan Carlos, born in 1938, attended several military academies and the University of Madrid. In 1969, he agreed to be Franco's successor, taking over on November 22, 1975. With the aid of a reform program he had introduced and owing to his personal authority, he was able to transform the Spanish dictatorship into a democracy without great political upheaval. Juan Carlos's greatest hour came during the attempted coup in 1981. With his appearance as the supreme commander of the military on television and with a speech unambiguously in favor of the new form of government, he was able to isolate the leaders, bring the military over to his side, and secure the new democratic system.

7 A homeless person in front of a bank in Madrid, 2002

1953 | ETA founded

1975 | Basque, Catalan, and Galician declared state languages

1977 | "Falange" dissolves

1978 | New constitution passed

The Regions of Spain

The Spanish regions gained more rights through democratization. At present, Spain is transitioning into a federal state.

In a concession to the desire for cultural identity in the Basque Region, Catalonia, and Galicia, King Juan Carlos granted the Basque, Catalan, and Galician languages the status of official state languages in the respective regions in 1975. However, this was not sufficient for those striving for autonomy. In September 1977, ⑩ Catalonia demanded self-governing rights that the region had already been granted once in 1931. Demonstrations in other regions followed. New parties were formed that raised the demand for autonomy.

A national solution was found in the constitution of 1978. Under Article Two, Spain was divided into 17 autonomous regions. The whole national parliament, the Cortes, from then on faced a Senate made up of regional chambers. The authority of the regions, as differentiated from the functions of the central state, is laid out in the text of the constitution.

The regions have the right to self-government in, for example, public works, environmental protection, and economic development; the national government regulates ⑧ defense and foreign policy, among other things. The particulars of power vary from region to region, but Catalonia, ⑪ Galicia, and the ⑨ Basque Region have had a high degree of autonomy from the outset.

Not all sections of the populace reacted favorably to this development. Even the process of democratization was threatened at first through acts of violence and terrorist attacks. The armed forces rejected the efforts toward decentralization, and many attacks by the extreme right took place. The right wing repeatedly called for the military to take over the government. On the other hand, the Basque separatist terror organization ETA continued to fight for complete sovereignty of the Basque Region by means of ⑫ assassinations and kidnappings.

Since 2002 there have been increased discussions in Spain over a new form of the power relationship between the regions and the central state. In addition, because the Senate has demonstrated itself to be rather weak until now, more independence continues to be demanded by the different Spanish regions.

9 The Guggenheim Museum in the Basque city Bilbao

10 Catalonian flags in Barcelona

11 Wind turbines on the Galician coast, 1998

12 An ETA car bomb attack in Santander, 2003

8 Spanish crown prince Felipe visits soldiers on a Spanish air force base, 2002

ETA

ETA ("Euskadi Ta Askatasuna"— Basque Country and Liberty) is an underground movement that developed as a students' group in 1953 from the Basque National Party (PNV) and reconstituted itself as ETA when the PNV seemed too moderate to them. Their goal is the formation of a Basque state out of the Basque regions in Spain and France. Their terrorist attacks increased after Franco's death. ETA has been blamed for about 800 deaths since 1968. Thousands demonstrated against ETA terror in 2000. The government refuses to negotiate with ETA as long as it refuses to lay down its arms.

Car bomb explodes, Madrid, 2002

23 Feb 1981 | Tejero's coup attempt

1982 | Felipe González becomes head of government

1982 | Spain joins NATO

1 Jan 1996 | Spain becomes member of EC

1996 | José María Aznar becomes prime minister

Portugal since 1945

The Tejo Bridge in Lisbon, built under the Salazar regime in 1966

The Estado Novo, the "new state" of the dictator ❶ Salazar, was an authoritarian, clerical, fascist system. The dictatorship was ended in 1974 by the peaceful "Carnation Revolution." The Portuguese colonies then gained their independence. After the first presidential elections in 1976, Portugal moved in the direction of a parliamentary democracy. In 1986, Portugal was accepted into the European Community, which improved the economic situation of the country.

The Estado Novo

The regime of Salazar followed a strict economic policy. In foreign affairs, it was oriented toward the Western camp during the Cold War and fought a brutal colonial war in Africa.

Following a coup d'état by the army in 1926, ❻ Antonio de Oliveira Salazar came to power in 1932. Under his dictatorial regime, Portugal maintained neutrality through most of World War II, but toward the end of the war, the dictator allowed the Allies to establish military bases on the Azores Islands. This alignment in foreign policy was maintained, and in 1949 Portugal was among the founding members of NATO. Entrance into the United Nations did not take place until 1955, and membership in the Organization for Economic Cooperation and Development came in 1961.

Domestically, the corporative governmental system based on privilege continued after 1945. Despite a few relaxations, censorship, the secret police, and the one-party system continued to keep the population suppressed. Although Salazar was able to reduce the state debt with his rigid economic policy, he did little to promote industry, and the agriculture sector remained in crisis. Only a few foreign investors were allowed into the country. Consequently, many ❹ Portuguese had to search for work abroad.

Catholic Baroque Church in Goa, India, built by the Portuguese in the 17th century

A unit of the rebel liberation army in the colony of Portuguese Guinea in West Africa, 1968

In 1951, Salazar declared the Portuguese colonies to be overseas provinces to prevent their independence. Despite that, in 1961 the Indian army occupied ❸ Portuguese possessions on the subcontinent, and in Angola, Mozambique, and Guinea ❺ demands for independence grew louder. A bitter and brutally waged colonial war followed, burdening the Portuguese national budget to such an extent that Salazar was forced to open Portugal to foreign investors.

Portuguese guest-workers in France build themselves provisional accommodations, 1963

In September 1968 Salazar suffered a stroke and stepped down from office. His successor, ❷ Marcelo Caetano, eased censorship laws and attempted a mild liberalization in the political sphere, but the reforms were halfhearted. In 1974 it became increasingly clear that the colonial war in Africa could not be won militarily, while there was no political solution in sight. The sense of crisis was exacerbated by the effects on Portugal's weak economy of the world economic recession that had begun in 1973. In this context the armed forces overthrew the government in a bloodless coup, with considerable support from the Portuguese people. The peaceful popular uprising was called the "Carnation Revolution" and signaled the end of both the dictatorship and Portugal's colonial empire.

Marcelo Caetano, 1973

Portuguese dictator António de Oliveira Salazar at his desk

1932 | Salazar comes to power
1949 | Portugal becomes a founding member of NATO
1955 | Portugal joins the United Nations
1960 | Portugal becomes a member of the OECD
1961 | Colonial war begins

The Carnation Revolution and Its Consequences

After the peaceful overthrow of the dictatorship, Socialist leaders launched a nationalization program, but it was reversed by subsequent governments.

The ❾ military coup of April 25, 1974, was carried out by a group of officers who called themselves the Movement of Armed Forces (MFA). The resulting two-year-long ⓫ Carnation Revolution, a period of liberalization and democratization, received its name from the flowers soldiers put in the muzzles of their rifles. In 1974, the MFA junta installed the conservative General Antonio de Spínola as president, but he resigned after only four months because he disliked the leftist direction of the revolution. In March 1975, he attempted an unsuccessful right-wing countercoup.

Socialist MFA officers then founded a revolutionary council and called an election for the constituent assembly that set Portugal on the road to socialism. Censorship was lifted and the ❼ secret police disbanded. The government nationalized the banks, transport, heavy industry, and the media. All of the colonies were given their ❽ independence by 1975, but this brought almost a million settlers back to the motherland, which greatly burdened the country's economy.

The moderate General Antonio Ramalho Eanes outpolled a radical left candidate in the first presidential elections after the adoption of a new constitution in April 1976. The chairman of the Socialist party, Mario Soares, formed a minority government that survived only two years. In 1979 a non-socialist party won the election for the first time after the Carnation Revolution. The governing party agreed with the Socialist opposition on the amendment of the constitution, which came into effect in 1982 and revoked some socialist elements dating from the days of the Carnation Revolution. The revolutionary council was abolished, and most of the nationalized industries were reprivatized. Following a process of reform and preparation, Portugal officially joined the ❿ European Community on January 1, 1986. Although Portugal today remains one of the poorer EU member states, it achieved ⓬ impressive rates of economic growth during the 1990s, and living standards rose significantly. Since 2004, the conservative Portuguese politician Jose Manuel Durão Barroso has held the post of president of the European Commission.

8 In the Portuguese colony of Guinea (present-day Guinea-Bissau), independence fighters declare their victory, 1973

9 A group of jubilant soldiers after the coup against the dictatorship, April 25, 1974

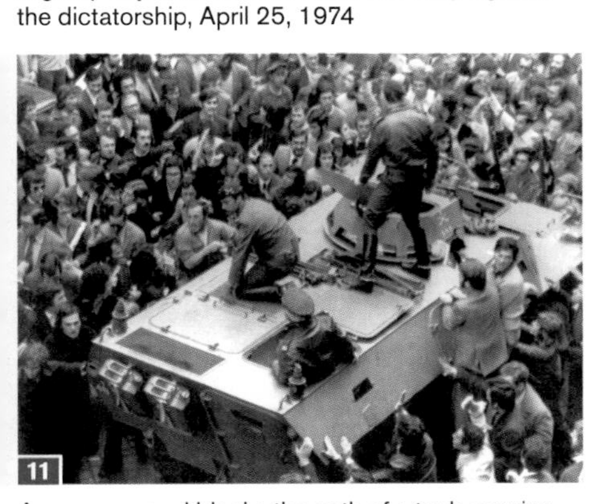

11 An angry crowd blocks the path of a tank carrying fleeing members of the government, April 26, 1974

7 During their arrest, three secret policemen from the Salazar regime are protected from an angry Portuguese crowd, Lisbon, 1974

10 Mario Soares (front) signs the treaty of Portuguese accession to the EC

12 The 1998 World Exhibition held in Lisbon

Fado

Fado, which means "fate" in Portuguese, probably dates back to the time when Portugal was a major seafaring power with distant colonies. African slaves in Brazil are said to have developed fado as a dance, and it was only later that it was sung in Portugal. Maybe it was sailors who sang these melodies because they were full of desire for their home. In the nineteenth century, singing fado was still considered indecent and heard only in shady harbor areas. It was only later that fado became socially acceptable, and famous "factistas" made it well-known internationally.

1968 | Resignation of Salazar
1973 | World economic crisis
1974 | Military coup by the MFA and "Carnation Revolution"
1974 | Regency of Antonio de Spínola
1975 | All colonies granted independence
1 Jan 1986 | Portugal enters the European Community

Northern Europe since 1945

The ❶ Scandinavian states became increasingly integrated into the world economy after 1945. Sweden and Finland remained politically neutral and strongly promoted understanding and peace in the world. To facilitate cooperation, the Scandinavians founded the Nordic Council. They were involved to varying degrees in the process of European unification. The Nordic countries, with their state welfare structures, are among the most prosperous nations of the world.

1 Oresund bridge between Denmark and Sweden, which also connects Sweden to the European mainland

The European North after 1945: The Commonalities

The plan for a Scandinavian defense alliance failed after 1945, but Northern Europe came together on a cultural and political level.

Of all the Scandinavian states, only Sweden did not suffer from the consequences of World War II. After the experience of occupation and deportation on a massive scale, the Northern European nations planned their own Scandinavian defense alliance to protect their coasts and hinterlands from attack. Though this failed in 1949, cooperation on other levels was intensified.

Sweden, Denmark, and Norway studied a possible customs union and founded the Nordic Council in 1952; ❺ Iceland joined the council in the same year and ❹ Finland joined in 1955. The Nordic Council is a common advisory body to which representatives are sent by the national parliaments. Its goal is working to promote cooperation among the Scandinavian states and the standardization of legislation in economic, social, and cultural areas. In 1971, the Nordic Council of Ministers was added to complement the committee. Although both are only advisory bodies, they have done much to promote the close collaboration of the countries. The strong social democracies in all the states played an essential part in bringing the political culture and living conditions into line. Due to this political stability, communism has played hardly any role in political life, except in Finland. There was a strong belief in the social market economy and the entire North set about building up welfare states, which are funded by high taxes.

❸ Liberalism in the Scandinavian countries led to a greater tolerance toward ❷ alternative lifestyles. Economic slumps brought on by world economic crises, among other things, have always been brought under control by the government. Concern for maintaining their regional achievements and autonomy has determined the relationship of the Northern European states to the European Union, to which they are tied by treaties.

3 Pippi Longstocking, the title figure of numerous books by the Swedish author Astrid Lindgren, embodies the ideals of freedom and an anti-authoritarian education; movie still

2 Hippy commune in the Danish capital Copenhagen, 1972

4 The senate house, built in 1822, in the Finnish capital Helsinki

5 The Icelandic capital Reykjavik, with around 115,000 inhabitants

Greenland

The world's largest island belongs to the smallest Scandinavian nation, Denmark. The United States built military bases on the western coast of Greenland in 1945, for which a defense treaty was signed with Denmark in 1951. The island gained self-rule in 1979 but remains a Danish territory. Together with Denmark, Greenland joined the European Community in 1973, but then left it following a plebiscite in 1985.

A fishing village in Greenland, 1990

1945 | American military bases built in Greenland

1951 | Danish-American defense alliance signed

1952 | Nordic Council founded

1960 | Denmark and Norway join EFTA

The European North after 1945: The Differences

Differences among the Nordic states exist in their military ties, their economic bases, and their relationship to the European Union.

Unlike Norway, in 1945 Denmark did not suffer widespread destruction as a result of the war. Both nations were able to benefit from the Marshall Plan program, Norway receiving as much as $35 million, and both were among the founding members of NATO in 1949. A plan for a collective military pact between all the Scandinavian nations had to be abandoned. Iceland and Greenland signed defense agreements with the United States within the framework of NATO. Sweden and Finland, on the other hand, decided on neutrality.

❼ Norway and Denmark's close trading partnership with Great Britain induced them to join the European Free Trade Association (EFTA) in 1960, but their paths diverged when it came to membership of the European Community. While Denmark became an EC member state in 1973 after approval in a referendum, the Norwegian population rejected membership first in 1972 and again in 1994. Norway is nevertheless tied to the European Union, which is its main partner in the European Economic Area (EEA). Its ❿ extensive oil deposits have made it one of the richest nations on Earth.

6 A British frigate collides with an Icelandic patrol boat thought to have destroyed its nets, 1976

8 The Soviet first secretary Leonid Brezhnev at the CSCE summit in Helsinki, 1973

10 A drilling rig in the North Sea oil fields that lie off the Norwegian coast, 2003

11 The Swedish royal couple, Carl Gustav XVI and Silvia, with their children, 2004

Iceland has not joined the European Union in order to protect its fishing industry. The extension of its waters triggered a fishing dispute in 1973 known as the ❻ "Cod War," in which Iceland and Britain came close to an armed conflict. Iceland has been a member of the EFTA since 1969 and the EEA since 1993. Since 2008 Iceland has been suffering the effects of a major financial crisis and currency collapse, which has led the government to apply for a full EU membership .

⓫ Sweden and Finland have been EU members since 1995, but there exists much skepticism in both countries regarding the community. As small nations, in terms of population if not geographical size, they are afraid of not having their concerns heard. While Finland nonetheless introduced the euro through the European Economic and Currency Union in 1999, the Swedish population declared itself against the introduction of the common currency in September 2003. Denmark has also maintained its national currency.

Finland and Sweden have both played important roles in overcoming supraregional conflicts. The first ❽ Conference for Security and Cooperation in Europe met in Finland in July 1973. The resolutions made there bolstered demands for civil rights around Eastern Europe, among other things. Sweden's ⓬ Dag Hammarskjöld was twice general secretary of the United Nations in the 1950s, and he was posthumously awarded the Nobel Peace Prize in 1961 for his numerous efforts in the cause of peace. Sweden produced yet another committed foreign diplomat in ❾ Olof Palme. Twice prime minister, Palme was involved particularly in disarmament initiatives and worked as a UN negotiator. His murder on February 28, 1986, was a great shock both nationally and internationally.

12 Dag Hammarskjöld with the Israeli Prime Minister Golda Meir, 1956

7 King Harald V of Norway and Queen Margarete II of Denmark in the Norwegian capital Oslo, 1997

9 Funeral procession for Olof Palme, 1986

1973 | Greenland and Denmark join EC

1973 | First CSCE in Finland

28 Feb 1986 | Olof Palme murdered

1995 | Sweden and Finland join EU

Eastern and Central Europe since 1945

After the end of World War II, the states of Eastern and Central Europe came under the communist control of regimes loyal to the Soviet Union. After the formation of popular front governments, power was taken over by the Communist party, whose rule was secured and protected by the Red Army. The economies of these so-called vassal states were geared to the requirements of the Soviet Union as were their political decisions. When the USSR was forced to carry out reforms in its own country and the regime could no longer find support within its sphere of influence, the regimes collapsed.

1 Destruction of the Stalin memorial in Budapest during the public uprising in Hungary, 1956

Hungary, 1945 to the Present

The Hungarian revolt of 1956 was brutally suppressed. Hungary was the first Eastern bloc country to open its borders to the West in 1989.

Nazi Germany's ally Hungary, which had declared war on the Soviet Union, was occupied by the Red Army toward the end of World War II. Budapest fell after a seven-week siege. Despite the relatively low proportion of pro-Communist votes in the elections of 1945 and 1947, the People's Republic of Hungary was proclaimed on February 1, 1946. Supported by the Soviet military, the Hungarian Communist party took over the administration, forced the parties into line, and united with the Social Democrats to form the Hungarian Workers' party. ❹ Mátyás Rákosi took the post of general secretary and followed a strict Stalinist course of "cleansings" and show trials, including those of Protestant and Catholic leaders.

2 Dismantling the border fence between Austria and Hungary, May 2, 1989

After Stalin's death in 1953, the new prime minister, ❸ Imre Nagy, attempted to relax the authoritarian system. He ended the forced collectivization of agriculture, eased the speed of industrialization, and put a stop to state terror. His program was thwarted, however, by the Stalinist resistance led by Rákosi. The population then ❶ revolted on October 23, 1956, out of discontent with the Communist party and the running of the government. Nagy formed a coalition government and announced Hungary's resignation from the Warsaw Pact. He paid for his commitment with his life in 1958 when he was executed.

Following the suppression of the revolt by the ❺ Soviet military, the new party leader ❻ János Kádár took control of the government in 1956. He eliminated internal party opposition and leaned heavily on the support of the Soviets. Individual economic initiatives were allowed at the beginning of the 1960s. This "Goulash Communism" brought about a certain economic rebound.

Following Kádár's resignation as party chief in 1988, reforms could no longer be halted. The opening of the Hungarian-Austrian ❷ border in September 1989 punched a hole in the Iron Curtain that had divided East and West and increased the pressure for reform in the entire Eastern bloc. After the first free elections in Hungary, the Democratic Forum took over the reins of government in 1990. Soviet troops left the country in 1991, and Hungary joined NATO in 1999. In 2004, the country was taken into the European Union along with nine other states.

3 Prime Minister Imre Nagy, 1954

4 Mátyás Rákosi, 1952

5 Soviet tanks in Budapest, 1956

6 János Kádár, 1956

1 Feb 1946 | People's Republic of Hungary proclaimed
1947 | Presidency of Gomulka in Poland
1953 | Death of Stalin
23 Oct 1956 | Hungarian people's revolt
1958 | Execution of Imre Nagy
Dec 1970 | Warsaw Treaty
1980 | Solidarity founded

Poland, 1945 to the Present

Poland's population repeatedly forced reforms and government change. The country was the first Eastern bloc nation to succeed in changing its political system.

Poland was forced to make especially great sacrifices in World War II: six million Poles died—including 90 percent of the Jewish population—and 38 percent of the national wealth was lost. After the war, in which the Polish government in exile continued the struggle from London, the Allies decided to place Germany's eastern territories under Polish administration, while at the same time Poland was forced to relinquish its eastern territories to the USSR. As Russian troops advanced into Poland, the Communist Party formed the Committee of National Liberation in Lublin. From 1944 onwards, this body held power in those areas not directly incorporated into Russia. The result was a massive resettlement that greatly changed the makeup of the population.

The Palace of Culture in Warsaw, Poland in the socialist style of the Stalinist era, modeled on the "Seven Sisters" in Moscow, built 1952–1955

Pope John Paul II is welcomed by the public in Warsaw, 1979

Lech Walesa, leader of Solidarity, 1981

After the first elections in 1947, the government led by ❾ Wladyslaw Gomulka tried to pursue a path to ❽ socialism in accordance with Poland's political and social distinctions, but the system was compelled to conform to the Soviet Union's guidelines in December 1948. The Polish Catholic Church was persecuted. After Stalin's death in 1953, unrest forced repeated attempts at reform and changes in leadership. Gomulka returned to power from 1956 to 1970.

In December 1970, Poland and the West German government under Chancellor Willy Brandt signed the Warsaw Treaty. This milestone in the history of reconciliation between Germany and Poland involved a nonaggression treaty and the recognition of the Oder–Neisse line as Poland's western border.

In 1978, Karol Józef Wojtyla, the Catholic cardinal of Krakow, was elected pope. His return to ❿ Poland as John Paul II in 1979 became a triumphal procession. It demonstrated the identification of the Polish nation with Catholicism, and accelerated the loss of power of the state party.

Poland's economic situation became increasingly critical in 1980. The rise in meat prices triggered a nationwide wave of strikes in July. The most significant demand of the interplant strike committee was to permit the existence of free, party-independent unions, and the government finally acquiesced. In October 1980, the independent trade union "Solidarity," under the leadership of ⓫ Lech Walesa, was officially registered. It soon represented 90 percent of the organized workers. In the summer of 1981, the Soviet Union threatened the Polish government with an invasion if it could not control the situation. In response, Prime Minister ⓬ General Wojciech Jaruzelski declared martial law on December 13, 1981, which lasted until July 1983. Solidarity was banned and its leading members interned. The Church could not be neutralized, nor could the union be intimidated over the long term.

In 1988, the government was compelled to hold ⓭ round table talks with the opposition to negotiate reforms. The first free elections in 1989 brought a victory for Solidarity. Poland became a parliamentary democracy, joining NATO in 1999 and the EU in 2004. The national conservative party "Law and Justice" won the 2005 election. After President Lech Kaczynski's death in a ❼ plane crash in Smolensk in 2010, it lost the majority.

President Bronislaw Komorowski at the memorial service for the 96 victims of the airplane crash of Smolensk, April 10, 2011

Wladyslaw Gomulka (right) talking with Leonid Brezhnev and Walter Ulbricht (left), ca. 1968

Prime Minister General Wojciech Jaruzelski, 1984

Representatives of government and opposition at the round table in Warsaw, 1989

13 Dec 1981 | Declaration of Martial law in Poland
1989 | First free elections in Poland
Sep 1989 | Opening of the Hungarian-Austrian border
1990 | First free elections in Hungary
1999 | Hungary and Poland join NATO
2004 | Hungary and Poland join the EU

Czechoslovakia and the Czech and Slovak Republics SINCE 1945

The "Prague Spring" reform experiment of Czechoslovakia's government was forcibly crushed. The "Velvet Revolution" of 1989–1990 led to the country's division three years later.

In 1945, Czechoslovakia, which had been dismantled by the Nazi regime, was restored to its previous borders with the exception of the region of Carpathian Ruthenia (Carpatho-Ukraine). The expulsion of the ❷ German and Hungarian minorities at the end of the war proved a long term economic loss.

Germans who were expelled from Czechoslovakia have retained their traditions and in some cases their claims to land, 2004

During a communist-organized rally, posters of Klement Gottwald and Joseph Stalin are carried through the streets, Prague, 1948

President Václav Havel (1993–2003)

Prime Minister Vladimir Meciar (1992-1998)

In 1947, the Soviet Union forced Czechoslovakia to reject the assistance offered by the Marshall Plan. In the meantime, the Communists under Klement Gottwald seized the key positions in the state. President Edvard Benes resigned in protest, and the non-Communist ministers stepped down in June 1948. ❹ Gottwald became the new president and formed a Communist government. In 1949, Czechoslovakia joined the Council for Mutual Economic Assistance (Comecon). In 1952, the country was shaken by show trials and the subsequent executions of prominent Communists.

❸ Alexander Dubcek was elected the new state and party head in 1968. He wanted to liberalize the system and implement "socialism with a human face." The Soviet Union was unable to stop the reforms through diplomatic political means, so on August 21, 1968, ❶ troops from the Warsaw Pact marched into the capital of the country and crushed the "Prague Spring." Under the new party leader, Gustáv Husák, Czechoslovakia became one of the Communist states most loyal to the Soviet Union party line. Nonetheless, in 1976–1977 a new opposition group, Charter 77, developed in the wake of the final resolution of the Conference for Security and Cooperation in Europe (CSCE) in Helsinki in 1975.

After the end of the Cold War, the effects of the process of change were evident in the entire Eastern bloc, including Czechoslovakia. The Communist Party's dictatorship was ended by the peaceful "Velvet Revolution" in 1989–1990. Dramatist and civil rights champion ❺ Václav Havel was elected president in 1990, and Dubcek was elected chairman of the Federal Assembly. The socialist state was on its way to becoming a federal state, but Slovakia, under its emergent leader ❻ Vladimir Meciar, sought independence. Since no agreement could be reached, the country was divided into two sovereign states on January 1, 1993. In 2004, the Czech Republic and Slovakia were accepted as EU members.

The tanks of the intervention troops are surrounded and blocked by the population during the "Prague Spring," 1968

Charter 77

The name of the most famous opposition movement in the Eastern bloc referred to the demand for civil rights in the final resolution of the CSCE. The charter quickly gained more than 800 signatories, including the writers Václav Havel and Pavel Kohout. They highlighted human rights violations in regular publications. The leading members became national political figures in the years of upheaval following 1989.

Václav Havel (left) in a discussion with other dissidents in his apartment in Prague, 1985

Alexander Dubcek, 1968

1948 | Edvard Benes resigns
1949 | Czechoslovakia joins Comecon
1965 | Ceausescu takes office
1968 | Alexander Dubcek's government
21 Aug 1968 | Prague Spring crushed

Bulgaria, Romania, and Albania, 1945 to the Present

The authoritarian Communist state systems of these three Balkan states collapsed in 1989. Despite their transition to democracy, these countries remain among the poorest in Europe.

After the end of World War II, the Communist Party in Bulgaria, led by its general secretary ❽ Georgi Dimitrov, began building up a Soviet-style "people's democracy." The opposition was violently eliminated. ⓫ Todor Zhivkov was first secretary of the Communist Party from 1954 to 1989. Between 1962 and 1971, he held the office of prime minister, and in 1971–1989 he was chairman of the council of state. Attempts to "Bulgarianize" the large Turkish minority after 1984 caused a mass exodus. The political upheaval of 1989 destabilized the government. An economic crisis in 1996–1997 led to major unrest. The parliamentary elections of 2001 were won by the party of the former king, ❾ Simeon II, who had promised an improvement in living standards.

In 1944, Communist partisans led by ❼ Enver Hoxha took power in Albania. As head of the party, he ruled autocratically and brutally eliminated any opposition. At first he turned toward Yugoslavia, then China from 1961 to 1977, and finally he completely isolated the country internationally. His successor, Ramiz Alia, cautiously began to open up the country to the outside world in 1985. The process of reform accelerated after 1989, and the first multiparty elections were held in 1991. After 1995, governments came and went in rapid succession. In 1997, hundreds of thousands lost what little money they had in a stock investment scam. In the subsequent disturbances, barracks were stormed and large numbers of weapons were stolen. Since 1989 people have been ⓮ emigrating on a large scale. Today poverty and corruption rates are high, while the relationship to the Albanian majority in Kosovo remains contentious.

Romania lost Moldavia to Ukraine after 1945 but gained Transylvania and with it a German and Hungarian minority. The Stalinist Communist Party head, Georghe Gheorghiu-Dej, made the country a part of the Eastern bloc, but after 1960, he sought greater independence from Moscow. His successor as state and party head after 1965, ❿ Nicolae Ceausescu, continued this policy and received ⓬ Western aid for breaking with the Soviets; however, the aid did not go toward alleviating the misery of the ⓭ starving population. His regime was primarily supported by the Securitate, the secret police. With its help, minorities were brutally resettled. Ceausescu was overthrown in 1989 and executed. In 1991 opposition demonstrations were crushed by pro-government coal miners and the security forces. Although governments have alternated rapidly, the pace of reform has increased since 1997.

All three countries were accepted into the NATO Partnership for Peace program. Bulgaria and Romania became EU members in 2007.

7 The Albanian dictator Enver Hoxha, statue in Tirana, 1989

8 Joseph Stalin (left) with Georgi Dimitrov, 1936

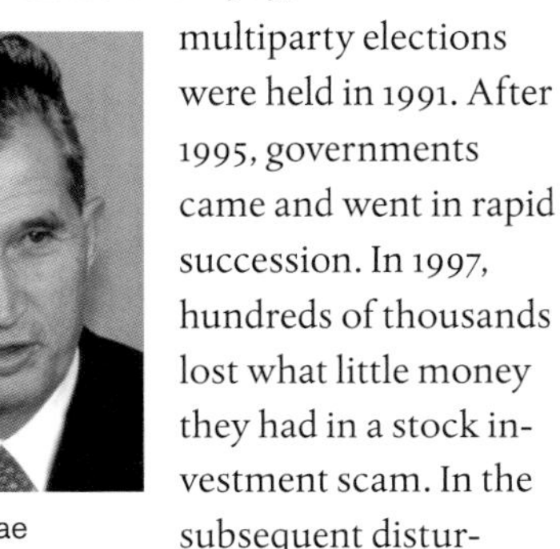
9 Simeon Sakskoburg-gotski, former king

10 Dictator Nicolae Ceausescu, 1984

11 General Secretary of the Bulgarian Communist party, Todor Zhivkov, 1987

12 Ceausescu wasted economic aid on costly, prestigious buildings such as the "People's House" in Bucharest

13 A group of Roma carriages on a road near the Romanian capital of Bucharest, 2001

14 Albanian refugees at a port in the Italian city of Bari, 1991

1976 | Charter 77 formed

25 Dec 1989 | Ceausescu executed

1990 | Václav Havel elected president

1 Jan 1993 | Czechoslovakia's "Velvet Divorce"

2004 | Czech Republic and Slovakia join EU

2007 | Bulgaria and Romania join EU

YUGOSLAVIA SINCE 1945

Yugoslavia, which was occupied by the German army in World War II, was liberated by a partisan army led by Tito and was not occupied by the Red Army. Tito was thus able to rebuff Stalin's intervention after 1945. He developed his own "path to Communism" and was a committed leader of the Nonaligned Movement. After his death, the state structure he had held together broke apart. The other parts of the republic set their own nationalist aspirations against the dominance of Serbia. A ❶ "nation-building war" followed and was characterized by appalling brutality.

1 Provisional bridge between the Croatian and Muslim parts of the city Mostar in Herzegovina, replaces the historic one which was destroyed during the civil war in the 1990s

Yugoslavia under Tito 1945–1980

Tito practiced a form of Communism independent of the Soviet Union. The country was a federation of republics and provinces, but the military was dominated by Serbia.

The Communist partisan army under its leader Josip Broz, widely known as ❸ Tito, was the victor in the war against the Italian and German troops that had occupied Yugoslavia during World War II. With Tito heading the National Liberation Council and then the government after 1945, Yugoslavia was given a Communist structure within a federal system, which achieved a large degree of unity. All nationalities living within Yugoslavia were promised equal rights. The king was deprived of his nationality.

Tito's government at first leaned toward the Soviet Union.

2 Head of the Yugolslav government Tito and his wife (right) as guests of the Iranian monarch, 1971

However, Stalin's attempts to assert control and ideological leadership over the Yugoslavian Communist Party were resisted by Tito, and a split resulted in 1948. Yugoslavia withstood an economic embargo imposed by Stalin with the help of Western aid, but 1955 brought a measure of ❺ rapprochement between the two governments. In 1961, Yugoslavia was a founding member of the ❹ Nonaligned Movement, an organization of states that belong to no military bloc and remained neutral in the Cold War conflict; thus the "Titoism" practiced in Yugoslavia stood for an independent form of Communism with self-governing workers and federal elements while at the same time building up good relations with ❷ non-socialist states.

3 Tito after the end of the war in Belgrade, 1945

4 Conference of the Nonaligned Movement in Bandung, Indonesia, 1955

To accommodate the separate nationalities, Yugoslavia was divided into six republics, plus the two autonomous provinces of Vojvodina and Kosovo-Metohiya. The Communist party was restructured in 1952 to become the Federation of Communist Yugoslavia, and the police were given a federal organization in 1966. Only the army remained under the central state, which was dominated by Serbia. Despite the federal structure of the country, nationalist demonstrations, such as the "Croatian Spring" between 1969 and 1971, sometimes occurred and were violently suppressed by Tito's regime.

The autonomy of the republics increased with the constitution of 1974. After Tito's death in 1980, the chairmanship of the state committee and the party was annually rotated among the nationalities— though this was not the case within the individual republics. The dissolution of the federal state became increasingly apparent, highlighting that Tito had held Yugoslavia together.

5 Tito (right) toasts Nikita Khrushchev, 1963

1945 | Tito's government takes power in Yugoslavia
1948 | Split with the Soviet Union
1961 | Yugoslavia joins nonaligned nations
1969–71 | Croatian Spring
1974 | New constitution

The Breakup of Yugoslavia, 1980 to the Present

Almost all of the Yugoslav republics declared their independence after the collapse of the Communist central state, which was accompanied by the bloody expulsion of minorities.

After 1945, the Albanian minority in Kosovo increased to a majority of 90 percent. Disturbances began in the region in 1981. ❻ Slobodan Milosevic, later to become president, made himself the spokesman for the Serbian minority. In 1986, he rose to become first secretary of the Yugoslav Communist party, later renamed the Serbian Socialist party. Milosevic annulled Kosovo's autonomy in 1989 and replaced the Albanian elite with Serbs.

At the end of the 1980s, nationalists took over power in all of the republics. Croatia and Slovenia declared their independence on June 26, 1991. The Yugoslav army marched into both countries but soon withdrew from Slovenia. A third of Croatia, however, remained occupied; the Serbian minority living there proclaimed the Republic of Krajina.

The elections in November 1990 in Bosnia showed a majority for the Muslim Party of Democratic Action under ❽ Alija Izetbegovic, who declared the country's independence in 1991. The reaction by the Bosnian Serb minority was the proclamation of a Serbian republic under Radovan Karadzic. The Serbs were able to occupy two-thirds of Bosnia with the help of the Yugoslav army. Brutal "ethnic cleansing" through expulsion and genocide took place. The violence only ended when NATO finally intervened in 1995. By that time, 2.2 million people had ❼ fled and 200,000 had been cruelly ⓫ murdered. The country was divided under UN supervision into a Bosnian-Croatian federation and a Serbian republic which together constituted a common state.

In 1995 Croatian forces retook Krajina. The Serbian population fled or was expelled, some into Kosovo. There, in 1992, the Albanians had proclaimed the Republic of Kosovo under Ibrahim Rugova. Escalating violence between the ❾ Kosovo Liberation Army and Serbian police led to the launch of a major ❿ Serbian offensive. NATO then intervened with air strikes against Serbia and the occupation of Kosovo.

Macedonia also declared its independence in 1991. The Albanian minority in Macedonia proclaimed the Republic of Illyria and created a liberation army in 2000. About 250,000 refugees from Kosovo further increased the tension. The presence of NATO and UN troops prevented the outbreak of another war.

Many thousands of Muslim Bosnians, also known as Bosniaks, flee from areas held by the Bosnian Serbs, 1995

Kosovo Liberation Army soldiers with an Albanian flag, 1999

Slobodan Milosevic (center) and his wife, 1997

Alija Izetbegovic presents a map of the regions in Bosnia where genocide took place, 1993

Albanian Kosovars killed and brutally mutilated by Serbs, 1999

Examination of a mass grave in Bosnia, 2002

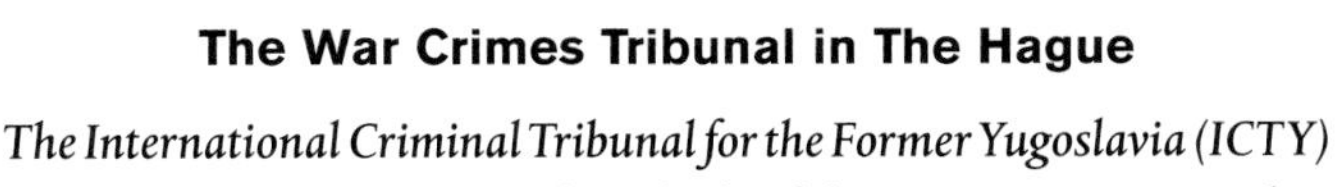

The War Crimes Tribunal in The Hague

The International Criminal Tribunal for the Former Yugoslavia (ICTY) was set up in 1993 as an auxiliary body of the UN Security Council. It deals with the prosecution of war crimes in former Yugoslavia. The Serbian leader Milosevic died in UN custody in 2006 before his trial could be completed. Karadzic was arrested in 2008 and his military commander Mladic was detained in 2011. As of 2010, 22 prison sentences had been handed down.

Bosnian Serb leader Radovan Karadzic (right) and military commander Ratko Mladic (left), 1993

from 1981 | Unrest and revolts in Kosovo

1989 | Milosevic annuls Kosovo's independence

26 Jun 1991 | Independence of Croatia and Slovenia

1991-95 | War in Bosnia

2001 | Milosevic is arrested

A wall separates the Greek and the Turkish parts of the Cypriot capital Nicosia, 1999

Greece and Turkey since 1945

Before the two neighboring states Greece and Turkey became democracies, both countries suffered under dictatorial regimes. After World War II, both countries became industrial and trading nations. Conflict-laden contentious issues between them have included the mineral resources of the Aegean Sea in the territory that lies between them, which is claimed by both countries, and claims to the island of ❶ Cyprus. While Greece had been part of the European Union since the 1980s, Turkey remains a candidate for membership.

Greek soldiers marching to a polling station in Athens, 1946

Greece: Kingdom and Dictatorship 1945–1974

After World War II and a civil war, Greece stabilized under conservative governments. The military carried out a coup against the first center-left government.

The Nazi army occupied Greece in 1943 after Greek forces had defeated Hitler's Italian allies. Various partisan movements, though also fighting among themselves, opposed the German occupation. After the war, the radical left boycotted the ❷ elections of 1946, allowing the conservative Alliance to win.This led to three years of civil war. In the 1947 peace treaty with Italy, Greece gained the ❹ Dodecanese Islands. Greece became a NATO member in 1952.

By 1952, 20 right-wing governments had ruled in succession. They were all rigidly anticommunist. The first stable government was formed by Field Marshal Alexandros Papagos with his Greek Rally party. In 1956, it became the National Radical Union, led by ❺ Konstantinos G. Karamanlis. After 20 years of a police state, the Greeks in 1963 voted into office the leftist Center Union Party led by Georgios Papandreou, who promised welfare reform in the country. However, in April 1967 conservative officers led by Colonel ❸ Georgios Papadopoulos organized a military coup and set up a dictatorial regime. A countercoup by King Constantine II in December 1967 failed. On June 1, 1973, a republic was proclaimed in Greece. Arrests, deportation, torture, and enforcement of the party line followed.

King Konstantinos II (center) with members of the government; to the far left: Georgios Papadopoulos, 1967

Konstantinos Karamanlis (right) with US President Jimmy Carter, 1978

Phaidon Gisikis became the new president in 1973 after a bloodless coup led by General Demetrios Ioannides. However, he soon came into conflict with the Turkish government over deposits in the Aegean Sea. A failed overthrow attempt against President Makarios of Cyprus, directed from Athens in 1974, eventually led to the downfall of the unpopular Greek military regime.

The monastery of St. John on the Dodecanese island Patmos, one of the holiest places in Greece

The Independence of Cyprus

In order to bring about the annexation of the British colony of Cyprus to Greece, the underground movement EOKA led by General Georgios Grivas began a war against the colonial power in 1955. This was accompanied by fighting against the Turkish minority. However, the island was granted independence on August 16, 1960, which was guaranteed by Great Britain, Greece, and Turkey. The first president, Archbishop Makarios III, altered the system of government to favor the Greeks. After a bloody conflict, the Turks withdrew from the government and set up a provisional administration. In 1964, the United Nations sent in peacekeeping troops.

right: Archbishop Makarios III, bronze monument

1941 | German army occupies Greece

from 1952 | Greece member of NATO

16 Aug 1960 | Cyprus becomes independent

1967 | Military putsch led by Georgios Papadopoulos

1 Jun 1973 | Republic proclaimed

The Greek Republic since 1974

Democracy was reestablished in Greece after the end of the dictatorship. The relationship with Turkey continued to dominate foreign affairs.

In 1974, ❼ General Gisikis was forced to turn over power to Karamanlis, who became prime minister. Greece returned to a parliamentary democratic form of government. Karamanlis and his New Democracy Party applied for membership in the European Community, and Greece's application was approved in 1981. In the same year, New Democracy lost its majority to the social-democratic PASOK, which appointed Andreas Papandreou as prime minister. His economic policies ignited severe social unrest in 1985, and an accusation of corruption forced him to resign in 1989.

6 Protected border crossing in Cyprus

After a close election victory in 1990, New Democracy under Konstantinos Mitsotakis carried out a reform program, and Karamanlis was elected president. The trade unions called a general strike in 1992 in protest over social problems. In 1993, PASOK won again with Papandreou, who had been found not guilty of the corruption charges. For health reasons, however, he stepped down in 1996 in favor of ❽ Konstantinos Simitis, serving until 2004.

The postwar economic growth of Greece was initially consistent. Marshall Plan funds played a large part in this, as did membership in the European Community. Yet in 2010, the world financial crisis and Greece's rampant black economy brought the country close to insolvency. Moreover, a cultural shift was running through Greece. Guest workers returning home from abroad brought not only technical know-how with them but also other concepts of living. A prolonged migration to the cities resulted in a third of all Greeks living today in the ❾, ⓫ Athens area. Through mass ❿ tourism, the Western lifestyle has come to have a permanent presence.

Animosity toward Turkey has remained the dominating foreign policy issue in the democratic republic. Disputes have arisen over rights to mineral reserves in the Aegean, issues of maritime traffic, and the rights to oil extraction. Even the NATO partnership of both states could not prevent military conflict within the context of the ❻ Cyprus issue.

The two states of Cyprus

A provisional administration founded by Turkish Cypriots in 1961 was meant to facilitate the realization of a federal form of government for the island. The attempted coup by Greeks in 1974 and the subsequent invasion by Turkish armed forces interrupted this development, however. Two settlement areas emerged, from which the respective minorities were expelled. The Turks established a federal state in 1975 under Rauf Denktasch, who proclaimed the Turkish Republic of Northern Cyprus in 1983. It was recognized only by Turkey, in contrast to the Greek-Cypriot government of Glafcos Clerides: The Greek Republic of Cyprus became a member of the European Union in 2004.

above: Glafcos Clerides (right) and Rauf Denktasch shake hands, 2001

7 Phaedon Gisikis (at the head of the table) with political leaders prior to the military rebellion, 1967

8 Konstantinos Simitis, 2002

9 Opening of the 28th Olympic Games in Athens, 2004

10 Tourists visit the Acropolis, 2001

11 Main road through central Athens, 2004

1974 | Konstantinos Karamanlis made prime minister

1981 | Joins EC

1983 | Turkish Republic of Northern Cyprus proclaimed

1992 | General strike

2004 | Greek Republic of Cyprus becomes member of EU

Turkey: On the Path to Democracy 1945–1970

Turkey became an industrialized state after World War II, but the path to democracy was not without numerous setbacks.

Anglo-French military guarantees to Turkey given just before the Second World War succeeded in keeping her neutral during the war, despite strong German pressure. Following the death of Kemal Atatürk in 1938, Ismet Inönüt became head of state. After 1945, as president, he sought support from the West, and Turkey was accepted into the Marshall Plan program. Membership in NATO followed in 1952. The allocation of Western aid was tied to the pursuit of democratic reform. Turkey therefore adopted a multi-party system, and in the elections of 1950 the newly founded opposition, the Democratic party led by Adnan Menderes gained a majority.

Execution of Adnan Menderes, 1961

The economic boom at the beginning of the 1950s was followed by an economic crisis that put the Democrats under pressure. In addition, the secularist elite criticized the pro-religious policies of the party. President Menderes reacted to the criticism with suppressive measures. In May 1960, a "Committee of National Unity" led by ❶ General Cemal Gürsel organized a coup against the Menderes government. Gürsel banned the Democratic party and arrested its leadership; ❷ Menderes was executed. Although the new constitution established in 1961 had liberal characteristics, governments were henceforth subject to the scrutiny of a National Security Council dominated by the commanders of the armed forces.

The Justice party, the successor party to the Democrats, won the elections of 1965. The new head of government, ❸ Süleyman Demirel, was confronted by growing social and economic problems and rising radicalism. Demirel oriented his economic policies toward the West and followed the advice of the World Bank. Consequently, industry outstripped the ❹ agrarian sector, though only a minority profited from this development. Numerous Turks ❺ emigrated. The workers organized into unions, and the extremist factions that emerged, some of them Islamist, were further to the right and left of the two major parties. Over the decades, terrorist acts by these groups contributed to Turkey's political destabilization.

Cemal Gürsel, center, after 1961

Leader of the Justice Party Süleyman Demirel, 2000

Turkish women and girls in a field harvesting cotton, a main product of the Turkish economy, 1989

Turkish immigrant workers waiting at a German airport, 1970

The Kurdish Minority

The Kurdish people live where Turkey, Iran, and Iraq meet. The Kurds feel oppressed by the Turkish government. A separatist organization, the Kurdistan Workers' party (PKK), has made itself the mouthpiece for Kurdish autonomy. These were expressed with increasing violence after 1984. By 1999, 37,000 people had died in fighting between the PKK and Turkish forces. It was not until 1991 that the Kurds were officially recognized as a minority. The violence has decreased since the arrest of the PKK leader, Abdullah Öcalan, in 1999. Since 2002 Turkey has eased restrictions on using the Kurdish language in education and broadcasting.

Turkish soldier with the corpse of a PKK member, 1996

1938 | Atatürk dies
1952 | Entry into NATO
1960 | Military coup under Cemal Gürsel
1961 | New constitution
1965 | Government of Süleyman Demirel

The Major Role of the Military since 1970

Turkey experienced two further military coups. Yet simultaneously Turkey made the transition from a developing country to a country on the threshold of economic takeoff.

6 Bülent Ecevit in front of a picture of Kemal Atatürk, 1998

8 Prime Minister Turgut Özal (right) with his Greek counterpart Andreas Papandreou, 1988

In 1971 President Demirel was ousted when the army took power. By suspending civil rights, the junta brutally but effectively fought radical and terrorist factions for two years. The political system remained untouched.

7 Prime minister Tansu Çiller, photo, 1997

In 1973, the social-democratic Republican People's party under ❻ Bülent Ecevit took over government. Ecevit formed a coalition with Necmettin Erbakan's Islamist National Salvation party. Ecevit was credited with the invasion of Cyprus that followed the attempted Greek coup of 1974, but this did not translate into support at the polls. In the following years, he and Demirel took turns in the leading offices of state but were unable to solve the continuing problems facing the country: ❾ economic crises, ❿ Islamism, and separatist terrorism. In 1975 there were 34 victims of violence, 1500 by 1980.

On September 12, 1980, there was a third coup. General Kenan Evren dissolved parliament and disbanded political parties and unions. Thousands were jailed and tortured, and executions were rife. He nonetheless succeeded in reducing the number of terrorist acts. After a new constitution was accepted by referendum in 1982, the military withdrew from power. The centralized government still allowed little autonomy to the country's provinces.

The centrist Motherland party won in the elections of 1983. Prime Minister ❽ Turgut Özal promoted democratization and market reforms, while reducing the influence of the military. In 1991, he gave the Kurds some cultural autonomy. Özal oriented himself politically and economically toward the West and in 1987 applied for membership in the European Community. In 1989 Özal was elected president, and Demirel became prime minister in the elections of 1991 as head of the True Path party. Demirel then became president after Özal's death in 1993, and his position as prime minister was filled for the first time ever by a woman, ❼ Tansu Çiller.

Since the 1980s, Islamic tendencies in Turkey have been increasing. The Islamic Welfare party first won a majority in the elections of 1995 but was banned in 1998. The electoral success of the newly founded conservative-Islamic AK party in 2002 was also a response of the populace to the economic crisis that was gripping the country.

Prime Minister ⓫ Recep Tayyip Erdogan managed to secure the opening of membership negotiations with the European Union, which began in late 2005. However, membership remains conditional upon the continuation of political and economic reform, together with fullfledged respect of human rights. Links between the European Community and Turkey began in 1963 through an association agreement, and since 1995 the country has shared a customs union with the EU.

9 Occupants of wooden houses, who have little hope of improvement in living conditions, in a slum area in Istanbul

10 Four Turkish Muslim women wearing chadors and a headscarf (right), in contemporary Istanbul

11 Recep Tayyip Erdogan after a visit to a mosque, 2003

1991 | Recognition of the Kurds as minority
Oct 2005 | Accession talks with the EU

1987 | Application for EC membership
1999 | PKK leader Öcalan arrested

The Soviet Union and its Successor States since 1945

After the Second World War, all of Eastern Europe came under the influence of Stalin's totalitarian system, which led the ❶ Soviet Union into the Cold War. The system was relaxed to a degree under his successors, who were increasingly bound to a "collective leadership." The party's claim to autocratic rule was not seriously questioned until Gorbachev. In the turbulent years of 1989–1991, the structure of the Eastern bloc crumbled, and then the Soviet Union itself collapsed, disintegrating into a federation of autonomous states. While the Central European countries sought bonds with Western Europe, autocratic presidential regimes established themselves in most of the former Soviet republics.

Military parade on the occasion of the 70th anniversary of the October Revolution on the Red Square in Moscow, November 7, 1987

The Soviet Union up to Stalin's Death

Joseph Stalin ensured Soviet domination of Eastern Europe after 1945 and oversaw industrial reconstruction. The USSR's increasing rivalry with the other victorious powers led to the Cold War.

In 1945, the Soviet Union was clearly one of the war's ❷ victors. At the conferences of Yalta in 1943 and Potsdam in 1945, Stalin, Roosevelt, and Churchill had agreed on the division of influence in postwar Europe. Over the next few years, Stalin systematically went about setting up Eastern European satellite states. By 1948, the Communists had taken over power almost everywhere, at first in alliance with non-socialist antifascists. The only exceptions were Greece and Yugoslavia. In 1949 East Germany was founded. ❸ Stalin had already developed his "two camp" theory of the contrasts between the Communist and Capitalist worlds by 1946, which the United States answered in 1947 with the parallel concept of the "Cold War." The relationship between the two former allies worsened steadily and reached its nadir in the Soviet blockade of Berlin lasting from 1948–1949.

Stalin in uniform, painting, 1949

Domestically, the terror of the Great Purges had passed, but the political pressure exerted by Stalin and ❹ Lavrenti Beria, the all powerful head of the Soviet People's Commissariat for Internal Affairs (NKVD), was relentless. All soldiers and officers who had had contact with the enemy—the West—during the war were eliminated or relegated to obscure positions, including war hero Marshal Zhukov. Stalin intensified the pace of the reconstruction of ❻ industry within the framework of his fourth Five-Year Plan, which proceeded rapidly, while the development of agriculture lagged behind. By 1948, the Soviet Union's industry had reached the prewar production level of 1940, and it had doubled by 1952, but there was no rise in the population's standard of living.

Portrait of the Russian leader Stalin, ca. 1945

Lavrenti Beria, the much-feared head of the Soviet secret police who enforced Stalin's reign of terror, 1953

The *Zhdanovshchina* carried out by cultural official Andrei Zhdanov in 1947–1948 established Stalin's ❺ personality cult and the nationalistic glorification of the Soviet Union. Writers and artists who did not adhere to this direction were vulnerable to repression and accusations of "formalism" and "cosmopolitanism." In 1952, the Stalin Note proposed to western leaders the reunification of Germany as a demilitarized and nonaligned neutral state. The Western powers quickly dismissed the offer, suspecting Stalin's motives.

Victory celebrations on the Red Square in Moscow: Soviet soldiers carrying flags captured from the Waffen SS, June 24, 1945

Workers in a locomotive factory, 1967

1943 | Yalta Conference
1945 | Potsdam Conference
1946 | Stalin outlines his "two-camp" theory
1947-48 | *Zhdanovshchina*
1948-49 | Blockade of Berlin
Mar 1953 | Death of Stalin

Life After Stalin: Power Struggle and Khrushchev's victory

After Stalin's death, the regime relaxed his hardline policies. At first Malenkov seemed to be prevailing in the struggle to replace him, but in 1955, he was brushed aside by Khrushchev.

In January 1953, Stalin denounced a plot against his life by the Kremlin's doctors, but before a wave of further purges could be initiated, ⑩ Stalin died on March 5, 1953.

Georg Malenkov, leader of the Soviet Union (1953–1955), shortly after Stalin's death in 1953

Party Secretary Nikita Sergeyevich Khrushchev, 1960

The power struggle for the succession as leader began immediately. At first Georg Malenkov, who had the government apparatus behind him, and Nikita Khrushchev, who had the support of the party, joined forces against Minister of the Interior Beria, who was deposed in June 1953 and shot in December.

⑨ Malenkov, who dominated at first, announced on August 8, 1953, a "new course" that would provide for the strengthening of the underperforming agricultural sector and the consumer industry, cultivation of new lands in the east, and "socialistic justice." A "thawing period" began in 1954 in which writers, creative artists, and intellectuals regained some freedom of expression. The first moves towards détente with the western alliance also took place. However, in May 1955, the Eastern bloc's Warsaw Pact was founded as a counterpart to NATO, and tensions returned.

In February 1956 Nikita ⑪ Khrushchev was able to win out over Malenkov at the 20th congress of the Soviet Communist party. He became party secretary and, by 1958, premier. During the 1956 congress Khrushchev famously denounced Stalin's crimes and the direction of the party under his leadership. During the wave of "de-Stalinization" that followed, revolts took place in Poland and Hungary, but both were militarily suppressed. Khrushchev relaxed ⑫ cultural policy, released many from the prison camps (*gulags*), and increasingly relied on agricultural production to improve the standard of living. He also promoted technology: The launching of ⑦ *Sputnik*, the first manmade Earth satellite, in October 1957 was a shock for the West. In 1961, ⑧ Yuri Gagarin, in his capsule *Vostok I*, became the first human in space.

In foreign affairs, Khrushchev fluctuated between competition with the US and the idea of "peaceful coexistence." He constantly tried to expand the Soviet Union's sphere of influence in the world. Khrushchev took advantage of the desire for independence of Asian and African countries. Following the 1956 Suez Crisis, he also gave military and financial support to Arab countries engaged in the Middle East conflict.

Stalin lying in state alongside Lenin in Moscow, March 7, 1953. Eight years later his body was removed

Nikita S. Khrushchev and his government at a reception for Soviet artists and writers, painting, 1957

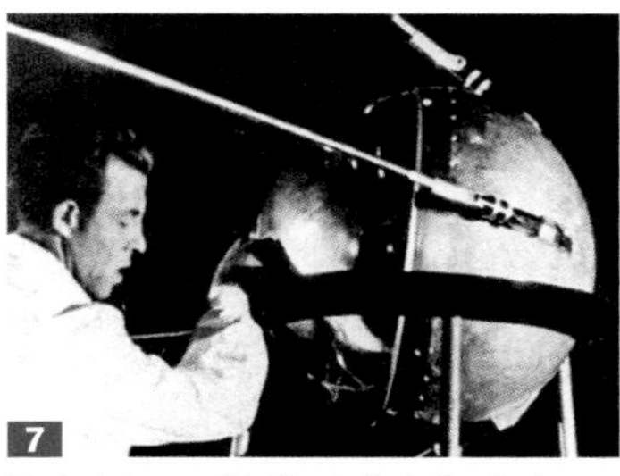

Technicians with *Sputnik 1*, the first man-made satellite to orbit Earth

Russian Cosmonaut Yuri Gagarin became the first human to orbit the Earth on April 12, 1961

Dmitry Dmitriyevich Shostakovich

The changing directions of Khrushchev's cultural policy are illustrated by the case of composer Dmitry Shostakovich. He composed many hymns glorifying Stalin and the Soviet Union in order to gain the freedom to do his own work. For a time he was a star of Soviet culture. In 1936, he was publicly denounced for the first time as being "decadent" and for "formalistic excesses." Later in 1948, he was forced to exercise "self-criticism" and ostracized. As first secretary of the Soviet Composers' Association, between 1960 and 1968, Shostakovich turned against "Western avant-gardism," again in line with party policies.

above: Dmitry Shostakovich

8 Aug 1953 | "New Course" under Malenkov
Mai 1955 | Warsaw Pact founded
1957 | *Sputnik* launched
1958 | Khrushchev becomes party secretary
14 Oct 1964 | Khrushchev deposed

Khrushchev's Downfall and the Brezhnev Era

After Khrushchev's demise in 1964, Brezhnev became the new Soviet leader; his power, however, was kept in check by other party members more than that of previous leaders. Gradually, a détente with the Western world took place in foreign policy.

In 1959 Khrushchev's foreign policy course began to lead to a growing ideological alienation from China. The stationing of nuclear missiles in Cuba brought the world to the verge of a third world war in October 1962, though escalation was avoided when the Soviet Union backed down. Khrushchev had increasingly been showing a tendency to sudden and often (for the party) unpredictable decisions and changes in course since 1961. This led to his overthrow on October 14, 1964, by the members of the Soviet presidium (Politburo).

The new strongman as general secretary of the Communist party was ❷ Leonid Brezhnev, in tandem with Premier Aleksey Kosygin as chairman of the Council of Ministers and President Nikolay Podgorny as chairman of the presidium. A one-man rule in the style of Khrushchev would not be tolerated in the future. The Brezhnev era is considered a time of "normalization" and "bureaucratization" of socialist everyday life. From the mid-1970s onward, the Soviet leadership increasingly became a ❶ political gerontocracy.

6 Worker in a factory producing locomotives in Tblisi, Georgia, 1967

1 The elderly Soviet leadership wave to the crowds during celebrations in Moscow on May 1, 1982; from left to right: Chernenko, N. Tichonow, Brezhnev, Grischin, and A. Kirilenko

The 23rd Communist party congress in 1966 cemented the dominance of ❻ heavy industry in the economy and the goal of ❺ arms parity with the United States. The immense expenditure for nuclear missiles and submarines in the 1970s resulted in, among other things, massive supply shortages for the population. The increasingly strong suppression of artists, intellectuals, and dissidents (Alexandr Solzhenitsyn and ❼ Andrey Sakharov, among others) was countered mostly with repressive measures by the state—deportation to work camps and the use of "political psychiatry."

5 Military procession taking part in celebrations marking the 50th anniversary of the Russian Revolution, Red Square, Moscow, November 7, 1967

After the Soviet leadership forcefully suppressed the "Prague Spring" in 1968, it greeted the ❸ policy of détente begun in 1970 by West German Chancellor Willy Brandt. From 1970 on, a series of agreements were negotiated between the Soviet Union and Western countries. These culminated in the ❹ Strategic Arms Limitation Talks (SALT I and II) in 1974 and 1979 with the United States and the 1975 Helsinki Accords on international security policy and arms control. The process of détente suffered repeated setbacks, however, including the NATO decision to counterarm in 1977, the Soviet invasion of Afghanistan in 1979, and the West's boycott of the ❽ Olympic Games in the city of Moscow in 1980.

Some domestic reforms were successful, such as the improvement of public education and the establishment of greater political and cultural autonomy for the various nationalities that made up the Soviet republics. On the other hand, the burden of the arms race with the US increasingly undermined the performance of the economy, with resources concentrated on the military and heavy industry sectors at the expense of consumer goods. Corruption inevitably followed these supply shortages.

7 Soviet dissident and physicist Andrey Sakharov during an interview given in March 1973

2 Soviet Premier Leonid Brezhnev, who presided over détente, 1980

3 The policy of détente: The West German Chancellor Willy Brandt (right) and Brezhnev on a speedboat during a diplomatic visit to the Soviet Union, September 17, 1971

4 US President Jimmy Carter (left) and Leonid Brezhnev (right) sign the Strategic Arms Limitation Treaty II, 1979

8 Poster for the 22nd Olympic Summer Games held in Moscow between July 19 and August 2, 1980

1968 | "Prague Spring"
1974 | SALT I Agreement
1975 | Helsinki Accords
1977 | NATO-decides to upgrade missile systems
1979 | SALT II-Abkommen/Sowjetischer Einmarsch in Afghanistan
1980 | Olympic Games in Moscow

Gorbachev and the End of the Soviet Union

In 1985, a radical change in direction took place with the election of Gorbachev as general secretary. His reforms led to the collapse of Soviet Communism between 1989 and 1991.

Following ❾ Brezhnev's death, first ⓫ Yuri Andropov in 1982 and then ⓭ Konstantin Chernenko in 1984 took turns to hold power. When Chernenko died on March 10, 1985, ❿ Mikhail Gor-

Yuri Andropov holding an end-of-year speech, December 21, 1982

Interim leader: Konstantin Chernenko ruled the USSR for just over a year before his premature death

bachev was elected general secretary of the Soviet Communist party the next day. Step by step, together with Foreign Minister Eduard Shevardnadze and his younger leadership cadre, Gorbachev carried out comprehensive reforms. He renewed the disarmament talks with the United States in Geneva right away and withdrew the Soviet army from Afghanistan in 1987–1989.

Domestically, the Soviet leadership began privatizing the economy in 1987 and legally established companies' independence in

Revolution from the top: Mikhail Gorbachev outlines his reform plans, involving *perestroika* (reconstruction) and *glasnost* (openness), to a Communist party conference, 1988

1988. However, rapid inflation often impeded the economic reforms. Cultural and educational policies were liberalized with the slogans *glasnost* (openness) and *perestroika* (reconstruction), and Western cultural influences flooded the country. Gorbachev's reforms immediately radiated to the allied socialist states, where the people in the countries of Central and Eastern Europe forced the fall of the Berlin Wall in 1989 and the dissolution of the entire Eastern bloc. For his rejection of any form of violent course of action in this process, Gorbachev was awarded the Nobel Peace Prize in 1990.

Meeting between Mikhail Gorbachev and US President Ronald Reagan, December 9, 1987

Gorbachev, however, came under increasing internal pressure. The traditional party cadre sabotaged his reform course, while his efforts did not go far enough to satisfy Western-oriented reformers. The catastrophic economic situation led to strikes, and the Soviet Union became increasingly dependent on extensive financial assistance from Western countries. To make matters worse, in April 1986 the worst nuclear power plant disaster to date occurred in Ukraine when the Chernobyl plant's ⓬ No. 4 reactor exploded.

In addition to these problems, separatist conflicts broke out. As early as 1986, unrest began in

Demanding freedom: more than 20,000 citizens demonstrate in Moscow on September 16, 1990

Kazakhstan. National reform movements and representatives of the people, particularly in the Baltic republics, sought to leave the Soviet Union in 1990. The same year, the first Russian ⓮ demonstrations against Communist rule took place. On August 19, 1991, conservative hardliners attempted to execute a coup and isolated ⓯ Gorbachev, who was absent from Moscow.

Brezhnev's funeral: leading representatives of the Soviet party and government carry his open coffin, November 15, 1982

Damaged reactor at the nuclear power plant in Chernobyl, 1986

Andrey Gromyko

For almost 30 years, from 1957 to 1985, Andrey Gromyko, an economist and long-standing ambassador to Washington and the United Nations, represented the interests of the Soviet Union on the world stage. The grim-mannered foreign minister became known as "Mr. Nyet" in the West. He was central to negotiations with the US over disarmament and nonaggression agreements, becoming a member of the ruling Politburo in 1973. In July 1985, Gorbachev sidelined him by making him chairman of the state council.

above: Soviet foreign minister Andrey Gromyko in 1985

Mar. 11, 1985 | Gorbachev becomes general secretary of the USSR
1986 | Nuclear disaster in Chernobyl
1987-89 | Soviet army withdraws from Afghanistan
1989 | Fall of the Berlin Wall
1990 | Gorbachev awarded Nobel Peace Prize

Russia under Yeltsin and Putin

In 1991, the Soviet empire broke down into a federation of former Soviet Socialist Republics. Sweeping reforms were carried out under Yeltsin, but the war in Chechnya also began.

Boris Yeltsin (right) humiliates Gorbachev in the Russian Duma, August 23, 1991

The Moscow coup on August 19, 1991, failed due to the resistance of the people and uncertainty in the army. When Mikhail Gorbachev returned, he found he had been ❶ deprived of virtually all power. The new leader as president of ❹ Russia was Gorbachev's former rival, Moscow mayor ❷ Boris Yeltsin. In September, Yeltsin recognized the

The most powerful man in Russia from 1991 on: Boris Yeltsin, 1990

Soldiers of a Russian honor guard, June 12, 1999, during a parade for Independence Day

independence of the Baltic States, and in November he disbanded the Communist party of the Soviet Union. The USSR was officially dissolved on December 21, 1991, when eleven former Soviet republics—Armenia, Azerbaijan, Belarus, Georgia, Kazakhstan, Kyrgyzstan, Moldova, Tajikistan, Turkmenistan, Ukraine, and Uzbekistan—withdrew and, together with Russia, formed the Commonwealth of Independent States (CIS).

In the next few years, President Yeltsin leaned heavily on the support of the West, particularly for economic assistance. He also advanced the disarmament process. Yeltsin imposed a new constitution on the parliament in 1993, strengthening the presidency and thwarting an attempted coup by conservatives. Russia joined NATO's Partnership for Peace program in June 1994 and signed a security agreement with NATO in May 1997.

❺ Russian troops invaded Chechnya in 1994 following separatist moves, and the heavy handed military campaign proved unpopular with the Russian people. A second Chechen war began in 1999 in the wake of assassinations and bomb attacks by Chechen rebels. The Russian military offensive soon became bogged down in a brutal occupation which attracted criticism from the international community.

Following a rapid devaluation of the ruble, the Russian government was forced to default on its foreign debts in 1998. Many Russians lost their savings as inflation soared and Yeltsin became increasingly unpopular. Beset by health problems, he stepped down in favor of the former chairman of the security services, Vladimir Putin, at the end of 1999.

Russian soldiers patrolling the region around the Chechen capital of Grozny, where Chechen rebels continued their attacks, July 1986

❸ Putin soon established himself as a popular and strong leader, announcing his intention to reduce corruption. However, critics inside and outside Russia have been alarmed by his curtailment of press and media freedom and his increasingly authoritarian leadership style. Putin has sought to restore Russia's international standing. After the head of the oil company Yukos, oligarch Mikhail Khodorkovsky, was arrested on tax evasion charges in 2003, Putin was reelected president with 71 percent of the vote in 2004. After serving the constitutional maximum of two consecutive terms, he endorsed his first deputy prime minister Dimitrij Medvedev as presidential candidate. Medvedev appointed Putin as prime minister after he won the election in 2008. Putin remains Russia's leading political figure, but Medvedev has gained influence.

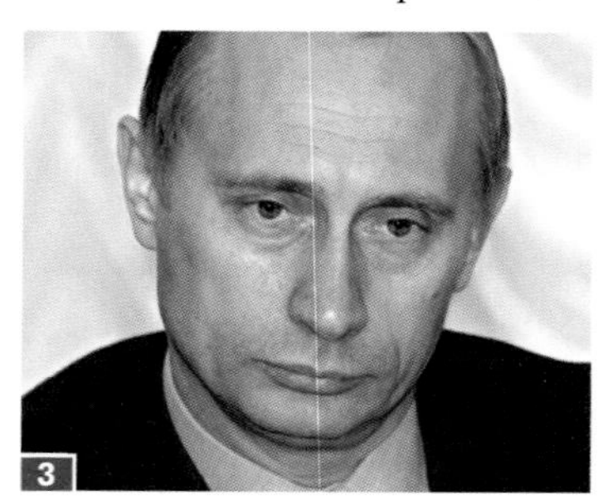

Vladimir Putin, June 7, 2000

The Chechnya Conflict

The violent conflict began in December 1994 with the occupation of Chechnya by Russian troops in response to the kidnapping of a Russian soldier by a separatist militia. After seizing the capital, Grozny, President Yeltsin declared the war officially over in May 1997. The elected president of Chechnya, Aslan Maskhadov, was not recognized by Russia and went underground. He was shot dead by Russian troops in Chechnya in 2005. A Second Chechnya War began in 1999 after a series of terrorist attacks against Russian targets by separatists.

Chechen woman in front of destroyed houses in the capital Grozny, December 30, 1994

Chechen sniper watching the area in front of the presidential palace in Grozny, January 10, 1995

19 Aug 1991	Moscow coup, Yeltsin's Presidency
21 Dec 1991	Formation of CIS
1993	New constitution
1994	Kuchma's presidency in Ukraine
Jun 1994	Russia joins NATO's "Partnership for Peace"
Dec 1994	Russian occupation of Chechnya

Ukraine, Belarus, and Moldova

While Ukraine and Moldova have developed functioning democratic systems, the political regime in Belarus (formerly Byelorussia) remains authoritarian.

Since the middle of World War II, Ukraine had been making efforts toward autonomy. The Ukrainian Insurgent Army waged bloody battles against Soviet authorities until 1954. With the breakup of the USSR in December 1991, Ukraine became a member of the CIS, and a majority of the Ukrainians voted for continued close cooperation with Russia. ❻ Leonid Kuchma, who ruled with a firm hand as president from 1994 to 2004, began to open up the country to a market economy. Politically he leaned decidedly toward Russia. Irregularities in the elections for Kuchma's successor in 2004 led to peaceful, long-running popular ❿ protests—the "Orange Revolution," resulting in a runoff election in January 2005. The election was won by reformist politician and former prime minister ❼ Viktor Yushchenko, who declared his intention to bring Ukraine closer to the West. Since 2010 his successor Viktor Yanukovych has continued this course and strives to find a balance between Russia and the EU.

6 President Leonid Kuchma (left) at a meeting with prominent regional political figures, November 29, 2004

8 Moldovans on a horse-drawn buggy

Byelorussia, which declared its sovereignty as the Republic of Belarus in July 1990 and has been a member of the ⓫ CIS since 1991, has also been politically close to Russia. ❾ Alexander Lukashenko has been president since 1994. Originally seen as a reformer, he increased his authority through a referendum in 1996 and since then has ruled as "Europe's last dictator." The press and opposition have been massively intimidated and political opposition suppressed. At the end of his term of office in 1999, Lukashenko simply refused to step down. Since 2007, he has mobilized his followers through mass party organization.

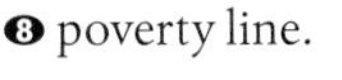

In Moldova, a member of the CIS since 1991, former Communist party members have been governing since 1994 in various alliances. There are tensions between the ethnic Moldovans, Russians, and Gagauz over the Dnestr region (Transnistria), which claims autonomy. The country is also struggling with economic problems, and approximately 80 percent of the population lives below the ❽ poverty line.

7 Viktor Yushchenko, November 22, 2004, elected president after a revote in Ukraine's 2004 election

9 Aleksandr Lukashenko, "Europe's last dictator," March 28, 1997

10 Supporters of Viktor Yushchenko demonstrating on the streets of Kiev during the "Orange Revolution," October 23, 2004

11 Lukashenko (Belarus), Nasarbajew (Kazakhstan), Putin (Russia), and Kuchma (Ukraine) during a CIS debate about a common free trade area

1996 | Lukashenko's dictatorship in Belarus
May 1997 | Security agreement with NATO
1999 | Second Chechen Conflict begins
2000 | Yeltsin resigns, Vladimir Putin takes office
March 2004 | Putin reelected President of Russia

The Baltic States and the Caucasus

Since gaining independence the Baltic States turned toward the West, establishing democratic structures and joining the European Union. Since 2003 Georgia has moved toward democracy.

Strong independence movements emerged in the Baltic States as early as 1987, recalling the countries' traditions of independence after 1918. In 1990, Lithuania and Latvia were the first Soviet republics to declare their ❷, ❸ independence; violent coup attempts in both states by Moscow loyalists were averted. In all three Baltic Soviet republics, the people voted for independence in referendums, and independence became a reality for them in the wake of the coup attempt against Gorbachev in August 1991.

The Baltic nations' transition to stable democratic conditions after the Western model was made easier through membership in the United Nations (1991) and the Council of Europe (1993–1995), as well as economic assistance and cooperation treaties with the West. The ❶ withdrawal of Soviet troops and border treaties with neighboring countries were completed by 1994. Latvia was the first Baltic country to apply for ❹ membership in the European Union, on October 27, 1995, and ❽ Estonia and Lithuania soon followed. After strengthening their economies and parliamentary systems, the three were among the ten new EU members on May 1, 2004.

1 Soviet troops withdrawing from Lithuania, March 3, 1992

4 Young Lithuanians celebrating their country's accession to the European Union at a concert on the Cathedral Square in Vilnius, April 30, 2004

5 Soviet forces on the border between Armenia and Azerbaijan, January 22, 1990

2 Demonstrators wave the Lithuanian flag in front of the parliament building in Vilnius, January 9, 1991

3 A young man waving the Latvian flag during a demonstration demanding independence from the Soviet Union, Riga, January 14, 1991

In the Caucasus, bloody fighting began as early as 1989 over the ❺ Nagorno-Karabakh region, whose predominantly Armenian population declared its independence from Azerbaijan in 1991. In 1993 Armenia invaded Azerbaijan in support of the enclave; the two CIS members finally agreed to a cease-fire the next year. In Azerbaijan, the former Communists, led by Heydar Aliyev, returned to power in 1993. Nagorno-Karabakh elected its own president in 1997, although he is not recognized by the Azerbaijani government and the situation remains tense. Armenia and Azerbaijan both became members of the Council of Europe in 2001.

Ethnic tensions also rose to the surface in Georgia during 1989, when Georgians and South Ossetians clashed; the same year, Soviet troops crushed pro-independence demonstrations in Tblisi. The national opposition, led by ❼ Zviad Gamsakhurdia, won the first multiparty elections in 1990 and declared Georgia independent in 1991. President Gamsakhurdia was deposed in 1992 after heavy fighting and the former Soviet foreign minister, ❻ Eduard Shevardnadze, was elected as his successor. Shevardnadze stabilized the economy with the earnings from oil exports and contracts with the West, but he also consolidated his own personal power through a presidential constitution. His regime was characterized by repression and corruption. Peaceful demonstrations following manipulated parliamentary elections in 2003, forced Shevardnadze to resign. New elections held in 2004 were won by opposition leader Mikhail Saakashvili, who then became president. A military conflict with Russia erupted in 2008, after Russia recognized the independence of South Ossetia and Abkhazia. Heavy battles led to casualties and destruction on both sides.

6 Eduard Shevardnadze, president of Georgia, addressing the national parliament, April 30, 2000

7 Zviad Gamsakhurdia, the first post-Soviet Georgian president

8 Tourists in the old town of Tallinn, capital of Estonia, 2001

1989 | War over Nagorno-Karabakh between Armenia and Azerbaijan
1990 | Presidency of Niyasov in Turkmenistan
1991 | Tajikistan becomes independent
1991 | Independence of Lithuania and Latvia / Both countries join the UN
1992 | Presidency of Shevardnadze in Georgia

The Central Asian States

The former Soviet republics of Central Asia formed authoritarian presidential regimes that combined modest economic reform with old political elites.

Like their Caucasus counterparts, the former Soviet republics of Central Asia experienced political turbulence after independence. They all share a resurgent and often politicized Islamic base, whose radical adherents gained access to weapons and propaganda material through the uncontrolled borders of Afghanistan. The regimes of these states exercised a virtual monopoly over political life in the state .

12 Emomalii Rahmon, the Tajik president, 1993

In Turkmenistan, Communist party head ❾ Saparmurat Niyasov was president and head of government from 1990–2006. He increased his authority with a new constitution in 1992 and appointed himself president for life in 1999 with a bizarre personality cult. His successor Gurbanguly Berdimuhamedov (since 2007) follows a less autocratic course.

9 Saparmurad Niyasov, president of the Central Asian Republic of Turkmenistan, 1997

10 Islam Karimov, the authoritarian president of Uzbekistan since 1990

Tajikistan became independent in 1991, and ⓬ Emomalii Rahmonov, who changed his name to Rahmon in 2007, assumed power as head of state a year later. He declared war on Islamists and called on CIS troops to help against armed rebels in 1993–1994. After Afghan supported rebels gained control of a part of the country in 1996, Rahmon concluded peace talks with them and even allowed them to participate in the government in 1998. A strong personality cult has supported his repeated reelection.

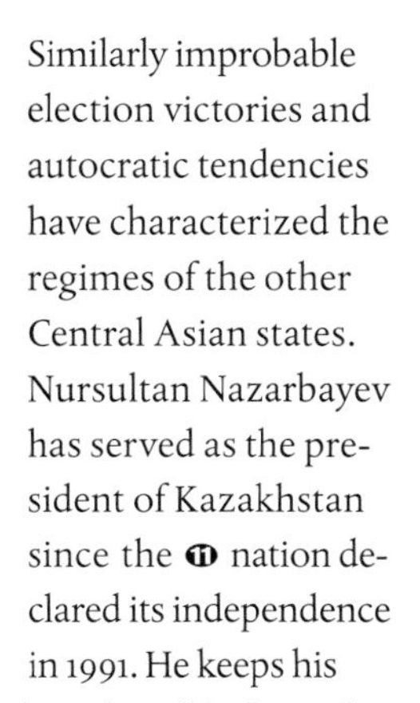

Similarly improbable election victories and autocratic tendencies have characterized the regimes of the other Central Asian states. Nursultan Nazarbayev has served as the president of Kazakhstan since the ⓫ nation declared its independence in 1991. He keeps his country relatively stable through economic ties with the West, cordial political relations with Russia and China, and the exploitation of the country's ⓯ oil and mineral reserves. In 2000, he was granted lifelong powers.

President ❿ Islam Karimov has held power in Uzbekistan since 1990, ruling over the ⓮ predominantly Muslim population with an iron hand. Uzbekistan provided bases for the American- led coalition during the invasion of Afghanistan in 2001. Kyrgyzstan, the smallest of the republics with perhaps 5 million citizens, was run by President ⓭ Askar Akayev from 1990 to 2005 and encouraged the development of a market economy. In 1998 Kyrgyzstan became the first former Soviet republic to join the World Trade Organization (WTO). After heavy fighting between government troops and Islamist rebels in 1999, Akayev began a severe crackdown against dissidents. During the Tulip Revolution in 2005, he was ousted by opposition leader Kurmanbek Bakiyev, who was also driven out of office and forced to flee the country amid violent antigovernment riots in 2010. The interim government has passed a new constitution that supports a parliamentary system and reduces the power of the president.

13 Askar Akayev, president of the Central Asian Republic of Kyrgyzstan

11 Memorial erected to mark the country's independence from the USSR in the Kazakh capital Astana, 2004

14 Uzbek Muslims praying in a mosque in the capital city Tashkent, 2001

15 Oil production in Kazakhstan: drilling platform in the Caspian Sea, 2005

Northwest Africa since 1945

Between 1956 and 1962, the Maghreb freed itself of its political ties to France, but not always peacefully; the war of liberation in Algeria was prolonged and bloody. Although Morocco, Tunisia, and Algeria all have somewhat authoritarian regimes today, they have frequently assumed a mediating role between Europe and Africa or the Islamic world and have made progress in economic modernization. Attempts to modernize along the lines of Western industrial society have often been accompanied by efforts to keep ❶ Islamist groups out of political power.

Fighting against Islamic fundamentalists: An Algerian soldier guards the village Ben Achour, July 23, 1997

Morocco and Tunisia

After winning independence in 1956–1957, both countries initially achieved political stability only at the cost of entrenching authoritarian regimes.

Morocco's fight for ❸ independence was fought by the Istiqlal (Independence) party. When Sultan ❹ Muhammad V endorsed its demands in 1953, the French exiled him. Subsequent protests accelerated decolonization, which was completed on March 2, 1956. Muhammad V became king and reigned with the support of the nationalists. In 1956, Morocco regained Tangier, which had been internationalized, and raised claims to the Western Sahara.

Women in Tangiers, Morocco, September 16, 2004

In 1961 Muhammad died and was succeeded by his son, Hassan II, who faced criticism from the left-wing opposition and the Istiqlal party. He took repressive action against his opponents and in 1965 imposed martial law. An attempted coup by military units in August 1972 resulted in a fresh crackdown. In 1976, the king annexed a section of the Spanish Sahara with the civilian "Green March," later occupying the area militarily. King Hassan eased domestic restrictions after 1977 and carried out cautious modernization. His son, ❺ Muhammad VI, has introduced reforms since taking the throne in 1999, pardoning thousands of political prisoners. Efforts have also been made to improve the ❷ legal position of women, while respecting the sentiments of Moroccan Islam.

In Tunisia, the Neo Destour Party under ❻ Habib Bourguiba led the nationalists in the fight for independence. Following the granting of autonomy from France in 1954, Tunisia became an independent republic on July 25, 1957. President Bourguiba pursued his own "path to socialism," introduced improvements in social and medical care, and sought to bring about the secularization of society. He worked for closer ties to the West and opened up Tunisia to ❼ tourism, although he took tough measures against dissi-

Grafitti demanding independence for the French protectorate, ca. 1944

dents. He was forced into retirement in 1987 by his successor, Zine el Abidine Ben Ali. After initially lifting restrictions on press freedoms, Ben Ali's rule has been characterized by the repression of dissenters, notably from Islamic political groups. After heavy riots that also spread to other Arab countries, Ben Ali fled to Saudi Arabia in January 2011. Under the interim government the country has still not come to rest.

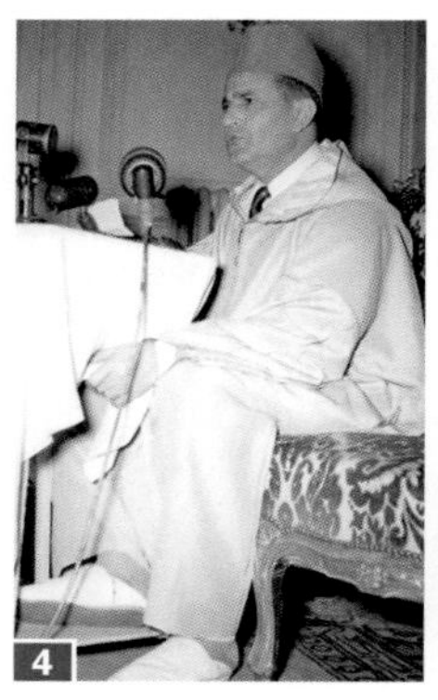

Muhammad V during a radio broadcast, November 14, 1955

The progressive king Muhammad VI, June 20, 2000

Habib Bourguiba at his residence in Tunis, July 1957

Tamerza, a village in one of Tunisia's oases

Nov 1954 | Formation of FLN in Algeria – Beginning of the Algerian War

2 Mar 1956 | Morocco becomes independent

25 Jul 1957 | Tunisia granted independence

from 1961 | King Hassan II rules in Morocco

Algeria

Following the violent war of independence that lasted until 1962, the country only briefly found peace. A new civil war between government forces and Islamic militia raged from 1991 to 1999.

The war of independence in the ⑨ French colony of Algeria was waged with increasing brutality by both sides. The various armed liberation movements joined together as the National Liberation Front (FLN) headed by Ahmed Ben Bellah in November 1954, and the ⑧ Algerian War began. As the violence escalated, the guerrilla warfare of the independence fighters was met by military repression from the French that further alienated the Algerian people. When the French government finally declared itself ready to make concessions to Algeria, the Fourth Republic in France was toppled by an alliance between French Algerians and the French army in May 1958. General de Gaulle used his prestige to resolve the crisis, preserving French democracy and preparing the way for the French withdrawal from Algeria.

On March 18, 1962, Algeria was granted independence. ⑩ Ahmed Ben Bellah became the country's new leader and let himself be elected president in September. In October, Algeria was accepted as a member of the United Nations and Bellah signalized Algeria's future neutrality concerning international affairs. His one-sided domestic politics, though, caused an ⑪ exodus of Europeans, leaving the country without an economic and technical elite. In June 1965, Ben Bellah was ousted by his defense minister, ⑬ Houari Boumedienne. He introduced a new socialist agenda, nationalizing French rural estates, industry, and oil companies, while relying on the military to prop up his rule. Extensive industrial projects were initiated, primarily with Soviet aid, and an "agrarian revolution" was carried out by distributing land to poor farmers. General Chadli Ben Dschedid became president after Boumedienne's death in 1979. The radical Islamic Salvation Front (FIS) was established at the same time.

In the December 1991 parliamentary elections, the FIS won the first round and looked certain to achieve an overall majority, but the military—with tacit international approval— intervened to prevent the FIS from taking power. Military repression and a state of emergency led to revolts and assassination attempts by Islamists. In June 1992 President Muhammad Boudiaf was the victim of such an attempt as the country plunged into a ⑫ civil war that killed ca. 95,000 people.

Charles de Gaulle after being elected French Prime Minister in June 1958, in Algeria

Deifen-Bacher, the prefect of Tlemcen, asks the population to stay

French soldier guards the University of Algiers during the Algerian war, February 28, 1962

The first president of Algeria, Ahmed Ben Bellah (left), and his later adversary Houari Boumedienne (right), September 10, 1962

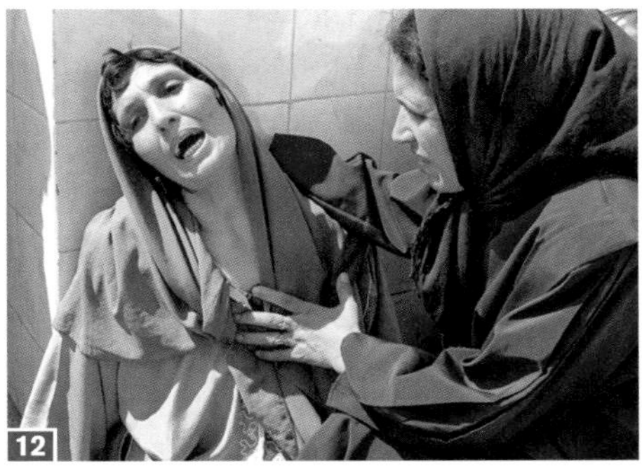

September 23, 1997: A woman cries for the victims of a massacre by Islamic fundamentalists, who, according to the official version, killed about 85 people in Bentalha on September 22, near Algiers

Houari Boumedienne (third from right), the former defense minister and leader of Algeria, gives a press conference on July 22, 1965 with members of his new government and participants in the coup against Ben Bellah

Algeria today

Peace did not return until Abdelaziz Bouteflika, president since 1999, began to pursue "national reconciliation." Though this policy has met with some success, relations between Islamist groups and the government remain tense, and sporadic violence continues. In September 2003, the army killed 150 Islamist fighters in the mountains east of Algiers, and in June 2004 security forces murdered Nabil Sahraoui, leader of the Salafist group. His second-in-command, Amari Saifi, who was captured in 2004, is presumed to be responsible for the 2003 kidnapping of 32 European tourists in the Sahara.

above: President Abdelaziz Bouteflika with his followers during an electoral campaign, April 10, 1999

18 Mar 1962 | Algeria becomes independent

1976 | "Green March"

1987 | Ben Ali comes to power in Tunisia

1991–99 | Civil war in Algeria

1999 | King Muhammad VI crowned in Morocco

ISRAEL SINCE 1948

The State of Israel's fight for ❶ existence determines its policies and identity to this day. Between the wars, and especially after 1945, many Jews settled in Palestine and cultivated and developed the country with determination and idealism. However, from the beginning, no satisfactory political solution could be found for the consequent expulsion of the Palestinians who were already living in the area. Relations with Israel's Soviet-backed Arab neighbors have long been strained to the breaking point. The US-Israeli alliance has become central to both countries' foreign policies, helping to ensure Israeli supremacy in the Middle East. After a series of military defeats, most Arab countries eventually reached an accommodation with Israel, leaving the Palestinians isolated in their struggle for a state of their own.

1 Behind barbed wire: An Israeli flag flutters over a kibbutz, 1988

Israel before the Six-Day War of 1967

In 1948 Zionists fought against the British colonial authorities, Palestinian inhabitants, and the neighboring Arab states to create a Jewish state. With US help it succeeded economically, militarily, and politically. Its military power brought security but not peace to the Palestinians.

The state of Israel was born in conflict. In 1939, in order to avert tensions with the Palestinians, the British mandate authorities reduced the immigration quota of Jews to Palestine to 75,000 people. Beginning in 1945, however, after the Holocaust in Europe, thousands of Jews ❷ poured into the country—most illegally, but supported by Jewish refugee organizations. They lived in communes and kibbutzim and were determined to fight for their survival. Until 1948 the British tried numerous repressive measures to stem the flow, to which the Jewish underground organizations responded with violent attacks.

3 First Prime Minister of Israel David Ben-Gurion, 1950

❸ David Ben-Gurion, the leader of the Workers' party (Mapai), proclaimed the ❹ independent state of Israel on May 14, 1948. In 1949 the Knesset met for the first time as a single-chamber parliament and began by electing Chaim Weizmann as president and Ben-Gurion as prime minister. By 1954 the number of immigrating Jews had doubled to 576,000; they seized 750,000 (303,514 ha) acres of Arab lands, which they rapidly ❺ developed. The conflict with the Palestinians remained unresolved, and Jerusalem became a city divided between Israelis and Arabs. By 1948, 500,000 Palestinians had fled to neighboring countries, especially Jordan; a further 300,000 followed in the next few years.

With extensive financial assistance from the United States, Israel experienced rapid economic growth and established a modern and powerful military defense. Israel triumphed in the Arab-Israeli War of May–November 1948 and occupied ❼ Gaza and the Sinai Peninsula along with Britain and France in October 1956. During the Six-Day War (June 5–10, 1967), Israel crushed a coalition of Arab states led by Egypt, in the process occupying Syria's ❻ Golan Heights, East Jerusalem, and portions of the Palestinian territories.

5 Tractor on a kibbutz, a collective farm community in Israel, 1962

6 The Golan Heights, occupied by Israel since 1967

2 Groups of Jewish immigrants make illegal night landings on the coast of Palestine, seeking to evade British patrols, December 1947

4 Leader of Zionist insurgency and first Israeli Prime Minister David Ben-Gurion proclaims the independence of the state of Israel in Tel Aviv, May 14, 1948

7 Mobilization for the occupation of Gaza and Sinai in Tel Aviv, October 1956

14 May 1948 | Proclamation of the state of Israel
1949 | Weizmann elected president
Oct–Nov 1956 | The Suez-Sinai War
5–10 Jun 1967 | Six-Day War
1972 | Israeli invasion of Lebanon

Israel from 1967 to the Present

The peace agreements with Egypt and Jordan were milestones in Israeli foreign policy. In the handling of the Palestinians's demands, numerous attempts at mediation have been undertaken, but the process remains contentious.

In 1972 under Prime Minister ❾ Golda Meir, Israeli troops occupied southern Lebanon, from which Palestinian guerrillas were conducting attacks into northern Israel. The Israelis were also able to repel Egypt and Syria's surprise attack in the Yom Kippur War of October 6–26, 1973. Since the Geneva Middle East Peace Conference in December 1973 and through the mediation of the United Nations, the United States, and other nations, gradual settlements have been cautiously reached with Egypt and later with Jordan, and temporarily also with Syria. The terror attacks and ⓫ militancy of the Palestine Liberation Organization (PLO) and other Palestinian groups nevertheless remained an urgent problem and led to various diplomatic initiatives.

In 1974 Israel stood at the point of a serious financial and economic crisis. At the same time, a rift opened within the leading Israeli parties concerning understanding and agreement with the Palestinians. In 1979 peace with Egypt was reached only by strenuous effort. The office of prime minister changed hands between hard-liners and moderates who sought a permanent accord with the Palestinians. The voices of ⓬ strict Orthodox Jews and of radical settler groups grew ever louder.

Growing US pressure and secret confidence-building talks led to Israel's acceptance of the PLO as a negotiating partner in the Camp David peace talks in 1992–1993. The peace process suffered its first serious setback when Israeli prime minister Yitzhak Rabin ⓭ was murdered by a Jewish fundamentalist on November 4, 1995. Palestinian self-government began in some communities in 1997. In 2000 Ehud Barak's Labor government seemed poised to offer more concessions to the Palestinians than any previous Israeli leader—including a Palestinian state—but could not clinch a deal. After the 2001 launch of the Intifada and suicide bombings, Prime Minister ❿ Ariel Sharon (2001–2006) answered with military retaliatory strikes. In 2002 he began the construction of a controversial ❽ separation barrier as protection against Palestinian terrorist attacks. In 2009 Prime Minister Benjamin Netanyahu (1996–1999, since 2009) endorsed for the first time the idea of a Palestinian state, but he has not stopped Israeli settlement construction in the West Bank.

9 Golda Meir, Israeli Prime Minister between1969 and 1974

10 Prime Minister Ariel Sharon at a press conference, 2004

8 Israeli workers constructing the security fence unilaterally announced by Israel in 2004; Kalkilia, West Bank, November 17, 2004

11 An armed militant from the radical group Hamas guards a Palestinian refugee camp in the Israeli-occupied Gaza Strip, October 1, 2004

12 An Orthodox Jew in traditional dress praying before the Wailing Wall in Jerusalem, 1992

13 Careful advances: PLO chief Arafat talks with the Israeli Prime Minister Yitzhak Rabin during a meeting in Madrid, 1994

Yitzhak Rabin

A long-serving Israeli army chief of staff and leading strategist of the victory in 1973, Yitzhak Rabin changed his hard-line politics to a policy of understanding. As prime minister in 1992 he forbade the building of further Jewish settlements in the occupied Palestinian zones and initiated talks with the PLO. On September 13, 1993, a historic handshake took place between Rabin and PLO Chairman Yasir Arafat in the presence of US President Bill Clinton, for which the two leaders received the Nobel Peace Prize. On November 4, 1995, he was assassinated in Tel Aviv by a Jewish right-wing fanatic.

above: Yitzhak Rabin

Dec 1973 | Geneva Middle East Peace Conference

4 Nov 1995 | Murder of Yitzhak Rabin

6–26 Oct 1973 | Yom Kippur War

1979 | Peace accord with Egypt

2001 | Ariel Sharon becomes prime minister

The Arab World and the Near East

SINCE 1945

After gaining independence from European colonial rule the Arab states looked to the USSR and Pan-Arabism as alternative paths to nation-building. However, ❶ authoritarian rulers soon established themselves in the region. Since the 1970s a growing educated population lacking employment opportunities has begun to undermine many regimes, and this frustration has been exploited by politically radicalized Islamic groups. Ironically, the only freely elected Arab government in the region is that of the Palestinians, who do not have their own state.

Jordan's King Abdullah II followed by his honorary guard

Palestine and Jordan up to "Black September," 1970

In 1948 thousands of Palestinians fled the Arab-Israeli fighting that accompanied the founding of Israel. The arrival of the refugees destabilized Jordan until King Hussein II reasserted control.

The "Palestinian problem" is intimately tied to the history of Israel. The UN decision on November 29, 1947, to divide Palestine into Jewish and Arab states failed. Following the founding of Israel, Palestinians fled en masse into the West Bank and Jordan, and their land was expropriated by Israel. Jordan, which was structurally weak with a small population and which had only become an independent kingdom in May 1946, struggled to cope with the waves of refugees. In 1950 it annexed part of the West Bank territory (now West Jordan). Clashes broke out between Palestinian guerrillas and Jordanian forces. While the grand mufti of Jerusalem, ❸ Amin al-Husayni, the political leader of the Palestinians, called for a war of annihilation against Israel, ❷ King Abdullah I of Jordan sought rapprochement with the Jewish state. He was assassinated by a Palestinian gunman on July 20, 1951, in al-Aqsa Mosque in East Jerusalem.

The increasingly radicalized Palestinians sought help from the rest of the Arab world and in the 1950s looked to Egyptian president Nasser above all. In the name of Arab solidarity, other countries in the region also became involved and armed Palestinian fighters. There were raids and skirmishes with Israel. Abdullah's grandson ❺ Hussein II had been ruling in Jordan since August 1952. In 1957, Great Britain withdrew its last soldiers from the country. Under pressure from the Palestinians, Hussein allied himself with Nasser while still maintaining contacts with the West. He survived several assassination attempts and attempted coups. His son, ❹ Abdullah II, succeeded him to the Jordanian throne in 1999.

During the 1967 Arab-Israel war, Israeli forces occupied all of Jerusalem and the West Bank, leading to a new influx of Palestinians into Jordan. Following the Arab defeat, ❼ Yasir Arafat, the head of the Palestine Liberation Organization (PLO), began organizing guerrilla attacks against Israel, operating out of Jordan. The Palestinian group threatened to take control of the capital ❻ Amman until, in 1970, after protracted and heavy fighting, King Hussein militarily broke the PLO's power during "Black September."

Amin al-Husayni, the grand mufti of Jerusalem, 1941

King Abdullah II of Jordan during his pilgrimage to Mecca, November 2004

King Hussein II of Jordan during his service as an air force pilot, 1955

The main street, named after King Talal, in the center of the Jordanian capital of Amman

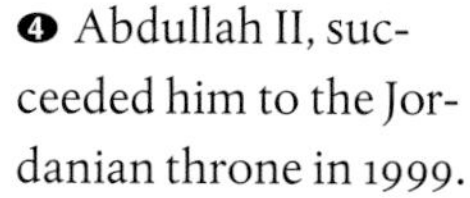

King Abdullah I (left) of Jordan, broke with the Palestinians after 1970

PLO leader Yasir Arafat, 1978

1947 | Division of Palestine
1948 | Palestine War
20 Jul 1951 | Murder of King Abdullah I
1964 | PLO founded
1969 | Yasir Arafat becomes PLO leader
Sep 1970 | "Black September"
1977 | Carter initiative
1987 | Start of the first Intifada

On the Path to a Palestinian State

After speaking at the United Nations, PLO leader Arafat began to gain international recognition for Palestinian claims to an independent state. Attempts at direct Palestinian–Israeli negotiations began in 1993 with the Oslo Peace Process but have yet to yield a comprehensive settlement.

In 1971 a general reconciliation took place between Jordan and the Palestinians, as well as between Jordan and its neighbors Egypt and Syria, both of which had sided with the Palestinians in 1970. From 1972 the Palestinian leadership began a series of spectacular attacks and airplane hijackings, such as the ⓭ 1977 Lufthansa seizure, with the aim of drawing international attention to their cause. After the Arab defeat in the Yom Kippur War of 1973 and Egypt's reconciliation with Israel, the Palestinians increasingly sought support from other Arab countries—especially Syria, Libya, and Iraq—while the PLO brought its goal of founding a Palestinian state before the United Nations. The United States shielded Israel from much of the pressure but also sought to mediate, notably with the 1977 "Carter Initiative." Arafat and the PLO leadership revised their thinking and increasingly sought to negotiate. However, this process suffered a major setback in 1982 when, following the occupation of West Beirut, Israel's ally, the Christian Falangist militia, carried out a massacre in the Palestinian refugee camps of Sabra and Shatila.

Intifada: Israeli policemen fire tear gas at Palestinian youths during the first Intifada, Eastern Jerusalem, December 21, 1987

Palestinian mourners at Arafat's funeral in Ramallah, November 13, 2004

Lufthansa flight hijacked by Palestinian militants on October 13, 1977, during a forced landing in Mogadishu, Somalia

The Palestinian ⓾ Intifada (national uprising) began in ❽ Gaza and the West Bank in 1987. Initially peaceful, it soon deteriorated into violent street clashes between stone-throwing civilians and Israeli troops. After recognizing Israel's right to exist in 1988, Arafat stepped up his demands for an autonomous Palestinian state. The Oslo Accords, signed in 1994, set out a framework for a negotiated peace. The following year, the Palestinian Authority was set up to administer the Gaza Strip and parts of the West Bank, and in 1997 ❾ Hebron was returned to the ⓬ Palestinians. But this process was increasingly undermined by continued violence on both sides. A second Intifada began in 2000, and after a wave of bombings, the Israeli army reoccupied the Palestinian autonomous territories in April 2001 and then besieged Arafat's headquarters. In April 2003, the United States proposed a "roadmap to peace" that envisaged a Palestinian state. President Arafat ⓫ died in November 2004, and many saw the election of his successor, the moderate Mahmoud Abbas, as an opportunity to break the deadlock. Since 2007 the growing conflict between two political factions has divided the Palestinian autonomous territories: the Gaza Strip is ruled by the radical Hamas and the West Bank by the moderate Fatah under Abbas. This disruption complicates peace initiatives for a united and independent Palestine.

Israeli military checkpoint in the southern part of the Gaza Strip

Rooftops in the Palestinian city of Hebron, occupied by Israel until 1997

Excerpt from the PLO founding Charter of 1964

"The Palestine Liberation Organization, representative of the Palestinian revolutionary forces, is responsible for the Palestinian Arab people's movement in its struggle—to retrieve its homeland, liberate and return to it, and exercise the right to self-determination in it—in all military, political, and financial fields..."

(Article 26)

Arafat supporters mourn his death, November 6, 2004

After signing the Hebron agreement Israeli President Benjamin Netanyahu and Yasir Arafat shake hands, 1997

1994 | Oslo Accords
1995 | Autonomous authority set up
1997 | Hebron handed over to Palestinians
2000 | Start of second Intifada
Mar–May 2002 | Siege of Arafat's headquarters
Apr 2003 | US announces "Roadmap"
Nov 2004 | Arafat dies

Egypt under Nasser and Sadat, Libya under Qaddafi

Under Nasser, Egypt achieved a position of supremacy in the Arab world. His successor Sadat ended the anti-Israel course, while Libya under Qaddafi continued the path of "Nasserism."

In Egypt, the corrupt regime of King Farouk I, though supported by the British, was toppled on July 23, 1952, by a group known as the "Free Officers Movement," which proclaimed a republic on July 18, 1953. In 1954 ❸ Gamal Abdel Nasser became premier of the republic; two years later he assumed the office of president as well, being the only candidate in presidential elections. Nasser suppressed the Communists and the Muslim Brotherhood and proclaimed a path to modernize the country based on socialism and nationalism. He established himself as the voice of Pan-Arabism and in 1955, along with Indian prime minister Nehru and others, became a leader of the Nonaligned Movement opposing the dominance of the superpowers.

Anwar el-Sadat, Egyptian head of state from 1970 to 1981

Distributor on a pipeline on the oil field As Sarah in Libya

By nationalizing the Suez Canal in July 1956, Nasser provoked the international Suez Crisis that came to a head in October. Despite Egypt's military ❺ defeat by Israel, Great Britain, and France, Nasser generally managed to maintain his political credibility while building up great prestige in the Third World. In 1958, as an experiment in Pan- Arabism, Syria and Egypt merged as the ❻ United Arab Republic; the union lasted only until 1961, however, although it existed officially until 1971. In the 1960s Nasser initiated major construction projects such as the ❼ Aswan Dam and power plants in Egypt.

Premier Gamal Abdel Nasser, 1955

Colonel Muammar al-Qaddafi, 1975

Gamal Abdel Nasser and his Syrian colleague Shukri el Kuwatli after the signing of the document uniting Egypt and Syria, February 1, 1958

Although weakened by his defeat in the Six-Day War against Israel in 1967, Nasser's state doctrine ("Nasserism") became an example for neighboring countries, particularly Libya, where the Revolutionary Command Council led by Colonel ❹ Muammar al-Qaddafi seized the government on September 1, 1969. Qaddafi adopted Nasser's principle of mass mobilization and personality cult with his institutionalized revolution and radically eliminated all potential opponents. He modernized the country and achieved a rise in living standards after 1969 through nationalized ❷ oil exports. His often unpredictable policies and his support of terrorist groups led to Libya's isolation in the 1980s and 1990s, which Qaddafi tried to overcome after 2000 through international compromises. An anti-government revolt in February 2011 has escalated into a bloody civil war between rebels and regime forces and Qaddafi was executed.

Warships on the Suez Channel during the Suez crisis, November 1956

Construction of the Aswan Dam, 1963

In Egypt, ❶ Anwar el-Sadat, Nasser's successor after his death in 1970, at first continued Nasser's policies, but decided in the mid- 1970s to move away from socialism. A peace treaty with Israel in March 1979 resulted in Egypt's isolation in the Arab world and its dependence on the West.

Qaddafi's Pan-Arabism

Colonel Qaddafi attempted to become the head of the Pan-Arab movement following Nasser's death. The movement seeks the unification of all Arab states. Qaddafi's ideology gave Islam a more central position. With the "Charter of Tripoli" in December 1969, he tried to bring about a merger of Libya with Egypt, Syria, and Sudan. In January 1974, he announced the impending union of his country with Tunisia, but this too failed, primarily due to Qaddafi's absolute claim to leadership.

1943 | Baath Party founded in Syria
23 Jul 1952 | King Farouk of Egypt deposed
18 Jun 1953 | Republic of Egypt proclaimed
1956 | Suez Canal nationalized
Oct 1956 | Suez crisis
1956–61 | Gamal Abdel Nasser's presidency
1963 | Amin Hafis leads putsch in Syria

Egypt under Mubarak, Syria since Independence

Mubarak continued the presidential regime in Egypt until 2011. In Syria, the Baath party prevailed under the Assad regime after initial instability.

Sadat's war against Islamism, his conciliatory stance toward Israel, and his authoritarian domestic policy, expressed in the 1978 ban on all political activities, were reasons behind his ❽ assassination during a military parade in 1981. His successor, ❾ Hosni Mubarak, continued Sadat's course, while at the same time endeavoring to reconcile with the Arab camp. He also opened up Egypt to more ❿ tourism. Egypt became a full member of the Arab League again in 1989. Mubarak's authoritarian presidential regime eased up the battle against the Muslim Brotherhood but was met with increasing criticism in the West for its lack of democracy. Inspired by the Tunisian revolution in January 2011, millions of Egyptian protesters demanded the overthrow of Mubarak who resigned from office in February 2011.

8 Security staff caring for victims lying injured on the floor after the assassination of Anwar el-Sadat, October 6, 1981

9 The President of Egypt: Hosni Mubarak (1981–2011), March 30, 1993

10 One of Egypt's many tourist attractions: One of the Memnon colossi, November 22, 2004

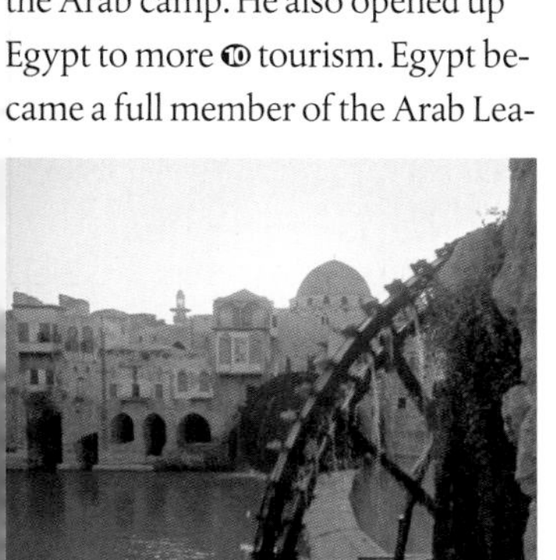
11 View over the Syrian city of Hama with a water wheel in the foreground

The conditions in ⓫ Syria, with its capital ⓮ Damascus, during the first few years after gaining independence from France in 1946 were very unstable due to the population's religious, ethnic, and political heterogeneity. After military coups in 1949 and 1951, the Baath (Rebirth) party, founded in 1943 and legalized in 1955, rose to become the leading power in the country. It propagated a Pan-Arab nationalism and socialism and cooperated with Nasser's Egypt. After the union with Egypt, driven by the Baathists, Syria withdrew again as a separate republic on September 30, 1961. In March 1963, the Baath party seized the government in a coup led by General Amin Hafis. Syria subsequently distanced itself from Nasser and turned more toward Iraq and the Palestinians. A move to the left within the Baath leadership in 1966 led to closer cooperation with the Soviet Union. In the Arab-Israeli war of 1967, Syria lost the Golan Heights to Israel.

Syria's support of the Palestinians in the "Black September" of 1970 resulted in a power struggle within the Baath party, which was won by the Alawite ⓬ minister of defense, Hafez al- Assad, in November 1970; he became president on March 11, 1971. Assad suppressed Islamic revolts, did away with possible rivals, and modernized the country on a socialist and nationalist basis. In 1976, he militarily intervened in the Lebanese civil war. The break with Iraq that had already begun in 1968 intensified through the 1970s, ultimately leading to Syria's entrance into the anti-Iraq coalition in the 1991 Gulf War. After Assad's death in 2000, the power went to his son ⓭ Bashar al-Assad. Following increasing international pressure over Syria's presence in Lebanon, Syria was forced to withdraw its troops. The revolutionary movements taking place in the Arab world since December 2010 also led to mass protests against the Syrian government. The regime responded with a violent crackdown on demonstrations and the forced detainment of protesters.

12 The Syrian defense minister, Colonel Hafez al-Assad, late 1960s

13 The Syrian president Bashar al-Assad, 8 April 2005

14 The old town of Damascus, in the center the Great Mosque,1991

1 Sep 1969 | Muammar al-Qaddafi seizes government in Libya
1967 | Six-Day War
1979 | Anwar el-Sadat takes office in Egypt
26 Mar 1979 | Peace treaty with Israel
6 Oct 1981 | Mubarak's presidency

Lebanon

Rising tensions between Lebanon's various religious communities led to a series of political crises. These culminated in a devastating civil war between 1975 and 1990. Despite the partial withdrawal of Syrian troops, the country is still marked by political unrest.

Since its independence from France on January 1, 1944, Lebanon has faced a number of problems. Proportional religious representation between Christians and Muslims was worked out in the National Pact of 1943, but subsequent developments polarized the population into the more prosperous and Western-oriented ❹ Christians in the north and the poorer, Arab-aligned Muslims of the south. An early civil war was waged from May to July 1958 after the reelection of the Christian president Camille Chamoun, whose government reestablished its authority with U.S. military assistance. The arrival of Palestinian refugees in southern Lebanon exacerbated sectarian tensions. A violent division of the country was prevented only by the establishment of a military administration in October 1969. Syria intervened on the side of the Muslims in the ❸ civil war that began in 1975 and in 1976 began a nearly 30-year occupation of broad areas of Lebanon.

The major fighting that destroyed Beirut and other Lebanese cities generally subsided after October 1976 through the mediation of the Arab League. In June 1982, following an assassination attempt against one of its ambassadors, Israel launched a full-scale invasion of the country, dubbed "Operation Peace for Galilee." The newly elected president, ❻ Bashir al-Jumayyil, was murdered in September 1982, which led to a ❺ massacre carried out by Christian Falangist militia in Palestinian refugee camps. Later in the month Jumayyil's elder brother ❼ Amin was elected his successor. The following year he oversaw peace negotiations in Geneva that included all parties involved in the civil war. Israel agreed to withdraw to a security zone in the south.

In 1988, combat flared again between the Christian militias of the north and the radical Shiite Hezbollah group. Maronite Christian general Michel Aoun declared a "war of liberation" against Syria in 1989. In 1991, Syria formally recognized Lebanon's independence but did not withdraw its military presence, citing the need to provide a counterbalance to the power of the militias. This left Lebanon occupied by two foreign powers. The 1975–1990 civil war took the lives of more than 144,000 people in all.

The situation generally ❶ stabilized after 1992 with the support of UN peacekeeping troops, but the only partially disarmed militias and the ❽ radical Palestinian movements in the country remained a problem. After the collapse of its ally, the South Lebanese Army, Israel unilaterally withdrew its forces from Lebanon in 2000. In reaction to the murder of former prime minister Rafiq Hariri in February 2005, Lebanese demonstrators demanded the ❷ withdrawal of Syrian forces. Despite extensive efforts in rebuilding the country, the peace between rivaling religious groups remains unstable.

1 Everyday life after the war: In front of the ruins of destroyed houses, boys play soccer in a Beirut suburb, October 2003

2 Hundreds of thousands of Lebanese demonstrators waving flags take to the streets to demand the withdrawal of Syrian forces, March 8, 2005

3 Lebanese Christian Falangists at a military post in southern Lebanon, 1978

4 Church in Beirut

5 Aftermath of the brutal massacre carried out by the Christian Falangist militia in a Palestinian refugee camp, September 19, 1982

6 Bashir al-Jumayyil after winning the Lebanese presidential elections, August 23, 1982

7 Amin al-Jumayyil on a state visit to the Federal Republic of Germany, November 25, 1987

8 Hezbollah guerrillas launching rockets at Israeli targets from southern Lebanon, September 1979

Dec 31, 1946 | Lebanon granted independence
Jul 1958 | Lebanese civil war
1962–69 | Civil war in Yemen
1964 | King Faisal in Saudi Arabia
1975–90 | Civil war in Yemen renewed
1976 | Syria occupies parts of Lebanon
1979 | Islamists occupy mosque in Mecca

Saudi Arabia, the Sheikhdoms, and Yemen

Saudi Arabia and the oil-producing sheikhdoms combine monarchical forms of rule with extraordinarily wealthy elites. Following a civil war, Yemen was politically divided between 1967 and 1990.

By virtue of the country's Wahhabism, Saudi Arabia is one of the most politically and ⓬ religiously conservative of the Islamic countries. The ruling al-Saud family and its clientele have a monopoly on power and are hugely wealthy. Democratic structures are entirely lacking. This conservatism stands in strange contrast to the enormous wealth of the elite and the modern infrastructure of the country, which has been financed by the exploitation of its ⓭ oil reserves, the largest in the world.

13 Oil refinery near Dhahran on the East Coast of Saudi Arabia

The founder of the kingdom, ⓫ Abd al-Aziz bin Abd al-Rahman bin Faysal bin Turki bin Abdallah bin Muhammad al-Saud, or Ibn Saud, died in 1953 and was succeeded in turn by his sons Saud, Faysal, Khalid, Fahd, and Abdullah. In 1964 ❾ Saud was deposed by his brother, Crown Prince ❿ Faysal. Faysal carried out cautious reforms and became the leader of the conservatives of the Islamic world that stood opposed to Nasserism. In 1975, Faysal was murdered by a member of his family and his brother Khalid succeeded him. Out of fear of the Islamic revolution in Iran as well as of the military dominance of Iraq, Khalid began to arm Saudi Arabia in 1980, primarily with the help of the United States. Saudi Arabia was America's most important ally in the region during the first Gulf War.

Despite growing demands for ⓮ democratic reform, the Saudi rulers have made few concessions. Similar political conditions reign in a more moderate form in Kuwait under the ruling family al-Sabah, as well as in the United Arab Emirates, Bahrain, Qatar, and Oman.

The seizure of a mosque in Mecca by Islamist extremists in November 1979, sternly dealt with by Crown Prince Fahd, was the first sign of a problem with Islamic radicalism. Today, the Saudi regime has come under pressure because many international terrorists are from Saudi Arabia.

9 The Saudi Arabian king Saud I, deposed by his brother in 1964

10 Crown Prince Faysal of Saudi Arabia, seized the crown in 1964

11 Founder and first king of modern Saudi Arabia, Abd al-Aziz ibn Saud III ruled until 1953, 1935

12 Thousands of Muslims circle the Kaaba in front of the Great Mosque of Haram Sharif seven times as part of their pilgrimage to Mecca, 2004

The United Arab Emirates

In 1971, seven emirates on the Persian Gulf, which had until then been British protectorates, joined together to form the United Arab Emirates (UAE). Among them, Dubai and the capital Abu Dhabi are the most important. They prosper through oil production and stand out for their modern ports, major building projects, and luxury hotels. Sheikh Khalifa of Abu Dhabi succeeded his father as UAE president in 2004; the sheikh of Dubai is also the prime minister.

The Marina Yacht Club in Dubai, a lavish oil-funded construction in the shape of a sailing ship, 2004

The special development of North Yemen's theocratic political structure ended in September 1962 with the overthrow of the absolute rule of the Zaidi imams, who had ruled the caliphate for a millennium. After the British withdrew from South Yemen in 1967, Marxist radicals seized power there, and in November 1967 the country was officially divided along lines similar to those drawn by British and Ottoman colonizers in 1849. South Yemen became a secular People's Republic on the Soviet model, supported by both the USSR and China; North Yemen remained an Arab republic. After periodic fighting, the two halves began negotiating a reconciliation in 1979. On May 22, 1990, the unified Republic of Yemen was created under President Ali Abdullah Saleh, who still holds office today.

14 Meeting of the Shura Council in Riyadh after the first democratic elections, February 10, 2005

1989 | Peace talks in Geneva

May 22, 1990 | Reunification of Republic of Yemen

1982 | Israel occupies southern Lebanon; Hezbollah formed

1983 | Syria proclams war of liberation

Apr 2005 | Syria announces withdrawal from Lebanon

Iraq to 1979

Following the revolution of 1958, a series of nationalist presidential regimes governed Iraq. In 1968, the secular nationalist Baath party came to power in the country.

1 King Faisal II swears an oath to the constitution in front of the Iraqi national parliament after his enthronement, Baghdad, May 2, 1953

2 The Golden Mosque in Kadhimain, near Baghdad, 1958

3 The new Iraq cabinet of General Abd al-Karim Qasim, second from left, and Abd al Salam Aref (left) in Baghdad before its first meeting, July 1958

After World War II, ❷ religious (Sunni–Shia) and inter-ethnic (Kurd–Arab) tensions grew in Iraq, where ❶ King Faisal II was controlled by his cousin, the regent Abd al-Ilah, and Prime Minister Nuri as-Said, both of whom were pro-British. Great Britain controlled a large part of the country's economy. A ❹ military coup deposed the monarchy on July 14, 1958, murdering the royal family. Brigadier ❸ Abd al-Karim Qasim, the leader of the coup, became prime minister of the new republic. He immediately undertook comprehensive administrative, social, and agrarian reforms, nationalized oil production, and in 1959 expelled the British from the country.

A revolt of the Kurds in the north began in March 1961 under Mustafa Barsani, who proclaimed a Kurdish state. All subsequent governments were compelled to negotiate with the Kurds, who were promised cultural autonomy and participation in the government in 1970.

Beginning in 1960, Qasim built up a personal dictatorship, and in 1961 he proclaimed Kuwait to be a province of Iraq. Qasim was defeated in a ❽ power struggle in February 1963 by his former second- in-command, Colonel Abd as-Salim Mohammed Arif, who seized power with the help of the Arab Socialist Baath party. Arif and the Baathists brutally persecuted Communists and other opponents, and then in November 1963, he eliminated the splintered Baathists and instead relied on traditional nationalists.

When Arif died in a helicopter accident in April 1966, his brother Abd al-Rahman Arif replaced him as ruler, but he was deposed by a military coup on July 17, 1968. Of the forces behind the coup, the revived Baath party headed by General ❼ Ahmed Hassan al-Bakr secured its supremacy over the army through numerous purges. After signing a ❺ peace deal with the ❻ Kurds in 1970, the government began to build up a socialist centralized state and initiated ambitious social projects. One major feature of this agenda was an accelerated program of land reform and irrigation projects aimed at bringing new areas into cultivation. While this process brought mixed results, the nationalization of the entire oil industry, which began in June 1972, guaranteed healthy state revenues that were further boosted the following year when prices soared. The conflict with Iran over the Shatt al Arab region on the Persian Gulf was settled in March 1975. At this point Iran withdrew its financial and military support from the Iraqi Kurds who had been rebelling in the North, forcing them to accept the government's cease-fire. Fearing renewed repression, 250,000 Kurds then fled to Iran.

4 After the fall of the monarchy: Soldiers collect furniture and other possessions thrown out of the fire-damaged royal palace following a military coup

5 Iraq president in the Kurd region: Abd as-Salim Aref (front) travelling by-donkey, July 1958

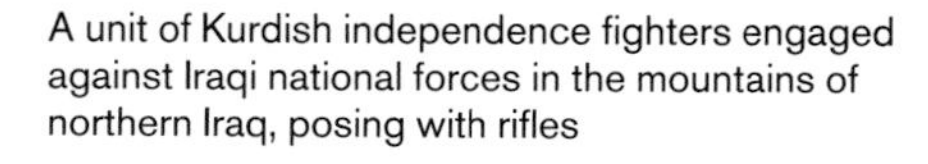

6 A unit of Kurdish independence fighters engaged against Iraqi national forces in the mountains of northern Iraq, posing with rifles

7 General Ahmed Hassan al-Bakr, head of the Baath party, 1968

8 A tank and soldiers on patrol in the streets of Baghdad two days after General Qasim was deposed in a coup, February 1963

1958 | Putsch led by Abd al-Karim Qasim
1959 | British expelled
1961 | Qasim declares Kuwait province
1961 | Kurdish revolt led by Mustafa Barsani
1963 | Putsch led by Abd as-Salim Mohammed Aref
1979 | Saddam Hussein becomes president

Iraq from Saddam Hussein to the Present

Saddam began to consolidate his personal power in 1979. After the war with Iran, he occupied Kuwait in 1990 but was defeated in 1991 and deposed in 2003.

10 Giant mural of the dictator Saddam Hussein, the kind of image that saturated the daily lives of the Iraqi people

General al-Bakr, the president of Iraq during the 1970s, came from Tikrit. In 1968, ❾ Saddam Hussein, who belonged to this clan, became al-Bakr's second in command, and from 1972 he dominated politics with a brutal single-mindedness. On July 16, 1979, he succeeded al-Bakr in the office of president and head of government and immediately set about eliminating possible rivals through numerous executions.

Using the general fear of an incursion by the Iranian revolution as justification, Saddam cleverly armed Iraq to become the strongest military power in the Arab world, largely with US assistance. He secured his rule through a ❿ personality cult, a skillfully devised surveillance system, and nepotism in the allocation of government offices—as was particularly evident in the roles given his sons Uday and Qusay. Saddam invaded Iran in September 1980, beginning a war that soon stagnated into a bloody stalemate and lasted until 1988. Saddam's forces also used ⓬ poison gas to kill thousands of rebelling Kurds in February 1988.

Taking up the claims of earlier governments, Iraqi troops occupied Kuwait on August 2, 1990, declaring it to be the 19th province of Iraq. Failure to observe UN demands to withdraw led to the first Gulf War (January 16–March 3, 1991), which ended with the Iraqis being driven out of Kuwait by a UN-mandated, US-led coalition. When the Shiites in the south and the Kurds in the north of Iraq took this opportunity to rebel against the defeated regime, Saddam brutally suppressed the rebellions, whereupon the Allies established protection zones for the Kurdish population. The Iraqi regime only hesitantly fulfilled the terms of commitment drawn up by a UN inspection team and the disposal of weapons of mass destruction agreed upon after the Gulf War. The trade embargo imposed by the UN affected the Iraqi people more than the leadership.

Following September 11, 2001, Saddam Hussein's regime again came into the eye of the United States as being a part of an "axis of evil." Citing Iraq's undisclosed weapons of mass destruction as the justification, mainly US and British armed forces invaded Iraq to depose Saddam's regime on March 20, 2003. Resistance soon broke and by May Iraq was ⓫ defeated, although no evidence of the alleged weapons was subsequently found. A governing council took over the political leadership of Iraq in May 2004, followed in June by a transitional government under ⓭ Ayad Allawi. The military presence of the Coalition and the looming power struggle between the Sunnis, who had ruled until then, and the Shiite majority led to almost daily attacks and suicide bombings since the end of the war. The first free elections, held in 2005 (which were boycotted by the majority of the Sunnis), were won by the United Iraqi Alliance, a Shiite alliance led by Ibrahim Jaafari, who was appointed prime minister. The Kurdish leader Jalal Talabani became the first non-Arab president of Iraq. Nuri al-Maliki followed Jaafari as prime minister in 2006. The withdrawal of international troops began in 2009 and was expected to be completed by 2012.

9 Saddam Hussein waving to a crowd of supporters in Kirkuk on April 2, 1988, one month after using chemical weapons against Kurdish civilians

11 US marines shortly after capturing Baghdad pass a statue of Saddam Hussein pulled down by an armored personnel carrier, April 10, 2003

12 A victim of the chemical weapons on the Iraqi-Kurd city Halabja, a father holds his dead child in his arms, between March 16 and 18 1988

13 The Iraq interim president Ayad Allawi, appointed after the invasion, 2005

since 1980 | Iran-Iraq war begins **Aug 2, 1990** | Occupation of Kuwait **20 Mar 2003** | Second US-led invasion of Iraq **2005** | Ibrahim Jaafari elected president

Aug 1988 | Ceasefire between Iran and Iraq **1991** | First Gulf War **Jun 2004** | Transitional government under Allawi

Iran to the Overthrow of the Shah

Shah Reza Pahlavi imposed an oppressively secularist vision of society and established an authoritarian and corrupt regime. This repression, and resentment at the perceived imperialism of western oil firms in Iran, provoked resistance in middle-class circles and among the Shiite clergy.

1 Mossadegh, leader of the nationalist Tudeh party, sitting in the dock at his trial in Tehran, September 9, 1953

2 A young Shah Muhammad Reza Pahlavi shortly after his accession in 1941

3 Oil mining in Iran, in the 1970s; the largest exporter of oil in the world

Iran was supported after 1945 by the United States and Great Britain, who had installed the young shah, ❷ Muhammad Reza Pahlavi, in 1941. As it was the most Western-oriented country in the Near East and, at the time, the main supplier of ❸ oil, the United States also armed Iran militarily, especially after a conflict developed with the Soviet Union over Azerbaijan in 1946. Mohammed Mossadegh, who assumed the office of prime minister in April 1951, opposed Britain's extensive involvement in the oil trade and nationalized the Anglo-Iranian Oil Company (AIOC). The shah fled the country on short notice in the subsequent power struggle, but then returned in August 1953 and toppled ❶ Mossadegh and his nationalist Tudeh party with the help of the US Central Intelligence Agency. The AIOC was restored and martial law imposed until 1957.

Beginning in 1960, the shah tried to regain control over the growing opposition within the country through a program of reforms. In January 1963, he instituted what was known as the "White Revolution" by taking land away from large landowners and initiating campaigns for literacy and ❹ women's emancipation. These initiatives primarily benefited the urban population. The ❺ Western lifestyle of the shah's family, his political ties to the West, corruption, and a disregard of Islamic traditions gradually alienated the ruler from his people. From the 1960s on, under Prime Minister Amir Abbas Hoveida, the direction became increasingly authoritarian. Regime opponents were tortured by SAVAK, the secret police, and in 1975 the de facto one-party system was institutionalized. In 1978, the shah attempted to pacify the massive opposition that had been forming since 1977 with promises of further reform. However he was undermined by regular mass demonstrations, particularly in Shiite holy cities, in support of the exiled Grand Ayatollah Ruhollah Khomeini, around whom the Islamic opposition in Iran had crystallized. In September 1978, Khomeini from exile began calling for an uncompromising war against the shah and for an "Islamic revolution," after which events took on their own momentum.

5 The Empress Soraya and Shah Reza Pahlavi, firm allies of the West, during a state visit to the Federal Republic of Germany, 1955

The upper class around the shah took their assets abroad and a wave of labor strikes brought oil production to a standstill. A military government installed in November could no longer control the situation. In Paris, Khomeini allied with the moderate "National Front" of the opposition, and they proclaimed the common goal of an Islamic republic. On January 16, 1979, the shah fled and, on February 1, the Ayatollah Khomeini returned from Paris, welcomed in Tehran ❻ by cheering crowds. The ❼ Iranian Revolution had begun.

4 "White Revolution": Women gather in front of the shah's palace, to demonstrate their support for his promise to extend the electoral franchise to women, February 1963

6 Upon his return to Iran, the Ayatollah Ruhollah Khomeini receives a triumphant welcome from the crowds in Tehran, 1979

7 The Iranian Revolution: Angry crowds of demonstrators protest against the regime, burning pictures of the Shah and chanting anti-monarchy slogans

1951 | Muhammad Mosaddeq takes office
1953 | Mosaddeq deposed by Shah Resa Pahlavi
1963 | White Revolution begins
1963 | Khomeini exiled
1975 | One-party system institutionalized
16 Jan 1979 | Shah flees

Iran since the Islamic Revolution of 1979

Under Ayatollah Khomeini, hard-line Islamic forces dominated the revolution and the country. Only after his death did some liberalization begin to take place. Traditionalists and moderate reformers continue to struggle over the future course of the country.

9 The spiritual and political leader of the Iranian revolution, Ayatollah Ruhollah Khomeini

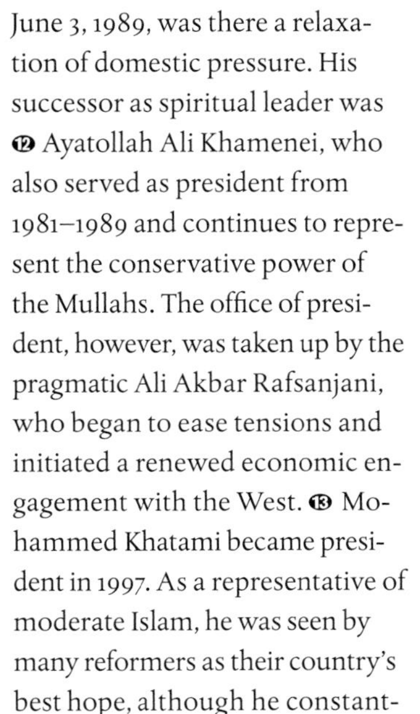

10 Devout women wearing full-length veils at a meeting to protest against trends toward women wearing "un-Islamic" ("provocatively revealing") clothing, Iran, 2004

Khomeini proclaimed the Islamic Republic of Iran on April 1, 1979, but did not immediately emerge as its political leader. At first, moderate opposition politicians were elected president, but the revolution was radicalized in November with the occupation of the US embassy in Tehran by students and the election victory of the strictly religious Islamic Republican party in the parliamentary elections in May 1980. A re-Islamization of public life began with the introduction of aspects of sharia Islamic law—the compulsory ❿ wearing of headscarves for women was popular among traditionalists—and a strong ideological orientation against the United States. ❾ Khomeini and the radical clergy leadership (the Mullahs) increasingly forced the splintered moderate forces out of the government or into exile. The ❽ Iran-Iraq War, launched by Iraq in September 1980, brought the final victory for the Mullahs. Even their opponents participated in the defense of the country, which Khomeini organized with the help of his fanatical "Guardians of the Faith." In 1988, Iran accepted the UN mediated cease-fire. In the meantime, the example of an Islamic revolution has inspired groups in other countries, notably the Hezbollah in Lebanon.

11 Mass public mourning at the funeral of Ayatollah Khomeini, leader of the Revolution, June 6, 1989

12 Ayatollah Ali Khamenei, President of Iran from 1981-1989

13 The Iranian president Mohammed Khatami, April 4, 2005

Only after Ayatollah Khomeini's ⓫ death on June 3, 1989, was there a relaxation of domestic pressure. His successor as spiritual leader was ⓬ Ayatollah Ali Khamenei, who also served as president from 1981–1989 and continues to represent the conservative power of the Mullahs. The office of president, however, was taken up by the pragmatic Ali Akbar Rafsanjani, who began to ease tensions and initiated a renewed economic engagement with the West. ⓭ Mohammed Khatami became president in 1997. As a representative of moderate Islam, he was seen by many reformers as their country's best hope, although he constantly had to struggle against the conservative-dominated institutions in the fight for power. Since his election as president in 2005, the hardliner Mahmoud Ahmadinejad has deeply polarized the Iranian people. Widespread anti-government protests arose after his reelection in 2009. His nuclear policies and his threat to destroy Israel have shocked the world and increased Iran's isolation from the international community.

8 The bodies of two Iranian soldiers killed in border clashes with Iraqi forces during the Iran-Iraq War, March 1985

Ayatollah Ruhollah Khomeini, describing his program for the establishment of an Islamic government

"It is our duty to work toward the establishment of an Islamic government. The first activity we must undertake in this respect is the propagation of our cause; that is how we must begin. It has always been that way, all over the world. A group of people came together, deliberated, made decisions, and then began to propagate their aims. Gradually the number of like-minded people would increase until finally they became powerful enough to influence a great state or even to confront and overthrow it.(...)"

Khomeini leads prayers at a mosque in Tehran, 1986

1 Feb 1979 | Khomeini returns from exile

1 Apr 1979 | Proclamation of the Islamic Republic of Iran

June 3 1989 | Death of Khomeini

1981–89 | Presidency of Ali Khamenei

1997 | Mohammed Khatami takes office

Afghanistan to the Civil War

Effective central government in ❶ Afghanistan has long been hindered by the powerful tribal culture. The monarchy was overthrown in 1973. In 1979, the Soviet Union invaded in support of an embattled left-wing regime, which led to a bloody occupation and civil war.

Two Afghan women carrying wood back to their village, ca. 1965

King Mohammad Zahir Shah of Afghanistan on a vist to the US in 1973

Training teachers in Afghanistan: prospective teachers taking classes, 1963

❷ Mohammad Zahir Shah ruled in Afghanistan, a country of traditional and autonomous tribal structures, from 1933, although the actual power rested with his three uncles, brothers of Nadir Shah who was murdered in 1933. Their efforts to ❸ centralize power failed due to the resistance of the tribes. From 1953, however, Prime Minister ❹ Sardar Mohammad Daud Khan, brother-in-law of the king, succeeded in introducing several social reforms with assistance from the Soviet Union. When Daud was ousted in 1963, moderate political forces introduced a constitutional monarchy in 1964, and in 1965 free parliamentary elections were held for the first time.

Daud deposed the king in a coup on July 17, 1973, and proclaimed a republic. As prime minister, he began a cautious program of land reform and the nationalization of banks. He secured the support of the Arab world and in February 1977 established an authoritarian presidential regime. Then in April 1978, the Communist-oriented People's Democratic party organized a coup with the help of the army, murdered Daud, and proclaimed the Democratic Republic of Afghanistan under Prime Minister Nur Mohammad Taraki. The new republic had close ties to the Soviet Union. The government's left-wing secularist course led to a 1979 revolt among many of the tribes and parts of the army, causing anarchy in many regions of the country. Increasingly under pressure, the new prime minister, ❺ Hafizullah Amin, called on the Soviet Union for aid. Soviet troops ❻ entered Afghanistan on December 27, 1979, and helped to install the loyal exiled politician Babrak Karmal as head of state and government. Although the new government generally respected Islam and Afghan traditions, a number of Islamic and nationalist groups were immediately formed to resist the Soviet occupation. Collectively known as the mujahideen, they began a ❼ guerrilla war against the regime in Kabul and the Soviet troops. The guerrillas were supported financially and militarily by the United States and many Arab countries.

The Afghan prime minister Prince Sadar Mohammad on a state visit to the Federal Republic of Germany, July 3, 1961

Embattled Afghan Prime Minister Hafizullah Amin requested Soviet aid

Soviet tank patrols the streets of Kabul looking for insurgents, February 1980

American-armed Mujahideen rebels fighting the Soviet occupation forces near the Pakistan border, February 14, 1980

1933	Reign of Mohammad Zahir Shah
1953	Mohammad Daud Khan seizes power
1965	First free parliamentary elections
17 Jul 1973	Proclamation of the Republic
1977	Presidential regime under Mohammed Daud
1978	Military putsch led by Mohammed Taraki
1979	Soviet invasion

Afghanistan from 1979 to the Present

After the withdrawal of the Soviet troops following heavy losses, the Islamic groups fought among themselves. First the mujahideen dominated the country and then the Taliban. The latter were driven from power in 2001–2002.

9 Mujahideen pose before a Soviet tank abandoned during the Red Army's withdrawal, 1988

The Afghan tribal council increasingly proved to be as powerless as the government, and the mountain regions in particular became centers of a radical Islamic resistance that had extensive ties to Pakistan and to underground fundamentalist groups. By 1983, 20 percent of the population had fled to neighboring countries, particularly Pakistan; several UN peace initiatives failed to end the conflict. Atrocities committed on both sides further damaged the prospects of a peace accord. In response to Soviet pressure, Karmal was replaced by Sayid Mohammad Najibullah as secretary-general of the People's Democratic party in 1986, and in 1987 Najibullah became president. He championed a policy of national reconciliation. With the radical Islamic mujahideen increasingly winning ground, the USSR under Mikhail Gorbachev, having suffered heavy losses, ❾ withdrew its troops in 1988–1989 following a peace treaty negotiated in Geneva.

With the Soviet troops gone, Najibullah's power base collapsed. Following an attempted coup in 1990, he was finally driven out of Kabul in April 1992 by the mujahideen. The new mujahideen government, with Sebghatullah Mujaddedi as head of state and Gulbuddin Hekmatyar as prime minister, failed to gain recognition from the other resistance groups in much of the rest of the country, and the civil war thus continued. In September 1996, the Islamist Taliban militia conquered Kabul and established an oppressive regime that enforced a ❽, ⓫ fundamentalist form of Islam through coercion, while also allowing ⓾ Afghan opium cultivation to reach 75 percent of the world's total production. The warlords in the north, who became known as the Northern Alliance, resisted Taliban attempts to conquer the remainder of the country.

10 Poppy farming in Afghanistan, April 2005

In 1997–1998, the Taliban, led by Mullah Omar, began to expel Western aid organizations and demonstrated their open support of Islamist terrorists, particularly Osama bin Laden. In August 1998, the United States launched ⓬ missile strikes against terrorist training camps in Afghanistan. After September 11, 2001, when the Taliban refused to comply with the US demand for bin Laden's extradition, coordinated ⓭ offensives were launched by US and British troops and the Northern Alliance, led by the Uzbek general Abdul Rashid Dostum. Kabul was retaken on November 13 and the Taliban were soon driven toward the border with Pakistan.

8 Colossal 170 ft- (52 meter-) high statues of the Buddha in Afghanistan, dynamited by the Taliban in 2001

NATO troops remain in the country to support the government of President Hamid Karzai. After 2007 the Taliban regained control of some regions and continued to attack Afghan police forces and ISAF troops.

Hamid Karzai

Hamid Karzai studied international relations in India. During the 1990s, he was deputy foreign minister in two mujahideen governments. As head of state, he has promised to halt opium cultivation and strengthen the rights of women. His government is still dependent on an international military presence in the main cities. His deputy, Hadji Abul Kadir, was assassinated in Kabul in July 2002, and he, too, barely escaped an attempted assassination in September of that year. He was reelected in November 2009. He is oriented to the West, but his regime has also been accused of nepotism and corruption.

above: Hamid Karzai, president of Afghanistan since the US-led invasion, November 4, 2004

11 A Taliban militia forcibly shaves the head of a passenger in a bus

12 A Taliban fighter carries a wounded comrade, 1997

13 US special forces on patrol in Afghanistan, November 15, 2001

1988–89 | Withdrawal of Soviet troops
1992 | Najibullah ousted
1996 | Taliban conquer Kabul
1998 | US airstrikes on Bin Laden's training camps
Nov 2001 | Northern Alliance forces conquer Kabul
2002 | Hamid Karzai becomes president

PAKISTAN AND INDIA SINCE 1947

From the successful war for independence against British colonial rule, India and Pakistan emerged as two self-contained states in 1947. Both countries' claims for the Kashmir region led to a continuous political and military conflict. While India developed a democratic parliamentary democracy domestically, Pakistan was ruled by an authoritarian military government. Religious tensions led to the separation of East Pakistan as Bangladesh in 1971.

Traffic jam in Dhaka, the capital of Bangladesh, November 2004

Pakistan and Bangladesh

In 1947, Pakistan established itself as a separate Muslim state on the Indian sub-continent. In 1971, the eastern part of the country seceded as Bangladesh

While ❻ India was struggling for independence, Muhammad Ali Jinnah called for a separate state for the Muslim minority. Bloodshed between Hindus and Muslims led to a partition of the subcontinent and a migration of the Hindu and Muslim minorities. The primarily Muslim regions on either side of Hindu India—East Pakistan (today's Bangladesh) and West Pakistan— became the state of Pakistan, a dominion of the British Commonwealth. Jinnah became the country's first president.

Tension between secularists and political Islamists over the role of religion, exacerbated by secessionist movements within the country and the conflict with India over Jammu and Kashmir, dominated politics. When the situation worsened in 1958, the secularist General Muhammad Ayub Khan seized power, stabilizing the country by imposing martial law. He followed a policy of a balance between the Cold War blocs, and in 1965 began a policy of détente with India.

Volunteers fight against the Pakistani army for an independent Bangladesh

Pakistani prime minister Zulfikar Ali Bhutto, 1976

The first free elections in East Pakistan were won by the Awami League with a large majority. Led by Sheikh Mujibur Rahman, the league sought autonomy for the region. When Rahman proclaimed the independent People's Republic of Bangladesh on March 26, 1971, the Pakistani government responded with force. India's ❷ military support ensured that ❶ Bangladesh became independent. Since then, democratic governments have alternated with military regimes in Bangladesh. Plagued by floods, the country is one of the poorest in the world.

After Bangladesh's secession in 1971, West Pakistan became Pakistan; it established relations with Bangladesh in 1974. Until 1977 the dictatorship of ❺ Zulfikar Ali Bhutto guaranteed a secular state, but General Zia ul- Haq seized power in a coup and planned the Islamization of society. Although the tension between secularists and Islamic forces continued to dominate politics, there was a return to free elections in 1985. ❸ Benazir Bhutto became the first woman to lead a Muslim country as prime minister from 1988 to 1990 and 1993 to 1996. She was assassinated in 2007. ❹ General Pervez Musharraf led Pakistan from 1997 to 2008. He was the United States' key ally in the War on Terror. Since 2008 reforms have strengthened Pakistan's democracy, but the Taliban continue to destabilize the country. In 2010 Pakistan was hit by a severe flood disaster.

Pakistani prime minister Benazir Bhutto after her second victory in November 1988

Pakistani prime minister Benazir Bhutto after her second victory in November 1988

Negotiating independence for India in 1947 under the leadership of the British Viceroy Lord Mountbatten and the leader of the Muslim League

14 Aug 1947 | Pakistan becomes independent
15 Aug 1947 | Indian independence
30 Jan 1948 | Mahatma Gandhi murdered
26 Nov 1949 | Foundation of the Indian Republic
26 Jan 1950 | First Indian constitution
1962 | Sino-Indian war
1966-77 | Indira Gandhi's rule

India

Since gaining independence in 1947, India has generally followed a policy of secular modernization, and political life has been dominated by the Nehru-Ghandi political dynasty. Despite numerous conflicts, the multiethnic state remains the world's largest democracy.

Shortly after independence was achieved, Muslim Pakistan broke off from India, but most of the 566 principalities of the subcontinent became a part of the new Indian state. Fighting poverty and integrating the various ethnic groups were the most pressing tasks of the country, along with the long-running conflict with Pakistan over the ❼ Kashmir region. Socially, the country fluctuated between secular modernization and traditional Hinduism. Mahatma Gandhi was murdered by a Hindu fanatic on January 30, 1948, and ❾ Jawaharlal Nehru, who had held the office of prime minister since 1946, became the dominant political figure in the country. Nehru pursued a socialist path, launching five-year plans to modernize the economically backward country. Constant unrest in the individual provinces and the Sino-Indian war of 1962–63 resulted in the loss of some border provinces. When Nehru died in May 1964, he was succeeded by Lal Bahadur Shastri. He too died in office in 1966, and Nehru's daughter ❿ Indira Gandhi then became prime minister. She continued the policies of her father, but shifted between delegation and centralization of authority. Gandhi presided over the Indo-Pakistani war of 1971, gaining support from the Soviets, France, and the United Kingdom in the UN Security Council. She was voted out of office in 1977, but regained power in a triumphant election victory in 1984. When in June 1984 she ordered military action against radical ❽ Sikhs who had barricaded themselves in the ⓫ Temple of Amritsar for two years, she was murdered by her own Sikh bodyguards. Her son Rajiv Gandhi then came into government, but he was killed in a 1991 bomb attack.

An evident radicalization of political Hinduism, separatist movements, natural catastrophes, local resistance to planned dam-building projects, and corruption scandals have led to repeated unrest in the country since the 1990s. In 2004, Sikh prime minister Manmohan Singh became the first non-Hindu to lead India's government.

Nomads in Jammu-Kashmir in the north of India

Young Sikh soldiers in Allahabad, 1993

Jawaharlal Nehru, 1962

Indira Gandhi, 1972

The Kashmir Conflict

India and Pakistan continue to dispute ownership of the region of Kashmir, in the northern part of the Indian subcontinent. The principality, inhabited by a majority of Muslims, had been governed by Hindu rulers since 1846. Over Pakistani protests, its rulers opted to join the Indian Union in 1947. Despite UN mediation since 1951, increasingly serious and violent conflicts over the region, ignited by revolts of Pakistan-backed Muslim rebels, culminated in a war in 1965. While the two countries remain in dialogue, the conflict has sparked an arms race between them, with both announcing the acquisition of nuclear weapons in 1998.

Indian soldiers at the border to Pakistan in Kashmir open fire on guerrilla positions in the mountains, May 31, 1999

Scene from Srinagar, Kashmir, India

Shrine of the Sikhs: The golden Temple of Amritsar, January 9, 2003

26 Mar 1971 | Bangladesh independence proclaimed

1977 | Putsch led by Zia ul-Haq in Pakistan

1984 | Indira Gandhi murdered

1988-90 | First presidency of Benazir Bhutto

1997 | Musharraf seizes government in Pakistan

2004 | Manmohan Singh is Prime Minister in India

Southeast Asia since 1945

After 1945, most of Southeast Asia was preoccupied with the struggle for liberation from colonial rule. Many of the region's countries including ❶ Malaysia and Singapore—and in particular Indonesia, with the largest Muslim population in the world—faced the problem of maintaining cohesion among various ethnic groups. The Cold War struggle was also played out in the Pacific arena, most notably in the Vietnam War. Since 1989, the region has tended more toward stability, and democratic systems have begun to emerge in most of the states.

View over a valley with terraced vegetable-growing in central Malaysia

Sri Lanka and Indonesia

Since its independence, Sri Lanka has been preoccupied with the conflict between the Sinhalese majority and the Tamil minority. After coming to power in 1966, Sukarno ruled Indonesia for the next 32 years. The country has had a functioning democracy since 1998.

On February 4, 1948, ❾ Sri Lanka (then the British colony of Ceylon) gained independence, becoming a member of the British Commonwealth.

From the outset, the nation's difficult economic situation was further complicated by the tense relationship between the Sinhalese majority and Tamil ❸ minority. In April 1956, the Sinhalese nationalist Freedom party under Solomon Bandaranaike won the national elections. He nationalized key industries, but his attempt to make Sinhalese the official language in 1958 escalated ethnic tensions, and he was murdered by a Buddhist monk in 1959. His widow, Sirimavo Bandaranaike, then continued her husband's policies. Their daughter, ❷ Chandrika Kumaratunga, was president from 1994 to 2005. As communal relations worsened, a Tamil paramilitary force known as the "Tamil Tigers" or LTTE was formed in 1976, and Sri Lanka experienced a civil war for much of the next three decades as the Tigers fought against government forces. The Sri Lankan military defeated the Tigers in 2009 and forced them to retreat to the northeast of the island.

Sri Lanka's President Chandrika Kumaratunga at a press conference, 1997

A Tamil fisherwoman and her child February 2005

Achmed Sukarno, June 1945

on his political philosophy ("Pancasila")

"The Indonesian people should not only believe in God; more than this, it should be clear that each Indonesian is allowed to pray to his own God. The Christians should serve God after the teachings of Jesus Christ. The Muslims after the teachings of the prophet Mohammed. The Buddhists should foster their religion after their books....The Indonesian state should be a state in which everyone can pray to his God without religious jealousy! The Indonesian state should be a state to which the belief in God belongs...on civilized way, on the path to mutual respect."

Sukarno visits the Technical University of Berlin, June 20, 1956

Change of government: Sukarno (left) points at Indonesia's new strong man General Suharto, September 1, 1966

Since Indonesia gained full independence in 1949, ethnic and religious conflicts have plagued the nation. While the majority of the population on the main island of Java is Muslim, Hindu or indigenous faiths tend to predominate on the other islands, such as Bali. The immediate postindependence leader was President ❹ Suharto, who looked to the USSR and domestic Communists for support and was prone to nationalistic posturing. After an attempted coup against the rule of the "Javanese" in 1960, Sukarno dissolved parliament and pursued an increasingly authoritarian course. In 1965 vio-

Megawati Sukarnoputri (right) president since 2001, with the former President Abdurrahman Wahid

1945 | Indonesia gains independence
Feb 1948 | Sri Lanka's independence
1957 | Achmes Sukarno's presidency in Indonesia
1960 | Parliament dissolved in Indonesia
1963 | "Federation of Malaysia" founded
Aug 9, 1965 | Singapore leaves federation

lence erupted against the pro-Communist Chinese minority, during which hundreds of thousands were killed. Isolated and under pressure, Sukarno ceded power to General Suharto in March 1966.

After becoming president in 1967, Suharto cultivated ties with the West while maintaining a military-backed regime. The government took a hard line against separatist movements and in 1976 forcibly annexed the newly independent region of East Timor. The issue resurfaced two decades later when the brutal actions of the Indonesian government in crushing a Timorese revolt attracted widespread international condemnation. East Timor only became an autonomous state in 2002 after Indonesia had released it from its rule in 1999.

Burning houses in Dili, the capital of East Timor, December 4, 2002

❻ Popular unrest in the wake of the Asian economic crisis of 1997 forced President Suharto to step down in 1998. After corruption allegations saw President Wahid forced out of office in 2001, ❺ Megawati Sukarnoputri, the daughter of the nation's independence leader Sukarno, held the office until 2004. She was succeeded by Susilo Yudhoyono.

The third largest earthquake ever recorded caused a severe tsunami in the Indian Ocean that devastated the shores of Indonesia and the surrounding countries in 2004.

Malaysia and Singapore

The Southeast Asian countries of Malaysia and Singapore achieved stability and economic growth under authoritarian governmental regimes.

Head of state of Singapore, Jusuf Ishak (middle), inspects a guard of honor during the celebrations for the new state Malaysia, September 15, 1963

In 1963, the Malay Peninsula, Singapore, Sarawak, and Sabah united to become the independent Federation of Malaysia, which consisted of nine sultanates and is an elective monarchy.

Political rivalries, ethnic tension, and competing economic interests caused ❼ Singapore to secede from the federation on August 9, 1965. The Sultanate of Brunei never joined the federation because of its reserves of oil; it is one of the wealthiest countries in the world. A Communist insurgency began in Sarawak in 1963 and continued until a peace was achieved in 1990.

Malaysia's head of state is the king, who is chosen every five years from the group of nine Malay sultanates, the other four states do not participate in the election of the king. The first prime minister, ❽ Abdul Rahman, sought to mediate between the Malay majority and the wealthier Chinese minority following race riots in 1969 by instituting a new economic policy intended to redistribute gains and known as the New Economic Policy. Prime Minister Mahathir bin Mohammed, who governed between 1981 and 2003, oversaw a period of political stability and rapid economic growth.

Lee Kwan Yew was Singapore's first prime minister, ruling until 1990. During his time in office, the country was transformed from an economically weak former colony into a prosperous high-technology ❿ powerhouse. Public life in Singapore is staunchly conservative and subject to strict regulation by the state and its stringent legal system. Lee's successor, ⓫ Goh Chok Tong, steered the country through the Asian economic crisis of 1997–1998, signing free-trade agreements with both Japan and the United States.

The first prime minister of Malaysia, Tunku Abdul Rahman, signs the constitution of federation, July 1963

The holy city Kandy in Sri Lanka, declared a world cultural heritage site by UNESCO in 1988

The center of high-rise offices of banks and business of the tiny island country of Singapore

The prime minister of Singapore, Goh Chok Tong at the Commonwealth summit in Australia

1966 | Suharto takes power in Indonesia
1976 | Indonesia declares East Timor a province
1981–2003 | Mahathir bin Mohammad's premiership in Malaysia
1998 | Suharto resigns
2001 | Regency of Sukarnoputris in Indonesia

The Philippines and Myanmar

A democratic system was first introduced in the Philippines after the fall of the dictator Marcos in 1986. Myanmar (previously Burma) has been ruled by a military junta since 1962 and has garnered increasing international criticism.

The Philippines was formally granted independence from the United States on July 4, 1946, although the US continued to exert significant military and economic influence over the country. For the first two decades, a pro-Western oligarchy ruled over the relatively poor population. The nationalist ❷ Ferdinand Marcos was elected president in 1965, promising land reform, but in 1972 he declared martial law and began to build up a personal dictatorship through the imprisonment of the opposition and censorship of the press. Only after Marcos's overthrow by popular protests in 1986 did the incredible extent of the corruption under his rule come to light.

Stronger democratic structures were established under President ❹ Corazon Aquino, who held office from 1986 until 1992. Under Benigno Aquino, Jr. ("Ninoy"), the Philippines continued to struggle with large public debt, and corruption scandals remained frequent. Since the 1970s, there have been repeated revolts and insurgencies by Muslim separatists seeking independence for the southern islands. Between 2000 and 2003, there was a renewed government offensive against the separatist terror group Abu Sayyaf, which kidnapped Western tourists on ❶ Sipadan.

The extremist Muslim group Abu Sayyaf meet in their hiding place with hostages in the southern part of the Philippines

Aung San Suu Kyi after the end of her house arrest, 1995

Since ❺ Burma's independence in 1948, governments have struggled to contain conflicts between Buddhists and Muslims, as well as between Communists and nationalists. For the first decade, Prime Minister U Nu dominated public life. He made Burma a founding member of the Non-aligned Movement and built up a welfare state. Concerned by the rise of separatist movements, the military seized power in a coup in 1962. The coup leader, General U Ne Win, declared a "Burmese path to socialism" with an extensive nationalization program. In December 1973, the Socialist Union of Burma was proclaimed. In 1988, the military moved again, this time to install U Saw Maung, who abandoned the socialist rhetoric. Burma changed its name to Myanmar as of May 26, 1989.

Free elections in 1990 were won by the democratic opposition coalition, but the military junta refused to relinquish power. General Than Shwe, the junta's leader, continued to head the government, despite anti-government protests led by Buddhist monks in 2007. The international community has accused the regime of grave human rights abuses, including the use of forced labor. ❸ Aung San Suu Kyi, the leader of the pro-democracy movement, was awarded the Nobel Peace Prize in 1991.

Ferdinand E. Marcos during a press conference in Manila, April 12, 1976

Former president of the Philippines, Corazon Aquino, 1986

Traffic on a busy day in the Burmese capital of Rangoon, 1997

Sithu U Thant

The third secretary-general of the United Nations was the Burmese statesman Sithu U Thant. Between 1947 and 1957, he was Burma's information minister and represented his country in the UN from 1957 until he was elected secretary-general in 1962. In 1967, he attempted to mediate in the Arab-Israeli conflict without success. Large-scale protests erupted in 1974 when the Burmese government refused to give him a state burial because of the UN's criticism of the regime.

above: Sithu Thant, third secretary-general of the United Nations

1946 King Rama IX in Thailand
1946 Formal independence of the Philippines
1948 Burma's independence
1949 Formal independence of Laos
1962 Ne Win in Myanmar leads coup
1965 Ferdinand Marco's presidency

Thailand and Laos

The kingdom of Thailand has experienced frequent periods of military rule, but since 1992 civilian government has prevailed. In Laos a socialist one-party regime has been in place since 1975.

After the murder of Rama VIII in 1946, his brother, ❻ Rama IX (Bhumibol), ascended the throne in Thailand. He remains the head of state and is now the longest-ruling monarch in the world. Shortly after King Rama IX came to the throne, Pibul Songahram established a military dictatorship with the assistance of the armed forces. He aligned the country with the West, before he himself was overthrown by a conspiracy by officers in September

Too much choice: In Bangkok a passer-by looks at the election posters of the different candidates

1957. The new prime minister, Sarit Thanarat, and his successors continued to rule through military power; while the needs of the people were largely ignored. During the Vietnam War, the United States was permitted to station troops in Thailand, a decision that brought some financial relief. Beginning in 1972, popular demands for democratic freedoms began to grow, and in 1973 student riots brought down the ruling Thai regime.

The system of rule from then on fluctuated between unstable ❼ civilian governments and interludes of ❾ military takeover. Following the parliamentary elections of 1975, the armed forces again seized power in 1977–78. Various coalition governments were in power between 1986 and 1991 and began to open up the country's economy to international trade. Prime Minister Thaksin Shinawatra was deposed by a military coup in 2006. His supporters, the "Red Shirts" continue to stage violent protests against the current government led by Abhisit Vejjajiva. Despite the rapid growth of the industrial and financial sectors over the last decade, agriculture and ❿ tourism remain the main sources of revenue.

The French colonial authority installed King Sisavang Vong in Laos in 1946 and expelled the leftist Lao Issara (Free Laos Movement) government; full independence as a constitutional monarchy came in 1954. The country was divided between right-wing royalists led by Prince ❽ Souvanna Phouma and the left-wing Pa-

The two princes of Laos: Prince Souvanna Phouma and Prince Utthong Souphanouvong

thet Lao movement led by Prince ⓫ Souphanouvong, who fought alongside the Communists in North Vietnam in 1950. The Pathet Lao began to conquer large stretches of the country in 1953 and in 1956 entered government. When they won the elections of 1958, a US backed coup by royalists and the military initiated a long-running and bloody civil war. Souvanna Phouma took power in the south in 1962, while the northeast remained in communist hands and was heavily bombed by the US Air Force. Negotiations in 1973 resulted in the formation of a government of national unity. Following the communist victory in Vietnam, leftist forces deposed the king and proclaimed a socialist democratic republic. In 1991, a new constitution was imposed, and the Pathet Lao, or People's Revolutionary Party, was declared the sole political party. Choummaly Sayasone has held the office of president and general secretary since 2006.

King Rama IX with his wife Sirikit under the canopy of the throne, ca.1977

Student unrest is violently suppressed after the renewed military takeover

Western tourists walking along the street of one of the holiday resorts along the coast of Thailand

"The red prince," Prince Utthong Souphanouvong giving a speech

1973 | Socialist Union of Burma proclaimed
1973 | Formation of Government of National Unity in Laos
1990 | First free elections in Burma
1991 | Aung San Suu Kyi awarded Nobel Peace Prize
1998 | President Khamtai Siphandon
2001 | Thaksin Shinawatra governs Thailand

Cambodia

The Cambodian king Sihanouk established socialist rule in 1955. The Communism propagated by the Khmer Rouge between 1976 and 1979 was accompanied by terror and genocide.

On March 12, 1945, ❸ King Norodom Sihanouk declared Cambodia (also known as Kampuchea) independent, but the French, colonial rulers of Cambodia since 1863, fought an increasingly vicious war with Communist insurgents before finally recognizing Cambodian independence at the end of the Indochinese War in 1954. Sihanouk abdicated in 1955 in favor of his father and, after a landslide election victory, became prime minister. As a socialist, he aligned with China, causing the Western powers to support the right-wing Khmer Serai. When the US Air Force began bombing border villages in 1965, intending to stamp out Vietcong bases and supply routes, the situation deteriorated.

A pro-Western group led by Prime Minister ❺ Lon Nol seized power in 1970, and the leftist factions went underground and formed the Communist ❶ Khmer Rouge. Together with the followers of Sihanouk, who had fled to China, they waged a violent civil war against the government of Lon Nol. Following the withdrawal of US troops from Vietnam, the Khmer Rouge advanced rapidly, and in April 1975 took the capital Phnom Penh.

The leader of the Khmer Rouge, ❷ Pol Pot, together with the nominal president, Khieu Samphan, came to power in April 1976. They subjected the country to a radical social reform process that was aimed at creating a purely agrarian-based Communist society. The city-dwellers were deported to the countryside, where they were combined with the local population and subjected to forced labor. About two million Cambodians died in ❹ waves of murder, torture, and starvation, aimed particularly at the educated and intellectual elite. Whole sections of the population were systematically wiped out. The terror gradually ended with the capture of Phnom Penh by invading Vietnamese troops in 1979, but the Khmer Rouge continued to fight on as guerrillas. Prince Sihanouk, in alliance with the Khmer Rouge, formed a government in exile against the Vietnamese occupation in 1982. In April 1989, a new constitution declared Cambodia to be an ideologically neutral state with Buddhism as the state religion, and a constitutional monarch where the executive power, however, is invested in the prime minister. Sihanouk was restored as King in 1993 and succeeded by his son Norodm Sihamoni in 2004. The leader of the leftist People's party, Hun Sen, staged a coup in 1997 and became prime minister after elections in 1998.

Guerrilla units of the Khmer Rouge in 1980

Cambodian dictator Pol Pot

Sihanouk, king of Cambodia, during a speech in 1966

The pro-American prime minister Nol (left) at a champagne reception with important military leaders, 1975

Skeletons of some 2000 victims, in the northwest of Cambodia, are reminders of the terror carried out by Pol Pot on the Cambodian population

Pol Pot

Pol Pot ("The Organizer") was born Saloth Sar. Little is known about his personal life. He studied electrical engineering in Paris, France, in 1949–1953, and then worked as a teacher in Phnom Penh. There he began his steady rise through the ranks of the Communist party. Between 1975 and 1979 he gave orders for the deaths of millions of Cambodians in an extraordinarily oppressive social experiment aimed at creating a totally communist society. He was convicted of genocide and condemned to death in absentia. After his arrest in 1997, a "people's court" changed the sentence to life imprisonment. Following an escape effort into the Cambodian forest, Pol Pot died on March 15, 1998, and was cremated with only close associates in attendance.

One of the major criminals of the 20th century: Pol Pot

1949–54 "Indochinese War"

1949 Ho Chi Minh president in Vietnam

1954 Ceasefire following Indochinese conference in Geneva

1957 Begining of the second phase of the Vietnam War

Vietnam War

War for the unity and independence of Vietnam was waged from 1946 to 1976. Through the military intervention of the United States in 1964, it became one of the ❼ bloodiest conflicts of the post–World War II period.

One year after the Communists proclaimed the Democratic Republic of Vietnam in the northern Vietnamese city of Hanoi in 1945, the Indochinese War (1946–1954) broke out. Although France had granted the state under the presidency of ❾ Ho Chi Minh the status of a Vietnamese "free state" within the French Union in 1946, it tried to restore its colonial rule over the country from out of Saigon in southern Vietnam. With that, France instigated a military conflict with the Communist rulers in the north, who put up bitter resistance against the foreign troops, primarily through the guerrilla troops of the Viet Minh. Through international mediation, a ceasefire was concluded in 1954 that included a division of the country in the Geneva Accords; the Communists controlled North Vietnam, and a pro-Western Republic of Vietnam was established in the South under the Catholic leader Ngo Dinh Diem. After the withdrawal of the French from Indochina, South Vietnam received financial and military support from the United States. Corruption and oppression in the Diem regime empowered the primarily Communist opposition National Liberation Front in South Vietnam, and its military wing, the Vietcong, began a guerrilla war in 1956. With the goal of preventing the further spread of Communism in Asia, direct US military intervention began in 1964.

7 The South Vietnamese head of police Nguyen Ngoc Loan shoots an officer of the Vietcong troops in Saigon on February 1,1966

9 Ho Chi Min, Vietnamese Revolutionary

Following the claim that two US destroyers in the Gulf of Tonkin had been attacked on August 2, 1964, the Vietnam War began. North Vietnamese cities and supply channels were systematically bombed by US aircraft beginning in February 1965. In the South, continuous bombardments were intended to destroy the Communist's' morale, and ❻ napalm and chemical ❽ defoliants were used to deprive the Vietcong troops of cover. Despite their military superiority, US forces were unable to defeat their opponents. The fighting that often involved civilians and incidents of excessive ❿ violence by the US troops—most infamously the My Lai massacre of hundreds of unarmed Vietnamese women and children civilians—incited international and US domestic protests against America's conduct in the war. Following the Communist's' Tet Offensive against Saigon in January 1968, the United States gradually began to withdraw from the war, shifting control of military operations to the South Vietnamese. A cease-fire was first agreed upon in January 1973, but North Vietnamese troops marched into Saigon in April 1975; on July 2, 1976, Vietnam was reunited as a socialist republic.

After Vietnam's involvement in Cambodia in 1978, violent border disputes with China followed until 1984. In 1986 the Communist regime began introducing economic reforms aimed at creating a capitalist-orientated market economy, without loosening the power monopoly of the Communists. Vietnam and the US resumed diplomatic relations in 1995.

6 Soldiers and terrified children flee a village following a Napalm attack by US military planes

8 American bombers spray defoliants over the countryside

10 US soldiers destroy a Vietcong camp

2 Aug 1964 | US involvement escalates

Feb 1965 | Bombing of North Vietnam cities

Jan 1973 | Ceasefire

Apr 1975 | FNL troops in Saigon

2 Jul 1986 | "Socialist Republic" of Vietnam reunited

China, Japan, and Korea since 1945

Following ❶ victory in the civil war, the Communists under Mao Zedong took power in China in 1949. In the years that followed, the most populous country on Earth underwent a dramatic transformation. After World War II, Japan transformed itself to become the world's second largest economy, although it has suffered from recession since 1990. Korea broke up into a Communist dictatorship in the North and a republic in the South, which became democratic in 1987.

1 Communists marching into Beijing are welcomed by crowds, 1949

Mao Zedong Comes to Power in China

Following the proclamation of the People's Republic of China in 1949, Mao initiated a restructuring of society along Communist lines that fundamentally altered China.

After the surrender of Japan in 1945, the united front between the Kuomintang under Chiang Kai-shek and the Communist troops under Mao Zedong quickly fell apart, and in 1947 civil war broke out. In 1949 the Communists occupied Beijing, and within a year a defeated Chiang had fled to Taiwan, where he declared himself president and ruled until his death in 1975.

In Beijing, ❺ Mao placed himself at the head of a Central People's Government and on October 1, 1949, proclaimed the People's Republic of China (PRC). He remained state premier until 1959, with ❻ Zhou Enlai as his prime minister. The ❷ new regime occupied Tibet in 1950 and a year later annexed it to the PRC; Tibet's Dalai Lama, was exiled in 1959.

3 A tribunal accuses Huang Chin-Chi of resisting collectivization

Mao introduced a radical domestic political reorganization within the state and society and enshrined the Communist monopoly on government in the ❹ new constitution of 1954. Sweeping aside the old elite, the government extended land reform through the ❸ collectivization of agriculture. Existing industries were nationalized and, with Soviet support, a state led industrialization program was launched. In this period, the economy grew, while education reforms improved literacy levels. The party rapidly came to dominate all aspects of public life through a network that reached even into remote rural areas. The powerful military and security forces were ideologically loyal to the party, which rapidly became synonymous with the state. In 1956–1957 the party leadership asked intellectuals to offer criticism in the "Hundred Flowers Campaign." After a few months in which increasingly hostile critiques were published, the party put an end to the experiment and arrested the dissidents.

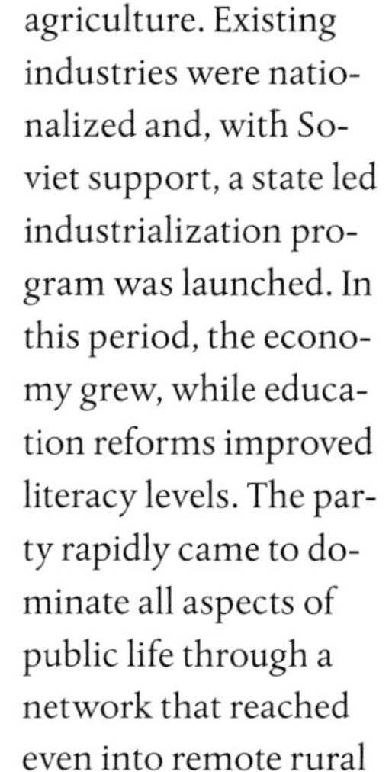

2 Chinese troops in Tibet, 1950–1951

4 The Central People's Government enacts the new constitution on June 14, 1954

5 Mao Zedong proclaims the People's Republic of China, October 1, 1949

6 Prime Minister Zhou Enlai, Mao's right hand man, 1957

The Dalai Lama

When the Chinese occupiers brutally suppressed an uprising of the Tibetan people in 1959, Tenzin Gyatso, the 14th Dalai Lama, fled into exile in India. Since then, the important teacher of Buddhism has gained a large international audience for his pronouncements on world peace. In 1989, he received the Nobel Peace Prize as the exiled leader of a neutral Tibet, despite Chinese protests.

The Dalai Lama in Berlin, 2003

2 Sep 1945 | Japan surrenders
1 Oct 1949 | People's Republic of China proclaimed
1950 | Chinese occupation of Tibet
1951 | Tibet annexed by China
1954 | Mao's Communists come to power
1958–61 | "Great Leap Forward" program

China from the Korean War to the Cultural Revolution

To counter internal party criticism, and in opposition to the Soviet Union, Mao intensified the socialist program from the mid-1950s on. The ❼ Cultural Revolution (1966–69) he initiated proved chaotic and ruinous.

7 Members of the Red Guard with flags and banners during a mass rally in Beijing, 1960s

The PRC's unsuccessful attempts to achieve the return of Taiwan to the motherland saw tensions with the United States grow, as the United States chose to recognize Chiang Kai-shek as the sole legitimate representative of all China. Sino-American relations reached a new low when China entered the Korean War on the side of the North and also became involved in the conflicts in Vietnam and Cambodia.

After the death of Stalin in 1953, China's relations with the Soviet Union deteriorated, building into an ideological and geopolitical split that remained until the collapse of the USSR. China contested the Soviet claim to leadership of the Communist world, and with the development of its own atomic weapons in 1964, clearly staked its claim to equal status with the two global superpowers, the United States and the Soviet Union.

8 Mao Zedong, left, together with his successor, Lin Biao, 1957

9 Heroic image of a young Chinese peasant working on a collective farm, propaganda poster, 1967

10 Propaganda painting of Mao Zedong, 1950s

In 1958 a program of collectivization and indoctrination, or "reeducation," was launched in what was billed as the "Great Leap Forward." In contrast to the Soviet focus on heavy industry, Maoist policy concentrated on collectivizing the ❾ agricultural sector and launching local small-scale steel production. To this end, the rural population was divided into more than 25,000 "people's communes," and "production brigades" were formed. Together with mass mobilizations for the construction of roads and irrigation systems, this was expected to complete the transition to true Communism.

The results of this policy were calamitous, with famines in 1960–1961 killing millions of peasants. As a result, criticism of the leadership grew within the party, particularly from Liu Shaoqi and Deng Xiaoping, who sought a more liberal, technology-focused policy. Mao Zedong stepped down in 1959 in favor of Liu, although he remained the ⓬ leading symbol of the party. With help from his "crown prince" ❽ Lin Biao, he turned the people's liberation army into the Maoist Guard and intensified the party struggle against those with "rightist" tendencies.

Toward the end of 1965, frustrated with the moderate direction of policy under his successor, Mao and his supporters proclaimed the "Great Proletarian Cultural Revolution" and publicly announced a campaign against representatives of the "capitalist way" and traditional Chinese thinking. The crusade was accompanied by a ❿ ritualized personal veneration of Mao. The ⓫ radical student Red Guards became a nationwide spy network. They terrorized and humiliated Mao's critics and harassed members of local officialdom. As their excesses increasingly grew out of control, the military and the party intervened with the approval of Mao, and by the end of 1967 order had been restored.

The Cultural Revolution led to anarchy, violence, and the displacement of much of the old party cadre. In 1969 Mao officially declared it over. Lin Biao became the designated successor of the increasingly frail Mao.

11 Young members of the Red Guard hold up copies of Mao's *Little Red Book* of quotes, Tiananmen Square, Beijing, 1965

12 "Long live our great teacher": Poster of Chairman Mao

1959 | Dalai Lama's exile begins
1959 | Mao steps down
1965 | Great Cultural Revolution
1969 | Cultural Revolution ends
1989 | 14th Dalai Lama wins Nobel Peace Prize

China 1969–1989

The power struggle between Mao and the reformers around Deng only ended with the death of the iconic leader. The group led by Deng then began to introduce reforms.

2 Tianjin, in the northeast of China, the second largest trading port in the world; in 1984 it became an "open city" for foreign investors, October 2001

After the Cultural Revolution, the moderate faction within the Communist party once again gained strength. Mao Zedong remained the highest authority in the state despite serious illness, although numerous party functionaries who had been expelled during the Cultural Revolution were rehabilitated. Following the unexplained death of Lin Biao in 1971, pragmatic forces within the party led by Premier Zhou Enlai and his protégé ❶ Deng Xiaoping emerged victorious for the first time. However, only after the deaths of Zhou and Mao in 1976 were the reformers around Deng finally able to have their way. The radical left-wing group called the "Gang of Four," including Mao's widow ❺ Jiang Qing, was stripped of power and condemned by a special court in 1981. Mao's successor as party chairman was Premier ❻ Hua Guofeng, while economic policies were decided by Deng. After Mao, ❹ Deng was the primary influence on the party, and he established new international economic ties. In June 1981 one of Deng's protégés, the reformer ❼ Hu Yaobang, replaced Hua as party chairman, thus clearing the path for Deng's new political direction.

5 Mao's widow, Jiang Qing, during her trial in Beijing, 1981

6 Hua Guofeng, Mao Zedong's successor as party leader

Deng then introduced economic modernization and liberalization in virtually all areas of society, and from 1979 he opened the nation to international trade with the establishment of "special economic zones." Deng also strove for a socialist but ❷ market-oriented economy, in which wage differences could exist and in which achievement had priority over other considerations. The country also liberalized politically. Everyday life became less and less dominated by ideological dogma and a Western-influenced legal system was slowly established, although freedoms of speech and assembly were forbidden and a move toward elections was not on the agenda.

3 Mao Zedong greeting Nixon, the first US president to visit China, 1972

In foreign policy as well, the pragmatic line held the upper hand. After serious border conflicts with the Soviet Union in 1969, a foreign political détente was evident through the admission of the People's Republic into the United Nations in 1971 and a ❸ visit from US President Nixon to China in 1972. Negotiations with the Soviets in 1982 led to a normalization of diplomatic relations and the reopening of their respective embassies in 1986. Regarding the question of Taiwan, however, the People's Republic remained adamant that only Beijing had the political right to represent China internationally and refused to recognize the government established on the island.

1 Deng Xiaoping

4 Deng Xiaoping is driven past a parade of Chinese soldiers

7 The reformer Hu Yaobang, June 16, 1986

1971 | Lin Biao dies
1971 | People's Republic of China joins UN
1972 | Nixon's visit to China
9 Sep 1976 | Death of Mao
1979 | Special economic zones set up
1981 | Condemnation of "Band of Four"

China since 1989

The refusal to allow political freedoms culminated in the massacre of Tiananmen Square in 1989. Despite worldwide protest, China holds to the strategy of ❿ economic liberalism without a parallel political liberalization and refuses to let Western demands shape its policy.

The easing of restrictions in the economy and lifestyle in China led to the growth of ❽ demands for a political voice for the people of China, particularly by students and intellectuals, and from both within and outside the party. The party's internal conflict concerning its future direction became more intense. In January 1987, following student protests, General Secretary Hu was dismissed as too liberal and was replaced by the previous premier of the State

10 The entrance to the Chinese stock exchange in Shanghai

Council, Zhao Ziyang; the new premier was Li Peng. In May 1989 in a number of cities, particularly in Beijing, students and civil rights activists demonstrated for freedom, civil rights, and democracy. Zhao was open to dialogue, but he was dismissed in June, and the hard line of Deng and Li triumphed. The months of peaceful protest in Beijing's Tiananmen Square were terminated on June 3–4, 1989, with the deployment of troops and tanks. The worldwide condemnation of this crackdown went largely unheeded and, despite economic sanctions against China from the majority of Western nations, death sentences and long prison terms were conferred on the leaders of the protests.

8 Chinese students demonstrating for freedom and democratic reforms, June 1989

Li and the new party general secretary, ⓬ Jiang Zemin, guaranteed the continuation of Deng Xiaoping's economic policies in the succeeding years and even after his death in 1997. They also held onto the right of exclusive power for the party, which was expressly confirmed in 1990. The hard line taken against members of the ❾ Falun Gong religious sect in 1999–2000 showed that the party's claim to power was unbroken. The creation of a "socialist market economy" was concluded in 1993, and economic and trade relations with the Western industrial nations were intensified. A new generation appeared in the political leadership in 2003 with Premier Wen Jiabao and President Hu Jintao, who has been general secretary of the party since 2002. In view of the enormous ⓫, ⓭ economic potential of China, Western voices critical of the human rights situation have been muted, but concerns about internet censorship remain. The imprisoned human rights activist Liu Xiaobo was awarded the Nobel Peace Prize in 2010.

12 Jiang Zemin, who continued Deng's economic reforms

In foreign affairs, China's tense relations with its neighboring states of Vietnam, Laos, and Japan were normalized between 1990 and 1993 through treaties and frontier agreements. The tone of comments relating to Taiwan became more severe after 1996; the possibility of an official Taiwanese declaration of independence has led to renewed tensions since 2004. The former British colony of Hong Kong was reintegrated into China on July 1, 1997. The fear of political pressure and the risk of a flight of capital from the financial center prior to the handover was countered by China with the concession of special "Western" rights for Hong Kong.

11 Chinese commuter sends a text message on his mobile phone

9 Falun Gong protest over the persecution of their Chinese members, 2001

13 Luxury apartments in the city of Shanghai, 2005

1982 | Diplomatic relations normalized with USSR
1987 | Hu Yaobang resigns
May 1989 | Demonstrations in Beijing
3–4 Jun 1989 | Tiananmen Square Massacre
1 Jul 1997 | Hong Kong reverts to China
1999–2000 | Persecution of Falun Gong Sect

Korea

The Korean Peninsula has been divided since 1948. The Communist dictatorship in the North has increasingly been isolated, while the republic in the South held its first elections in 1987.

After the 1945 defeat of Japan—which had occupied Korea since 1910—Korea was occupied by the Soviets in the north and by the Americans in the south. In February 1946, Kim Il Sung, formed a government along Soviet lines in the north, and on September 9, 1948, he proclaimed the People's Democratic Republic. When the Soviet troops withdrew, Korean troops from the North invaded the South in June 1950, beginning the Korean War. Under a UN mandate, ❷, ❸ US and allied troops repelled the North Korean attack, but China intervened on the side of the North. The armistice signed on July 27, 1953, ended a conflict that cost millions of lives.

3 US Marines bearing the flags of Korea, the US, and the UN, 1950

Politically, North Korea aligned with the Soviet Union and China. A ❶ state doctrine of self-sufficiency was proclaimed in 1955 by the Communist regime with a cult of personality centered on ❹ Kim. Since 1989, the dictatorship has sealed the country off from the world and the populace faces massive human rights abuses and starvation. In 1997 Kim Il Sung's son, ❺ Kim Jong Il, took power. He reportedly suffered from severe health problems and died in 2011. His son Kim Jong Un took over. Due to the continuation of its nuclear program since 2001 despite international protests, North Korea has become a concern for East Asian security.

In 1948, South Korea established an authoritarian regime aligned with the West. The president of this First Republic, ❻ Syngman Rhee, was deposed in April 1960. In August the Democratic party took over the government and established the Second Republic, which was replaced by a military government in 1961. General Park Chung Hee established the Third Republic in December 1963.

Continuing animosity between North and South Korea decreased after 1971. Various forms of military regimes followed after the assassination of General Park in October 1979. In October 1987 a new constitution introduced democratic reforms, although President Roh Tae Woo continued to counter the protests with authoritarian methods. It was only in 1997 with the election of Kim Dae Jung that democratic conditions were established and national reconciliation between North and South Korea was pursued. These policies were continued by his successor ❼ Roh Moo Hyun. Lee Myung-bak, who has been president since February 2008, follows a more hardline strategy toward North Korea.

1 Kim Il Sung, who developed the doctrine of self-sufficiency, raising economic autarky to national policy, 1966

2 US artillery fires on attacking North Korean troops to cover their retreat, April 27, 1951

4 The "great leader" of North Korea: Kim Il Sung, July 1976

5 The "much loved leader:" Kim Il Sung's son, Kim Jong Il, in 1988 during a meeting with members of the Korean People's Army

6 Syngman Rhee awards a military order of merit to US General Douglas MacArthur in Seoul, October 5, 1950

7 The president of South Korea, Roh Moo Hyun, during a press conference in Seoul on June 23, 2004

Kim Dae Jung

Kim Dae Jung, who died in 2009, was an activist of the Democratic party since 1956. He stood as an opposition candidate to President Park in 1971 and had to flee to Japan in 1972. The following year he was abducted and taken back to South Korea. In 1976 he demanded the reinstatement of basic rights, and for this he was sentenced to five years in prison and, in 1980, sentenced to death; after international protests, the government withdrew the sentence. From 1987, Kim led the democratic opposition, and he won the presidential elections in 1997. In 2000, he was awarded the Nobel Peace Prize.

above: Kim Dae Jung, who supported the dialogue between the two Korean states, March 9, 2000

1945 | Occupation of Korea
1946 | North Korea under Premier Kim Il Sung
3 Nov 1946 | Japan proclaims parliamentary democracy
1948 | First Republic under Syngman Rhee in South Korea
9 Sep 1948 | Proclamation of "Democratic People's Republic" in North Korea

Japan

In Japan after 1945, the US occupation forces installed democratic structures that proved to be robust. Through rapid economic expansion, Japan became the world's second largest economy.

9 The emperor of Japan, Hirohito, and his wife during a walk through the Japanese countryside, 1964

After US forces secured Japan's capitulation on September 2, 1945, following the dropping of atomic bombs on Hiroshima and Nagasaki, the American occupation forces oversaw the rapid installation of a civilian democratic government in Japan. In January 1946, ❾ Emperor Hirohito renounced his "divine" birthright, and on November 3, Japan established a parliamentary democracy under a new constitution. Democratic political parties and worker's syndicates were established, and various coalition governments were formed. In April 1952 Japan was officially returned to full sovereignty. Administrations were often only briefly in office, but on the whole the new system proved to be stable and effective. In November 1955 the Liberal and Japan Democratic parties united as the Liberal Democratic party, which has been the ❿ majority party ever since, ruling the country in shifting coalitions. However, corruption scandals and financial dealings among its own members continue to cause difficulties. The socialists, with their various groupings, form the perennial opposition, but are nevertheless often included in the government as a result of the coalition-style government. In foreign policy, relations with neighboring states have been shaped to some extent by Japan's imperial legacy, its conduct during World War II, and the way these topics are taught in Japanese schools; these are particularly sensitive issues for China and Korea. With the end of the Cold War and the growth of economic interdependence in the 1990s, regional relations have improved somewhat. After the rapid reconstruction of the country with US financial assistance, Japan experienced a massive market-oriented ❽ modernization and industrialization drive. This led to the rejection of many ⓬ traditional society structures and therefore did not go uncriticized. The 1990s have seen the rise in the political influence of conservative religious groups.

11 Business buildings in the Japanese capital Tokyo with billboards, December 2004

Japan developed into one of the ⓫ leading Asian nations and competed successfully with the Western nations on the world market, but it has experienced a drawn-out recession since 1990 and has been affected by the vicissitudes of the global economy. It also suffers financially from earthquakes.

After the 1989 death of Hirohito, whose role prior to 1945 is not yet subject to a national consensus, his son ⓮ Akihito took office as constitutional monarch without religious legitimization. Since 1992, economic problems in Japan have shaken the postwar political consensus, resulting in rapidly changing governments.

On March 11, 2011, Japan was struck by a massive earthquake setting off a devastating tsunami. This natural catastrophe caused extensive damages, many casualties, and ⓭ severe reactor accidents at the Fukushima nuclear power plant.

8 Tradition and modern technology:Three Japanese women wearing traditional kimonos and using mobile phones, 1999

10 Toshiki Kaifu, left, paints a lucky token on the day of the election, which he won on February 18, 1990

12 View over a stone bridge of the Emperor's Palace in the Japanese capital Tokyo, 1994

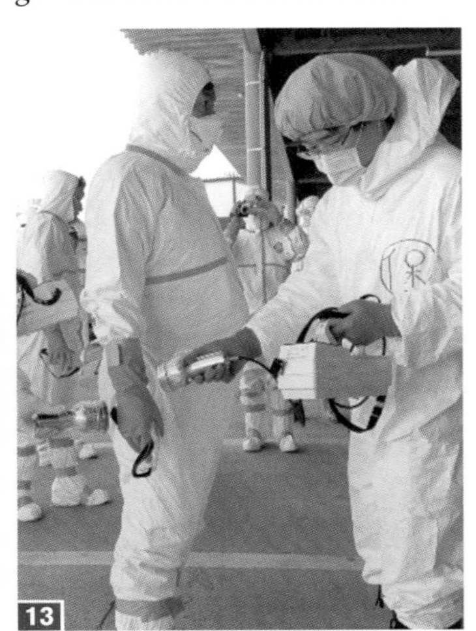

13 Japanese chief cabinet secretary Yukio Edano in the evacutation zone of Fukushima, April 14, 2011

14 Japanese Emperor Akihito during the inaugural meeting of the newly elected Japanese parliament on January 21, 2005

1955 State doctrine of "independence" in North Korea **1997** Kim Dae Jung's government in South Korea **2000** Kim Dae Jung awarded Nobel Peace Prize

Jun 1950 Korean War begins **1987** New constitution in South Korea **1997** Kim Jong Il takes power in North Korea

Australia, New Zealand, and Oceania since 1945

❶ Australia and New Zealand are wealthy and stable democracies based on the Anglo-Saxon parliamentary model, in which conservatives and social democrats alternate running the government. The original inhabitants in both countries—the Aborigines in Australia and the Maori in New Zealand—demand greater recognition of the centuries-long suppression of their cultural identities. As colonies of settlement in the British Empire, their transition to independence was smooth, and both voluntarily maintain strong links to Great Britain as members of the Commonwealth.

Symbol of the Australian capital: The Sydney Opera House, 1996

Australia

Since 1945, Australia has been a stable democracy, firmly aligned with the West during the Cold War. Its pluralistic society has yet to achieve a full reconciliation with the Aborigines, who remain economically and socially marginalized.

Australia, a constitutional monarchy and member of the ❹ Commonwealth, was threatened by Japan in 1942 in the Pacific War—an experience that brought the country closer to the US. This relationship was maintained after the war, and in April 1952 Australia entered into the ❺ ANZUS pact with New Zealand and the United States for security in the Pacific region. It sent troops during the Korean and Vietnam wars. Since 2001, Australia has been one of America's closest allies.

Elizabeth II, Australia's official head of state, March 22, 2000

Over the last two decades, Australia has looked to forge better relations with its Asian neighbors. The Australian government has worked to establish free-trade agreements with China and ASEAN (the Association of Southeast Asian Nations). It has also tried to prevent conflicts in Papua New Guinea and the Solomon Islands.

Native of Australia: An Aborigine prepares for a traditional dance

Liberals, conservatives, and social democrats compete in shifting coalitions over the formation of the government. After long periods with Labor (1983–1996) and the Liberals (1996–2007) in power, Labor politician Julia Gillard became the first female prime minister in 2010. The proposal of the constitutional assembly of 1998 to transform Australia into a republic was rejected in a referendum in November 1999, and Queen Elizabeth II remains the head of state.

Meeting of ANZUS members's representatives, August 1952

Economically, Australia is a major exporter, and since 1966 Japan has been the country's largest trading partner. Mineral resources (bauxite, nickel, oil) began to be mined more intensively in the 1950s. Liberal and competitive economic policies have attracted substantial foreign investment, especially from Europe and the United States.

Since the late 1970s there has been a growing recognition of the need to reconcile with the island's native inhabitants, the ❷, ❸ Aborigines, whose culture has long been suppressed and their living space progressively encroached upon. They have been granted wide-ranging cultural autonomy and targeted economic assistance, and in 1993 a law was passed opening the way to land restitution. Environmental issues arouse strong feelings in Australia and massive ❻ protests have taken place against nuclear tests carried out in the Pacific.

Aborigine plays in a Brisbane street, June 3, 2004

An Australian demonstrates against nuclear weapon tests, August 2001

1942 | Japanese attack in the Pacific War
25 Nov 1947 | New Zealand gains independence
Apr 1952 | ANZUS Treaty
1971 | South Sea Forum founded
1979 | Federated States of Micronesia proclaimed

New Zealand and the Islands of Oceania

New Zealand is a stable and prosperous democracy. The islands of the Pacific region gradually gained their independence after 1945 but for the most part maintain strong economic and political relationships with the major powers.

New Zealand became a sovereign state within the British Commonwealth on November 25, 1947. It has remained close to Australia, the United Kingdom, and the United States in its foreign policy, although there was a period of strained relations with the United States after New Zealand declared itself to be a nuclear-free zone in 1987. It joined the United States and Australia in the ANZUS defense pact. Domestically, the National Party and Labor are the two major political parties in the parliamentary system. The Labor party has led most of the governments since 1945. Labor prime minister ❾ Helen Clark was succeeded by John Key from the National Party in 2008. Although New Zealand has diversified significantly since the 1980s, ❿ animal husbandry, especially sheep farming, remains a key economic sector.

9 Helen Clark, first female prime minister of New Zealand, November 28, 1999

8 Men in Papua New Guinea wearing necklaces and headdresses made of plants

Most of the islands of Oceania fought for and won their independence after 1945. Relationships with former colonial powers often proved problematic. Today, most of the islands are ruled by elected governments. Conflict between ethnic groups sometimes erupts into violence, as happened on Guadalcanal in the Solomon Islands in 1998. Most of the island groups of Oceania formed the South Sea Forum with Australia and New Zealand in 1971 to promote further economic and cultural cooperation in the Pacific region.

The United States took over the administration of ⓫ Micronesia in 1947. After proclaiming the Federated States of Micronesia in 1979, the islands joined an association agreement with the United States in 1983. In 1986, the Marshall Islands also voted for a "free association" with the United States but declared independence in 1990.

In 1956–1957, the French-controlled territories of Oceania and Polynesia were given their own constitutions. Many former British territories, including Tonga and Fiji, have declared their independence; in the face of protests from Great Britain, a military regime seized power in ❼ Fiji in 1987 and declared a republic. A June 2001 peace deal put an end to a conflict between the central government of ❽ Papua New Guinea and militant separatists on the island of Bougainville that had raged since 1988–1989 and cost more than 10,000 lives.

7 Contrasts: Arcades from the colonial era next to a modern multi-story building on the Fiji island of Viti Levu

The Kingdom of Tonga

The Kingdom of Tonga, which is comprised of about 170 islands, was ruled by King Taufa'ahau Tupou IV from 1965–2006. He was succeeded by his son George Tupou V. Although the king supports traditional lifestyles and economic structures, the government strongly promotes economic investment in the islands with tax policies designed to attract foreign companies. In 2001, a biotechnical company was granted permission to record and research the genetic makeup of the native population, which is considered to be one of the most homogeneous in the world.

King Taufa'ahau Tupou IV

10 View over the green mountains of New Zealand, used for the sheep breeding that is the focus of the country's agriculture

11 Young women and girls wearing traditional headdresses and dancing costumes, Micronesia

1983 | Micronesia association agreement with the US
1987 | New Zealand declared nuclear-free zone
1988–89 | Civil war in Papua New Guinea
1990 | Marshall Islands's independence
from 1996 | Regency of John Winston in Australia

1 Famine: Undernourished child in a Sudanese refugee camp

Africa since the Independence of its Nations since 1945

The nations of Sub-Saharan Africa that became independent after 1957 have continued to suffer the consequences of their continent's experience of colonialism. The optimism of the early years of independence soon gave way to repeated military coups, violent conflicts, and popular disillusionment with promises to end poverty and improve living conditions. Other problems faced in parts of the region include ❸ drought and ❶ famines, limited access to drinking water, and the alarming growth of HIV/AIDS since the 1980s. These problems are compounded by authoritarian and frequently corrupt regimes.

Decolonization: Background and Problems

After World War II, weakened European colonial powers and an increased self-awareness of the native peoples led many African colonies toward self-government. Since independence, however, most have struggled to overcome serious economic, political, and social challenges.

Powerful ❺ independence movements began forming in the African colonies following World War II, leading to the creation of many new African nations since 1957. The main reason for the success of the Pan-African movement after 1945 lay in the increased self-awareness of the African nations. World War II, in which troops from many ❹ colonies fought alongside their colonial rulers, precipitated the end of European supremacy. The development of new forms of ❻ Islam, and especially of Christianity, that distinctly differed from the Western forms and were closely tied with concepts of national identity also played an important role. Most important of all, though, was a rethinking in the approach of the weakened European powers after the war.

The majority of the ❷ initiators of African independence came from the groups of native intellectuals and professional elites who had been educated in the colonial motherlands and who admired the functioning administration and material progress they encountered. They hoped that self-rule would help to create these conditions in the former colonies, too. However, on the threshold of independence, Africa was confronted by problems that were difficult to resolve and were often a legacy of colonialism. The gap between the educated elite and the ❼ illiterate majority of the populace was often vast, and the economies of these nations were intricately bound to the needs of the colonial metropoles. Furthermore, many of the former colonies were not "nations" as such, but zones of European influence. Abstract borders arbitrarily divided and grouped linguistic and ethnic groups, making it difficult for the inhabitants to identify with the resultant countries. Tribal solidarity and majority-versus minority struggles often undermined the new democratic structures. An extreme case of societal breakdown was the 1994 genocide in Rwanda. With a colonial legacy of political instability, unclear borders, poverty, and no infrastructure, the odds were against the new states.

2 Julius Nyerere, who studied in England, became the first prime minister of Tanzania in 1964

3 Herdsman leads his emaciated cattle through a landscape marked by drought, 1985

4 Senegalese soldiers on the side of Allied forces, in German captivity, 1940

5 Members of the Senegalese population demonstrate for independence

6 A group of African Muslim men pray in Senegal, ca.1950

7 Night school for the education of illiterate adults, Cameroon

1946 | Abolition of forced labor in the colonies

1957 | Ghana's sovereignty

1960 | Independence of Nigeria and Cameroon

from 1960 | Independence of French colonies

1961 | Wars of Independence in Angola and Mozambique

The End of Colonialism

From the late 1950s, the colonial powers of Great Britain, France, and Belgium saw their rule in Africa gradually come to an end. Where possible, they sought to retain their commercial interests.

9 Sunset over the Niger River in Bamako, the capital of Mali

The three countries responded in different ways to African desires for independence. The British initially used indigenous social structures and elites in order to "indirectly" administer their colonies cheaply and efficiently. The British slowly resigned themselves to African self-government, although African independence movements forced the pace. This was the case in ⓫ Ghana, which became the first independent nation in Sub-Saharan Africa in 1957. One after another, colonies became sovereign members of the British Commonwealth: Nigeria and Somalia in 1960, Uganda in 1962, Zanzibar (which joined with Tanganyika in 1964 to form Tanzania) and Kenya in 1963, and Zambia in 1964. Rhodesia and South Africa were exceptions, as the white populations seized power to prevent black majority rule.

11 Kwame Nkrumah waving to the crowd after having become the first president of the Republic of Ghana

France attempted at quite an early stage to grant civil rights to its Sub-Saharan African colonies and thereby to bind them to the motherland. In 1944, in order to ensure assistance in the struggle against the Vichy regime, General de Gaulle, the leader of the French government-in-exile, assured some of the ⓭ African leaders that civil rights would be granted to all inhabitants of the French colonies. In 1946 forced labor was abolished, but as the promised benefits failed to materialize, demands for independence grew louder. De Gaulle's plan for a union of states under French leadership failed. With the exception of Algeria, the French African colonies—including the ❿ Ivory Coast, Guinea, Cameroon, ❽ Niger, Senegal, Chad, and the Central African Republic—gained their ❾ independence peacefully after 1960; the strategically important Djibouti became politically independent only in 1977.

13 De Gaulle meets regional leaders fighting for independence in Brazzaville

Of the Belgian colonies, the Congo, considered a "model colony," underwent a particularly traumatic decolonization experience via intervention by the United States. Rwanda and Burundi became independent in 1962.

12 Civil war in Angola, 1976

8 Independence, Nigeria, 1965

10 The first prime minister of the sovereign Ivory Coast, Felix Hophouet-Boigny, gives a speech, ca. 1965

Portugal employed mercenary troops to stifle the independence movements in its colonies, ⓬ Angola and Mozambique. Bloody fighting raged through the 1960s, and they did not win their independence until 1975.

Ghanaian President Kwame Nkrumah

"Our Way to Freedom," 1961

"The African independence movement, which after the Second World War gained more importance, spread far and wide across Africa like a bush fire. The clear, echoing cry for freedom . . . has become a powerful hurricane, that will sweep away the old colonial Africa. The year 1960 was the year of Africa. In that year alone, 17 African states came into being as proud and independent, sovereign nations."

Kwame Nkrumah, the spiritual leader of Pan-Africanism and of African socialism

1962 | Rwanda and Burundi gain independence

1963 | Sovereignty of Kenya and Zanzibar

1964 | Sovereignty of Zambia

1975 | Angola gains independence

1977 | Djibouti gains independence

West Africa

Of the West African countries, Nigeria has had the most turbulent postcolonial history. Ghana, Senegal, and the Ivory Coast have slowly consolidated since their independence.

John Kufour at his swearing-in ceremony as the new president of Ghana, January 7, 2001

The name of the Biafra region became synonymous with misery, hunger, despair, and suffering

On March 6, 1957, ❶ Ghana became the first independent nation in sub-Saharan Africa. Kwame Nkrumah, one of the intellectual leaders of Africa's liberation and Ghana's prime minister since 1952, became president and installed an increasingly autocratic regime. In February 1966 he was deposed by a military coup d'état and emigrated to Guinea. After a short democratic period lasting until 1972, the military repeatedly took power in sequence of coups. At the end of 1981, Flight Lieutenant Jerry Rawlings took power in a coup, introduced democratic structures, and liberalized the economy. He then won two successive presidential elections before peacefully handing over governmental power to the victorious opposition leader ❷ John Kufuor, who was followed by John Atta-Mills in 2009.

After Nigeria's independence in 1960, intense clan wars took place, leading to the separation of national regions and parallel governments. From 1966 to 1999, several military coups and regimes followed one another, interrupted by short phases of democratization. A civil war broke out from 1967 to 1970 over the ❸ Biafra region, which declared itself provisionally independent. Under the leadership of President ❻ Olusegun Obasanjo (1999–2007), Nigeria began to stabilize and seek relations with the international community. However, corruption and religious conflicts continue to afflict the country.

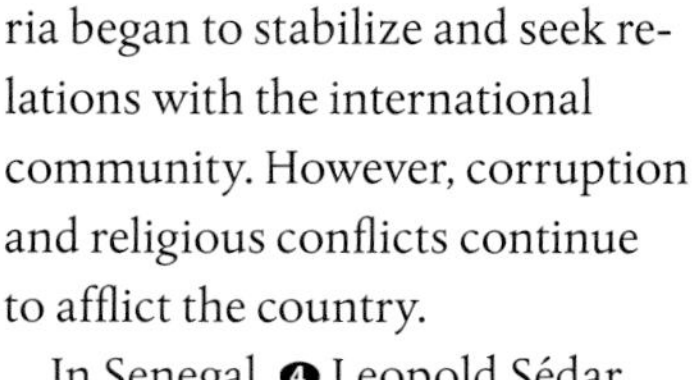

In Senegal, ❹ Leopold Sédar Senghor ruled from 1960. He was a socialist and acclaimed poet who was greatly respected as a spokesperson for the continent and as an international mediator. Senghor ruled as president until 1980 in a surprisingly liberal presidential system. His successors, Abdou Diouf (1980–2000) and Abdoulaye Wade maintained the internal political stability of the Senegalese state.

Ahmed Sékou Touré, who was president of Guinea from 1958 to 1984, established a socialist presidential government. His regime survived several coup attempts and was characterized by brutal suppression of the civilian population. His successor ❺ Lansana Conté continued this dictatorial rule. Corruption and human rights abuses have discouraged international donors and foreign investment, and in January 2005 Conté narrowly escaped an assassination attempt.

The Ivory Coast (Côte d'Ivoire) was led by President Félix Houphouet-Boigny until 1993. During this period, the country was one of the most economically prosperous and politically stable in Africa, although it fell short of a democratic system. Both his successor Henri Bédié, who ruled for seven years before being ousted in 2000, and the socialist ❼ Laurent Gbagbo used rigged elections to bolster the legitimacy of their rule. A civil war from 2002 to 2007 split the country along political and sectarian lines. Renewed fighting broke out after Gbagbo refused to recognize the victory of Alassane Outtaras in the presidential election in 2010. Gbagbo was arrested in April 2011.

Shrine of an Asafo company of the Fanti at the coast of Ghana, painted cement, 1952

Leopold Sédar Senghor, 1986

Laurent Gbagbo, October 2000

Guinea's president Lansana Conté

Olusegun Obasanjo

1958–84 | Authoritarian government of Ahmed Sékou Touré in Guinea

from 1960 | Leopold Sédar Senghor president of Senegal

1967–70 | Civil war in Nigeria

1973 | Jean-Bedel Bokassa's regime in the Central African Republic

1981 | Jerry Rawlings's government in Ghana

Central Africa

Since 1960, authoritarian governments have predominated among Central African states.

9 Libyan tanks bomb a street in the Aouzou border area in the northern part of Chad, April 7, 1987

In Niger, President Hamani Diori established single-party rule in 1960 and tied the country firmly to France, as did his successor Seyni Kountché. Unrest led to a military coup in 1996. In 1999 the military handed back power to President ❽ Mamadou Tandja, who introduced a multiparty system. In 2010 he was overthrown by Salou Djibo.

Chad suffered from religious tensions that emerged between its Islamic north and Christian south. The conflict escalated, following revolts by the Muslim population over taxes, into a ❾ civil war in which France and Libya intervened between 1984 and 1988. In 1993 Idriss Déby was elected, and his government slowly stabilized the country and wrote a national constitution. In 1994 Libya withdrew its troops from the country after the International Court of Justice rejected its claim to a disputed strip of territory between the countries.

The Central African Republic was initially ruled by President David Dacko as an authoritarian state. In January 1966 he was toppled by army chief Jean-Bedel Bokassa, who established one of the cruelest regimes in Africa. Bokassa made himself president for life in 1973 and then in a ❿ megalomaniacal ceremony in December 1977 crowned himself Emperor Bokassa I. He was deposed in September 1979 with international approval, and Dacko returned to power, but the country remained unsettled. Even President ⓫ Ange Félix Patassé, emerging from a controversial election in 1993, was unable to ensure stability in the country. François Bozizé, who came to power in 2003, has struggled to achieve political consolidation.

In Cameroon between 1960 and 1982, the Francophile president Ahmadou Ahidjo presided over a one-party system. His successor, Paul Biya, initially followed the same policies but was forced to introduce a multiparty system in 1990 following popular protests. Violent clashes had occurred in Rwanda since 1959 as the ethnic ⓬ Hutu majority rebelled against the Tutsi minority that had served as the ruling and privileged elite during the colonial era. Around 150,000 Tutsis fled from Rwanda to Burundi and other neighboring states. After independence in 1962, Hutu military leaders ruled for the most part. However, recurring conflicts with Tutsi rebels led to appalling massacres in 1994. After the genocide the Rwandan government established reconciliation tribunals that aimed to restore peace and unity.

8 The democratic president of Niger, Mamadou Tandja, 1999

10 Jean-Bedel Bokassa during his coronation ceremony in Bangui, December 4, 1977

11 Ange Félix Patassé brandishes a gun at a press conference, Sept. 26,1979

Genocide in Rwanda

After 1990, the tension between the Tutsi rebels and Hutu holders of power increased in Rwanda. When President Habyarimana was killed in an airplane crash under suspicious circumstances in April 1994, Hutu extremists began—with propagandist support from the government— systematically to massacre Tutsis and moderate Hutus throughout the country. Within only a few weeks, 800,000 people fell victim to a genocide in which virtually all layers of society took part. At the beginning of July, Tutsi troops were able to establish order and take control of the country.

A girl searches for her parents among the bodies of Rwandans who have been trampled to death, July 18, 1994

12 A group of young soldiers of the Hutu militia at a military exercise, 1994

1993 | Idriss Deby's government in Chad
1999 | Mamadou Tandja's presidency in Niger
since 2002 | Civil war in the Ivory Coast
1990 | Introduction of the multiparty system in Cameroon
1994 | Massacre of the Tutsi in Rwanda
2001 | John Kufuor elected president of Ghana

The Republic of the Congo and the Democratic Republic

Since their independence, both of these French-speaking former colonies in the ❶ Congo region have been unable to find lasting peace.

At the end of the 19th century, both Belgium and France claimed the Congo region. Belgium took the territory around the capital of Léopoldville, while France claimed the area around Brazzaville.

After World War II, Fulbert Youlou established himself as the leader of the independence movement in Brazzaville. When the former French Congo became a sovereign state in 1960, Youlou became its president and quickly installed a brutal regime. He was deposed in 1963, and Alphonse Massamba-Debat, introduced a socialist state. After a power struggle, Marien Ngouabi then triumphed in 1968, setting up the Congolese Workers' Party (PCT), and in 1970 proclaimed the Communist People's Republic of the Congo. Following his assassination, Denis Sassou-Nguesso was appointed president by the PCT in 1979. In 1990 he established a multiparty system and introduced democratic reform. The first election in 1992 was won by the opposition, whereupon violence erupted and a three-year civil war began. Sassou-Nguesso has held power in the Republic of the Congo since his forces seized Brazzaville in 1997, although fighting continues.

The Belgian Congo, whose ❷ mineral resources were exploited by Belgian mining companies, has been crisis-ridden since gaining ❹ independence in 1960. The leaders of the independence movement, ❸ Joseph Kasavubu and ❻ Patrice Lumumba, became president and prime minister of the new Democratic Republic of the Congo, whose capital was Léopoldville. Lumumba became an international figure in the liberation movement with his demands for a complete decolonization of Africa. In 1960, the mineral-rich province of Katanga, led by ❺ Moise Tschombé, announced its secession; a simultaneous mutiny by the army left the government helpless. The UN Security Council sent troops to oversee the disarmament of the Katangan forces. The army remained a threat and were suspected of the abduction and murder of Lumumba in January 1961.

In November 1965 General ❽ Mobutu Sese Seko led a military coup. He ruled dictatorially. Mobutu renamed the country Zaire and the capital Kinshasa, and he lavished patronage on his own clan. The corruption that enriched Mobutu and his clients was disastrous for the economy. In the early 1990s Mobutu began to share power by forming a coalition, but this imported power struggles into the government. In May 1997, while Mobutu was abroad for medical treatment, an alliance under ❼ Laurent-Désiré Kabila seized power. In 1998 the country, renamed the Democratic Republic of the Congo, became a war zone, as five neighboring states sent their own rebel fighting groups into the country. The war ended with a tentative peace in 2002 but is thought to have cost more than two million lives.

1 Traditional village huts, Belgian Congo

2 Industrial plant refining copper mined in the region of Jadotville, Zaire, 1959

3 Joseph Kasavubu, independence leader, 1965

4 During the ceremony marking the independence of the Democratic Republic of Congo, King Baudouin of Belgium (left) gives a speech; Joseph Kasavubu (seated) is also in attendance

5 Moise Tschombé, prime minister of the mineral-rich Congolese province of Katanga, 1961

6 Freedom fighters for the independence of Congo: Patrice Lumumba in Brussels in January 1960

7 The Zairan rebel leader Laurent Kabila, 1997

8 Mobutu Sese Seko, 1994

1960 | Fulbert Youlou's regime
1963–78 | Jomo Kenyatta's government in Kenya
1970 | "People's Republic of Congo" proclaimed
1960 | Katanga cedes from "Democratic Republic of Congo"
since 1965 | Putsch led by Mobutu Sese Seko
1971 | Belgian Congo renamed Zaire

East Africa

While Somalia and the Sudan have experienced violence and political chaos, relatively stable political systems have emerged in ❾ Tanzania and Kenya.

Zebras grazing on a savanna in Tanzania

Premier Milton Obote during a conference in Nairobi of the Organization of African Union in the 1980s

After Tanganyika and the island of Zanzibar were granted independence from Great Britain in 1961 and 1963, they united to form Tanzania in 1964. The first president, Julius Nyerere, stayed in office until 1985 and developed a socialist one-party system. After his resignation, Ali Hassan Mwinyi oversaw the transition to multiparty politics. Despite poverty and reliance on foreign aid, the country has remained stable under his successors Benjamin William Mkapa and Jakaya Kiwete (since 2005).

Uganda became independent in 1963. Premier ⓬ Milton Obote founded a socialist one-party state in 1966. After an army coup in 1971, ❿ General Idi Amin established one of Africa's bloodiest regimes; at least 200,000 people fell victim to his security forces. In April 1979 he was toppled, and Obote returned to power. President Yoweni Museveni, in office since 1986, has brought some stability to the country despite the rebel groups that continue to operate in the north.

Kenyan politics were dominated by the rule of Jomo Kenyatta from independence in 1963 until his death in 1978. Under growing pressure, his successor Daniel Arap Moi permitted multiparty elections after upheavals in 1991. Moi was defeated in the 2002 elections, and his successor Mwai Kbaki has pledged to fight Kenya's major corruption problem.

In 1969 military forces under General Siad Barre seized power in Somalia. Heavy fighting with rebel groups led to the flight of Barre in 1991 and to the secession of the Republic of Somaliland. In 1992–1994, US and ⓭ UN troops intervened unsuccessfully in the civil war, and since then no central government has established effective control over the country.

In Ethiopia, Emperor Haile Selassie was overthrown by the military in 1974. Between 1977 and 1979, thousands died under the "Red Terror" regime of Mengistu Haile Mariam, who also instigated a program of forced collectivization. He was overthrown in 1991 after the secession of the provinces of Eritrea and Tigray. The country suffered a famine in 1985 that led to a major international relief effort. Following a war with neighboring Eritrea in 1999–2000, border tensions remain.

Ever since its independence in 1956, Sudan has suffered from conflicts between Muslims, Christians, and members of African faiths. A military coup in June 1989 brought to power Islamic forces, whose attempts to introduce religion into public life caused conflict with other groups. Since 2003, a ⓫ campaign of ethnic cleansing and massacres against the population by government-backed Arab militias in Darfur has led to accusations of genocide. Southern Sudan voted for its secession from the North in a referendum in 2011.

In Baidoa, a Somalian child runs towards a rescue convoy; on the left, a French soldier watches closely, holding a weapon to cover the child's dash for the safety of the convoy, December 17, 1992

General Idi Amin, who later became known as the "Butcher of Africa"

Sudanese secret police intervening against rebels from the opposition, October 14, 2004

AIDS in Africa

More than 25 million Africans are infected with the human immunodeficiency virus (HIV). More than 70 percent of all HIV-infected people worldwide live in sub-Saharan Africa. Resources for prevention and treatment are lacking, although some countries, notably Uganda, have reduced new infections through educational initiatives.

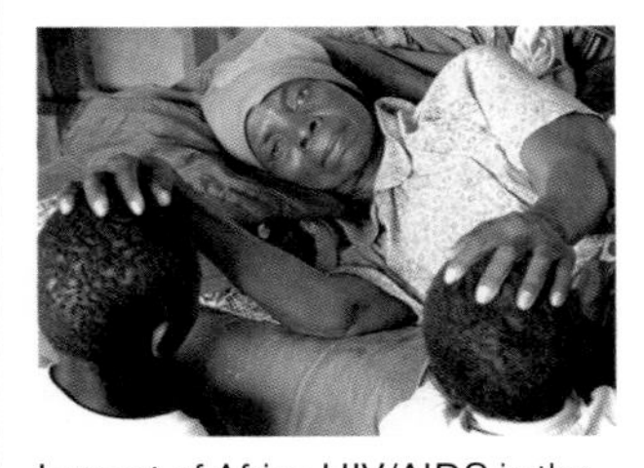

In most of Africa HIV/AIDS is the leading cause of death

1971	Idi Amin's regime in Uganda
1974	Emperor Haile Selassie deposed in Ethiopia
1977	Marien Ngouabi murdered
1991	Somaliland secedes from Somalia
1991–95	Civil war in Somalia
1991	Zaire renamed Democratic Republic of Congo

Southern Africa

With the exception of Zambia, the anticolonial liberation struggle in southern Africa was both protracted and bloody. An apartheid system was established in Rhodesia.

1 The president of Mozambique, Samora Machel, October 10, 1986

In the Portuguese colonies of Angola and Mozambique, the struggle for independence took more than a decade. In Angola, three divergent liberation movements led an armed struggle against the colonial rulers beginning in 1961. In 1975 Portugal allowed the Communists under ❻ Agostinho Neto to form an independent state. Neto, supported by the USSR and Cuba, sought to establish a socialist people's republic but was opposed by the US-backed UNITA resistance forces under Jonas Savimbi. After 1987, Neto's successor José Eduardo dos Santos abandoned Marxism and began to negotiate with Savimbi. Since 2002 a precarious peace has held.

Mozambique became independent in 1975, and the Communists under ❶ Samora Machel attempted to set up a socialist system while fighting against rebel groups backed by the apartheid regimes of Rhodesia and South Africa. Machel's successor ❷ Joaquim Alberto Chissano, president since 1986, won free elections in 1994 and 1999.

Zambia belonged to the British-administered Central African Federation from 1953 to 1963 as Northern Rhodesia, along with Southern Rhodesia (now Zimbabwe) and Nyasaland (now Malawi). After Zambia's independence in 1964, Premier ❽ Kenneth Kaunda became the country's president. He nationalized large parts of the economy and in 1972 established a one-party system. In the multiparty elections in 1991, Kaunda lost to ❸ Frederick Chiluba, who survived attempted coups in 1997 and 1998. After the death of President Levy Mwanawasa, Rupiah Banda came into office in 2008.

As a reaction to the independence of Zambia, the radical white settlers' party of Southern Rhodesia declared their nation ❼ independent despite the protests of Great Britain. In 1970 Rhodesia was declared a republic, and Ian Smith installed an apartheid regime similar to that in South Africa. This was resisted by the African liberation forces of ZAPU under ❹ Joshua Nkomo and ZANU under ❺ Robert Mugabe. As surrounding countries were drawn in, the struggle destabilized the region. Through British mediation, negotiations took place in 1978–1979 between Smith's government and the liberation movements (who merged in 1976 to become the Patriotic Front). After guarantees for the white settlers, ZANU won elections held in February 1980. Rhodesia became the independent Republic of Zimbabwe on April 18, 1980, and since then Mugabe has been president. Subsequently competition occurred between Mugabe and Nkomo. Since 2000 he has received much international criticism due to his tacit support for the occupation of white-owned farms by black veterans of the liberation movements. All opposition is brutally suppressed and the population is thought to be close to starvation.

2 The President at the ballot box: Joaquim Chissano, December 1, 2004

3 Frederick Chiluba

4 Joshua Nkomo, 1978

5 The Zimbabwean President Robert Mugabe, April 2, 2005

6 Agostinho Neto, Communist and poet, 1973

7 Prime Minister Ian Smith (middle) signs the Southern Rhodesian Declaration of Independence, November 11, 1965

8 The first president of Zimbabwe, Kenneth David Kaunda

since 1950s	ANC begins work
1960	Massacre of Sharpeville
1964	Zambia's independence and Nelson Mandela condemned
1970	Republic of Rhodesia proclaimed
1976	Formation of the "Patriotic Front"
18 Apr 1980	Mugabe's presidency in Zimbabwe

South Africa

In South Africa, a harsh apartheid regime ruled until 1990. In 1994, after a period of relatively peaceful political upheaval, Nelson Mandela, the formerly imprisoned leader of the opposition movement, became the first black president of South Africa.

10 Police operation using guns, tear gas, and dogs in the poverty-stricken black township of Soweto, near Johannesburg, May 12, 1986

11 Pieter Willem Botha gives a speech, February 1989

12 Hendrik Verwoerd, who was assassinated in Capetown in 1996

The white government of South Africa began implementing comprehensive apartheid laws in 1949 that segregated the black majority from the white minority and sought to reserve power for the latter. The apartheid policy of racial segregation was implemented through the creation of reservations, or "homelands," which were intended to prevent black Africans from entering the white-inhabited areas. In 1950 the African National Congress (ANC) began a campaign of civil disobedience and sought to activate mass resistance. Faced with violent repression from the security forces, the ANC fell increasingly under the influence of Nelson Mandela as the militant faction increasingly prevailed over the moderate pacifists. In 1960 there were riots and reprisals in the black townships, notably the "Sharpeville Massacre," in which scores of black demonstrators were killed by police. In the aftermath the government outlawed the ANC. From then on the ANC operated as an underground organization using guerrilla tactics. In 1964 several ANC leaders, including Mandela, were sentenced to life in prison.

In 1966 Prime Minister ⓬ Hendrik Verwoerd (1958–1966) was assassinated. His successor, Balthazar J. Vorster, enlarged the security apparatus and in 1976 several hundred blacks were killed during the uprising of the Soweto township. Such atrocities brought growing international criticism and isolation on the South African regime. After 1978, under external pressure, Vorster's successor ⓫ Pieter Botha abolished many of the apartheid laws while increasing the de facto repression of the black population. After bloody ⓾,⓭ uprisings in 1985–1986, he declared a national state of emergency. Not until Botha's successor ⓮ Willem de Klerk came to power in 1989 was the ban on the ANC lifted. Negotiations began, paving the way for apartheid's abolition. De Klerk organized a peaceful transition to democracy with Mandela, who had by then been released from imprisonment. In 1992 the last whites-only referendum voted against apartheid and in 1994 the first elections with black participation took place. The ANC won with a clear majority and Mandela became president. He pursued a policy of reconciliation. His former comrades-in-arms and successors ❾ Thabo Mbeki (1999–2008) and Jacob Zuma (since 2009) have continued Mandela's political course.

13 Demonstration in Middelburg against the apartheid regime, March 9, 1986

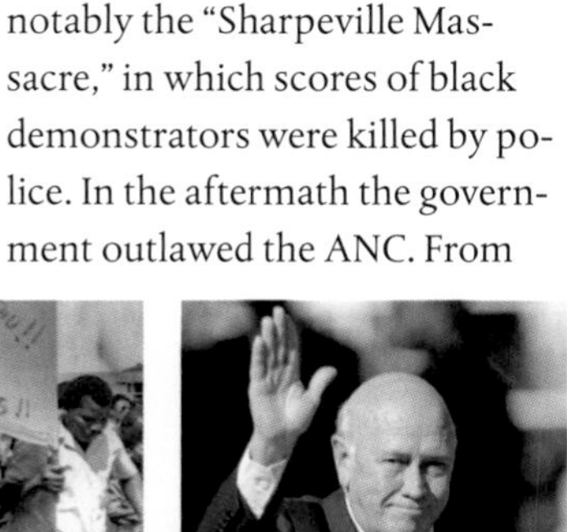

14 Frederik Willem de Klerk, April 27, 2004

9 The third free election, ten years after the end of apartheid: President Thabo Mbeki casts his vote in Pretoria on April 14, 2004

Nelson Mandela

A onetime lawyer sentenced to life imprisonment in 1964, Nelson Mandela became the international face of black resistance to apartheid. In February 1985 he refused release from prison and demanded instead the abolition of racial segregation. He was finally released after 26 years in prison as the apartheid regime began to crumble. In negotiations with the government, Mandela secured the nonviolent handover of power, and he was subsequently elected president. He and former president de Klerk shared the Nobel Peace Prize in 1993. Mandela continues to enjoy worldwide respect as an international mediator.

Nelson Mandela, a statesman respected throughout the world, December 27, 2004

1987 | Introduction of the free market in Angola
1990 | Apartheid abolished in South Africa
1992 | Free elections in Angola
1993 | Nelson Mandela awarded Nobel Peace Prize
1994 | Free elections in Mozambique
1994 | Mandela's presidency in South Africa

The Toronto skyline, with the CN Tower (right)

CANADA SINCE 1945

Since 1931, Canada has been a sovereign nation within the framework of the British Commonwealth. It has become a ❶ modern industrial state that, as a stable democracy, has been tightly tied into the Western alliance system and the peace missions of the United Nations. The imbalance between the culturally dominate Anglophone majority and the Francophone minority has repeatedly led, particularly in the province of Quebec, to separatist aspirations. With laws and changes to the constitution, the federal government must constantly seek a cultural and linguistic balance.

Canada into the 1960s

Canada has constituted an integral part of the Western political world since 1945. As a result of the existence of two cultures in the country, domestic problems have sometimes arisen.

Since Canada fought on the side of the Allies in World War II, the sovereign member of the Commonwealth has become politically and economically closer to the United States, although it made loans and supplied grain to Great Britain during the war. Canada has entered into several economic and defense treaties with the United States, such as agreements on the joint use of nuclear energy, and in 1963, after the Nuclear Test Ban treaty, the storage of US atomic weapons on Canadian territory. Mining of raw materials has increased, 75 percent of which is done by US firms.

As a result of the immensely rapid growth resulting from industrial mobilization during the war, Canada's growth required improved infrastructure, and in 1965 the Trans-Canada Highway, which connects all of the provinces, was completed. Through industrialization, cities experienced a rapid economic boom in the ❻, ❼ 1950s, which slowed again in the 1960s.

Winner of the Nobel Peace Prize Lester Bowles Pearson, June 25, 1962

Franco-Canadian leader of the cabinet, Pierre Elliott Trudeau, June 10, 1982

Conservative and Liberal governments have alternated. After a long period of Liberal government, Progressive Conservative John Diefenbaker became prime minister in 1957 and exiled the Liberals to the opposition benches until ❷ Lester Pearson took over government in 1963. For most of the 1968–1984 period, a Franco-Canadian, ❸ Pierre Trudeau, led the cabinet and promoted a bilingual culture. In 1969, English and French were both declared official languages.

Only an uneasy balance was possible with the separatist forces in the Francophone province of Quebec. In 1967, General de Gaulle had to cut short his visit when he made a speech in which he cried, "Vive le Québec libre!" Against the background of growing social and economic dissatisfaction among French-speaking Canadians in the 1960s, especially in ❺ Quebec, strong autonomy movements formed. ❹ Militant extremist organizations made attacks on politicians. The murder of Quebec's labor minister, Pierre Laporte, in 1970 led to the declaration of a national state of emergency.

Militant protester vandalizes property, Quebec, 1968

The old town of Quebec City

The skyline of Montreal

City of Montreal, Quebec

1957 | Pearson awarded Nobel Peace Prize

1959 | Agreement with the US on joint use of nuclear energy

1963 | Agreement with the US on basing nuclear weapons in Canada

1963–65 | Construction of the Trans-Canada Highway

1970 | Pierre Laporte murdered

Canada since the 1960s

The Canadian government has politically championed world peace. Internally the separatist tendencies of the province of Quebec are ever-present.

Since the 1960s Canada has worked, in foreign and economic politics, toward a careful disentanglement from its lopsided partnership with the United States. With its "third-opinion politics," it has sought closer relationships with Europe and Japan, and in 1970 also with the People's Republic of China, once economic agreements had been made. In the 1970s and 1980s, Canada took part in the Conference for Security and Cooperation in Europe and its successor conferences as well as in the ❾ summits of the leading industrial nations (G7).

As a founding member of the United Nations, Canada has consistently supported UN peace efforts with ❿ military troop contingents, for example, in the Congo in 1960 and in Cyprus in 1964. Diplomatically, Canada has also successfully worked to solve numerous conflicts. For his mediation efforts in the Suez Crisis, Foreign Minister Pearson was awarded the Nobel Peace Prize in 1957.

The separatist desires of the Quebec people remain a domestic flashpoint. In 1976, the radical separatist Parti Québecois, under the leadership of Rene Lévesque, won an absolute majority in the province but failed in its 1980 referendum to secede from Canada. The 1987 Meech Lake Accord gave Quebec special rights, but the agreement was scrapped due to protests from other provinces. The "Quebec Charter of the French Language" in 1992 ultimately defined a binding language agreement for the state offices and more autonomous rights for the provinces. In 1995, the ⓬ vote for separation failed closely once again; with just 50.56 percent of the votes against secession, the unity of Canada was maintained for the time being.

Prime Minister Trudeau put forward the Constitution Act in 1982 requesting full political independence from the United Kingdom. The British parliament responded with the Canada Act, which severed virtually all the remaining constitutional and legislative ties between the two countries.

Under Conservative Prime Minister ⓭ Brian Mulroney, who governed from 1984 to 1993, tensions with the original inhabitants of Canada, the ❽ Inuit and the ⓫ Indians, became prominent. After long unrest, in 1988 they were promised parts of the Mackenzie Valley in a preliminary treaty which was signed by representatives of the Canadian government. In 2008 conservative Prime Minister Stephen Harper officially apologized to the native peoples of Canada for the policy of forced assimilation.

The growing significance of the ⓮ Northwest passage as a trade route has led to conflicts between the USA and Canada during the last years. While the USA see the passage as international territory, Canada claims it as internal waters.

8 Two young Inuit girls in traditional dress, 1996

9 Paul Martin (second from left) and the ministers of finance of the leading industrial nations, Frankfurt, 1999

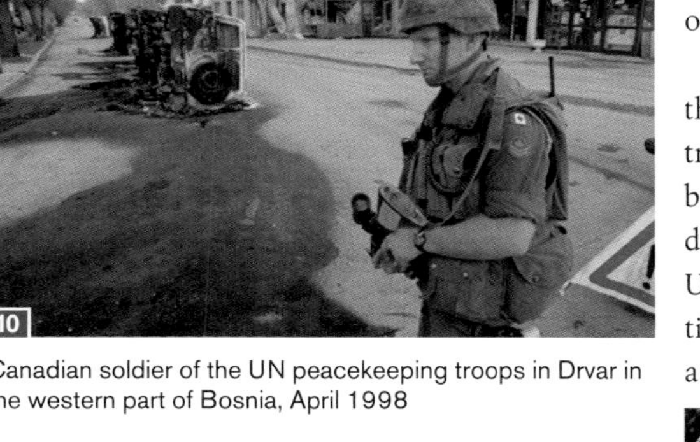

10 Canadian soldier of the UN peacekeeping troops in Drvar in the western part of Bosnia, April 1998

11 Canadian Indian wearing traditional clothes and headdress during a display of cultural traditions, 1990

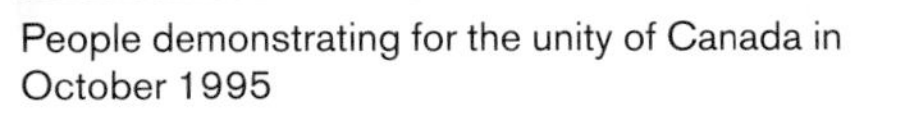

12 People demonstrating for the unity of Canada in October 1995

13 Prime Minister Brian Mulroney, May 1989

14 Icebreaker of the Canadian Coast Guard in the Northwest passage

1982 | Constitution Act severs link with Great Britain

1984–93 | Brian Mulroney's government

1987 | Meech Lake Accord

1988 | Territories transferred to Canadian native inhabitants

The United States: Global Power since 1945

The ❶ United States emerged economically strengthened from World War II and, in the postwar years, became the political and cultural leader of the West as the two-state bloc system began to take shape. It stood in opposition to the Soviet Union during the Cold War, which lasted until 1991. Internally, the civil rights movement and protests against the Vietnam War ushered in a liberalization of society in the 1960s. As a global superpower, the United States has since 1991 seesawed between global cooperation and efforts toward hegemony. Since the terrorist attacks of September 11, 2001, the United States and the Western world are confronting the challenge of international terrorism.

Flags in the streets of Manhattan, New York, 2001

The United States under Truman

After 1945 and at the beginning of the Cold War, the United States became the leading economic and political power in the Western world.

World War II demonstrated the enormous economic and military might of the United States. The war economy created full employment and a self-sustaining economic boom that seamlessly transitioned after 1945 to a prospering peacetime economy. The development of a consumer society, which had been interrupted by the Great Depression that followed the Wall Street Crash of 1929, gained pace again in the 1950s and ❷ healthy economic growth continued into the 1960s.

The car, symbol of prosperity: poster advertising a Cadillac limousine, 1953

United States nuclear weapons test, April 22, 1952

Domestically, Democratic ❸ President Harry S. Truman (1945–1953) attempted to build on the social welfare policies of the "New Deal," which had been initiated by his predecessor Franklin D. Roosevelt.

One of the most significant developments in US foreign policy after 1945 was that the "unnatural" war alliance with the Soviet Union broke apart in the face of the expansion of Communist power in Eastern Europe. The new postwar order in Europe and Asia was characterized by the onset of the Cold War between East and West. The United States definitively abandoned its isolationist stance and took over political and ideological leadership of the countries within its sphere of influence. After 1947, the "containment" of Soviet expansion became the central tenet of US policy. President Truman promised all free countries military and economic aid in order to preserve their independence. The reconstruction of Western Europe was generously supported and led to an economic boom there, most notably in West Germany.

American soldiers in Korea, wearing protective clothing against the rain during a cease-fire

The United States had a monopoly on ❺ nuclear weapons until the Soviets tested their atomic bomb in 1949. That same year, the states of Western Europe concluded a military alliance under the leadership of the United States, the ❻ North Atlantic Treaty Alliance (NATO), which commited its signatories to a joint military defense strategy in the event of an attack on one of the member countries. During the Korean War of 1950–1953, American ❹ troops fought alongside the forces of South Korea in conflict with North Korean and Chinese forces, directly engaging Communist armies for the first time.

US Democratic President Harry S. Truman gives a speech

US Secretary of State Dean Acheson signs the NATO pact; Truman (center) and Vice President Barkley

since 1947 | Policy of "containment" towards USSR
1949 | Soviet atomic tests
1949 | NATO founded
1950–53 | Korean War
1953–61 | Eisenhower's presidency
1954 | American intervention in Guatemala

The United States in the 1950s

Both internally and externally, the United States of the 1950s was absorbed by the conflict with the Soviet Union. At the same time, the civil rights movement registered its first successes in the quest for equal rights for African-Americans.

Between 1953 and 1961, Republican ❽ Dwight D. Eisenhower, a popular war hero, held the US presidency. During this period, the Cold War intensified until it dominated the foreign policy agenda. With the first atomic test by the Soviets in 1949 and the circumnavigation of the Earth by the Soviet satellite *Sputnik I* in 1957, the military and technological supremacy of the United States was brought into question; the response was a large-scale rearmament program. The US government began developing space and weapons programs and increased its atomic clout. Secretary of State ❼ John Foster Dulles followed a policy of undermining Soviet influence in the Eastern bloc, known as the "rollback" strategy. In 1954, the United States intervened in Guatemala. The Suez Crisis of 1956 and the Hungarian uprising of the same year increased tensions between East and West without bringing about a direct conflict. In 1959, the US admitted Alaska and Hawaii as the 49th and 50th states of the union. In the same year a crisis developed in "America's backyard" in the form of the communist revolution in Cuba.

7 John Foster Dulles addresses the press, ca. 1953

9 Senator Joseph Raymond McCarthy, 1950

The Cold War was also pursued domestically during the 1950s. Senator ❾, ⓫ Joseph McCarthy and the House Committee on Un-American Activities were the driving forces behind an anti-Communist wave of persecution in United States administration and public life. Unprecedented in American history, a climate of mass hysteria developed as liberals, artists, and intellectuals were defamed and fear of "treason" spread in government circles. In 1954, McCarthy was censured by his fellow senators for "bringing the Senate into dishonor and disrepute" during this period.

8 Dwight David Eisenhower, painting by Thomas E. Stephens

The continuing boom ushered in an era of affluence. A "baby boom" occurred. Cars, washing machines, and consumer goods became ❿ normal household possessions for the average family. Together with a new youth culture in ⓭ music and ⓬ film, the model of the "American way of life" spread throughout the Western world.

In the 1950s the struggle for African-American civil rights against continuing racial discrimination and segregation advanced under leaders such as Martin Luther King, Jr. In 1954, racial segregation was abolished in public schools, and in 1956 so, too, were separate seating arrangements on public transport.

Martin Luther King, Jr.

Martin Luther King, Jr. was a Baptist preacher from Atlanta who was a charismatic leader and advocate of nonviolent resistance against racial discrimination. Actions, such as the "March on Washington," made him a symbol of the protest movement at the beginning of the 1960s. As an advocate for peaceful integration, he was awarded the Nobel Peace Prize in 1964. On April 4, 1968, he was assassinated in Memphis, Tennessee, as he prepared to lead a march.

above: Martin Luther King during a speech at a rally against discrimination, ca. 1966

10 Living area with terraced houses in a suburb of Los Angeles, ca. 1958

11 McCarthy explains the spread of Communist sympathizers in the United States, ca. 1950

12 The face of the 1950s: Marilyn Monroe

13 The musical idol of the 1950s: Elvis Presley

1956 | Suez Crisis
1956 | Hungarian revolution
1959 | Alaska and Hawaii gain statehood
1964 | Martin Luther King, Jr. awarded Nobel Peace Prize
4 Apr 1968 | Martin Luther King, Jr. murdered in Memphis

Reform and Crisis: The US under Kennedy and Johnson

At the beginning of the 1960s, President Kennedy became the hope for a young and dynamic America. After his assassination, Johnson continued to implement Kennedy's domestic reforms but also escalated involvement in Vietnam.

1 US President John Fitzgerald Kennedy, October 1961

2 A modern first lady in the White House: Jackie Kennedy, 1950s

Campaigning on a platform of promises of social reform and concessions on the race issue, ❶ John F. Kennedy won the close election of 1960. Promoting his vision of a revitalized America setting out for "new frontiers," the young and dynamic Democrat became the hope for a new generation. With his elegant wife ❷ Jackie at his side, Kennedy brought a modern style of government to the White House. His time in office, however, was not characterized by domestic change but by foreign policy crises.

The Soviet construction of the Berlin Wall and the unsuccessful invasion of communist Cuba attempted by US-backed Cuban exiles in 1961 increased tensions between ❹ East and West. After the discovery of Soviet missiles in Cuba in 1962, the world teetered for days on the brink of a nuclear war. After this, Kennedy attempted to reduce tensions with the Soviet Union. The "hotline," a set of high-speed teleprinters linking Moscow and Washington, was set up. The United States, the Soviet Union, and Great Britain agreed in August 1963 on the Nuclear Test Ban Treaty to end atomic weapons tests, although China and France refused to sign the treaty. The ❸ assassination of Kennedy in Dallas on November 22, 1963, shocked the nation.

6 Racial unrest in Cambridge, MA, June 21, 1963

Under the slogan "Great Society," Kennedy's successor, ❺ Lyndon B. Johnson, partly implemented Kennedy's social welfare programs, including increased spending on education, Medicare, urban renewal, and a war on poverty and crime. The Civil Rights Act of 1964 guaranteed African-Americans protection when carrying out their right to vote, encouraged integration in schools, and banned racial discrimination. Economic disadvantages for blacks remained, and even President Johnson supported racist delegates from Mississippi. The black protest movement radicalized in 1964–1968, and in the inner cities ❻ unrest was not uncommon. Organizations such as the Black Panthers and the Nation of Islam, which propagated the superiority of the blacks and saw violence as legitimate, won increasing influence

Externally, Johnson decided on direct military intervention in the Vietnam conflict in 1964. The fighting continually escalated until the beginning of the 1970s. Military failures, and the ever stronger protest movement against the war, forced the domestic reform policy into the background and forced Johnson to renounce a run for reelection. The murders of King and popular Democrat ❼ Robert F. Kennedy in 1968 constituted a bloody end to the US reform period.

4 Kennedy and Khrushchev meet following the Cuba crisis in Vienna, 1961

3 A moment when the American nation held its breath: After President John F. Kennedy is shot, Jackie Kennedy jumps out of the car, Dallas, Texas, November 22, 1963

5 Kennedy's successor, the Democratic President Lyndon B. Johnson

7 Attorney General Robert Kennedy talks to demonstrators, June 14, 1963

1960	John F. Kennedy elected president
Oct 1962	Cuban Missile Crisis
Aug 1963	Nuclear Test-Ban Treaty
22 Nov 1963	Kennedy assassinated
1964	US involvement in Vietnam escalates
1964	Civil rights law banning racial discrimination

Division of the Nation: The United States under Nixon

The polarization between the protest movement and the Establishment destroyed the internal consensus within the United States at the end of the 1960s. Failure in Vietnam and the Watergate scandal caused a reevaluation of the country's identity, particularly by the young.

President Richard Nixon in the White House, January 1971

Protests against the Vietnam War grew into a rebellion of the young against the "Establishment," and this spread throughout the entire Western world. Through nonconformist clothes, haircuts, and music, the young rejected the traditional order. The pacifist ❽ "hippie" movement rebelled against paternalistic government, corporate business, and traditional social mores, and taunted the representatives of middle-class values through their glorification of "free love" and drugs. The protest movement divided the mainly conservative American society. With the 1968 election of the Republican Richard Nixon, a staunch anti-Communist became president. With the slogan of "Law and Order," he proceeded aggressively against those at the heart of the protest movement.

During the ❾ Nixon Administration, a milestone was achieved in space travel: on July 20, 1969, the first human landed on the ❿ moon.

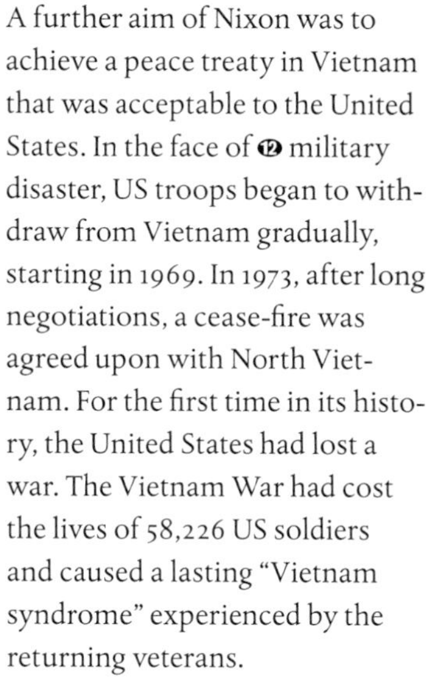

A later moon landing in April 1972: US astronaut Young puts up the American flag

Internationally, Nixon and his advisor ⓫ Henry Kissinger sought an improvement in relations with the leading communist states. In 1972 Nixon visited China—the first US president to do so—and in the same year the Strategic Arms Limitation Talks (SALT) with the Soviet Union, which had started three years earlier, resulted in an interim treaty. These historic visits ushered in a new phase of trade relations with both countries.

Washington Post journalists Carl Bernstein (left) and Robert Woodward who uncovered the Watergate scandal, May 7, 1973

A further aim of Nixon was to achieve a peace treaty in Vietnam that was acceptable to the United States. In the face of ⓬ military disaster, US troops began to withdraw from Vietnam gradually, starting in 1969. In 1973, after long negotiations, a cease-fire was agreed upon with North Vietnam. For the first time in its history, the United States had lost a war. The Vietnam War had cost the lives of 58,226 US soldiers and caused a lasting "Vietnam syndrome" experienced by the returning veterans.

Henry Kissinger, NSA and secretary of state under Nixon, September 9, 2001

A hippie in San Francisco, 1967

In addition, the ⓭ Watergate scandal shook public confidence and trust in the presidency. In May 1973, it was revealed that Nixon had authorized a break-in at Democratic party headquarters to mount listening devices during the presidential election. Attempts by the president to hide this fact after May 1974 led to impeachment proceedings against him. On August 9, 1974, Nixon resigned the presidency.

US soldiers carrying the body of a soldier killed in action, Vietnam,1966

Woodstock

An open-air music festival in Woodstock, New York, on August 15–18, 1969, became the symbol of a hippie generation hoping for cultural and political renewal. As many as 500,000 participants peacefully celebrated the greats of rebellious pop, blues, and protest music. Joe Cocker, Jimi Hendrix, Janis Joplin, and Joan Baez gave famous performances there.

Celebrating music and the peace and love lifestyle at the Woodstock festival, film still

1968 | Robert Kennedy assassinated
1968 | Nixon elected president
1969 | US withdrawal from Vietnam
15–17 Aug 1969 | Woodstock festival
1973 | Cease-fire agreement in Vietnam
1973 | Watergate Scandal
9 Aug 1974 | Nixon resigns

Consolidation and Détente: The US under Ford and Carter

Under Ford, the tarnished office of the presidency was rehabilitated to a certain extent. His Democratic successor's term was marred by unfortunate involvement in international events.

American drivers stand in line at a gas station in Los Angeles

James Earl "Jimmy" Carter, 1983

Republican President Gerald R. Ford, August 11, 1974

With Nixon's resignation in 1974, Vice President ❸ Gerald R. Ford became his successor. Ford attempted, through a rigorously correct administration, to improve the flawed image of the presidential office. Congress was given greater powers, and from 1975, many formerly covért operations of the Central Intelligence Agency came under the scrutiny of the public and the media.

During the Ford era, many domestic problems, such as unemployment and inflation, worsened. The international ❶ oil crisis of 1973–1974 illustrated the dependence of the Western industrial nations on Arab oil exporters. In the mid-1970s, public awareness grew of environmental damage done by industrial firms which had not been properly monitored by the government. The opportunities and risks of the peaceful use of nuclear energy were discussed and generated much controversy. In foreign affairs, further SALT negotiations continued the détente policy with the Soviet Union.

In 1976, the Democratic Party candidate ❷ Jimmy Carter won the presidential election. Carter strengthened the international efforts of the United States in the areas of human and civil rights—both traditional Democratic party concerns—which was also visible in the improved relations with the regimes of Latin America, although his approach was somewhat naive and often based on trust in corrupt and brutal regimes. His greatest foreign policy success was the ❹ mediation of a peace agreement between Israel and Egypt in 1979. After the signing of ❺ SALT II in 1979, the détente policy suffered a crisis in 1980 due to the invasion of Afghanistan by Soviet troops. American wheat shipments to the Soviet Union were suspended, and the Olympic Games in Moscow were boycotted by the United States and the majority of its allies.

The Islamic Revolution in Iran in 1979 also caused serious difficulties for the United States, which had supported the Shah. In November 1979, more than 50 US citizens were taken hostage in the ❻ US embassy in Tehran. An unsuccessful military rescue attempt in April 1980 significantly contributed to Carter's electoral defeat in the presidential race against the conservative Ronald Reagan.

Signing of the peace treaty between Israel and Egypt at the White House, March 26, 1979

First encounter between Carter and Brezhnev: Signing of the SALT II treaty for the reduction of strategic weapons, Vienna, June 15, 1979

American hostages are led to the site of the US embassy in Tehran; the hostage-takers demand extradition of the deposed Shah Reza Pahlavi, November 1979

The Reactor Accident at Three Mile Island in 1979

A failure in the cooling system of the Harrisburg, Pennsylvania, nuclear power station on March 28, 1979, was the worst accident in the history of the peaceful use of atomic energy up to that time. As a result of a technical mistake, radioactive gas was released. At a time when public opinion was very much divided over the issues of nuclear energy, the accident was a public relations catastrophe, as popular skepticism of atomic energy grew and awareness of the risks increased, giving impetus to the antinuclear energy lobby, particularly in the West.

View of two cooling towers at the Harrisburg. Pennsylvania, nuclear power station

1973–74 | International oil crisis
1976 | Treaty on mutual nuclear inspection
1976 | Jimmy Carter's presidency
1979 | Separate Egyptian-Israeli peace treaty
1979 | Islamic revolution in Iran

Anti-Communism and Disarmament: The US in the 1980s

Both internally and externally, Reagan followed a strictly anti-Communist policy. With Gorbachev coming to power in 1985, the two superpowers were able to begin disarmament talks.

7 Diagram of a Soviet orbit shuttle, from a study on the military strength of the Soviet Union, April 1985

8 Republican President Ronald Reagan, ca. 1984

Former California governor and Republican party candidate ❽ Ronald Reagan's promise to reinstate the military and political global supremacy of the United States helped him win the presidency in 1981. With his election, a more conservative America emerged both domestically and internationally. The traditional Christian lobbies, whose power had declined in the 1960s and 1970s, gained in influence. Reagan successfully boosted the economy through cutbacks in public spending, particularly for welfare programs, while simultaneously lowering taxes. This also increased the gap between rich and poor, however. Concurrently, Reagan sharply increased military spending. The planning of a ❼ space-based defense system—the Strategic Defense Initiative (SDI)—cost billions of dollars.

Reagan's rhetoric against the Soviet Union, which he described as the "Evil Empire," was backed up by his policies. He imposed economic sanctions following Soviet support of martial law in Poland in 1981. The United States supported anti-Communist movements worldwide, particularly in Latin America and the Near East, regardless of their governance and human rights records. In Nicaragua, the Contras who worked against the leftist Sandinistas were supported by US funds and weapons via the CIA. This led to much controversy following journalistic investigations of the administration's involvement in this proceeding.

9 Ronald Reagan (right) and the Soviet party leader Michail Gorbachev sign the INF treaty, 1987

US troops in 1982 intervened in the ⓬ civil war in Lebanon and in 1983 overthrew the leftwing government of the Caribbean island of Grenada. After failed disarmament talks with the Soviet Union in 1983, new nuclear intermediate-range ballistic missiles were stationed in West Germany as a reminder of US military power in Europe.

After his 1984 reelection, Reagan took advantage of the opportunities for adjustment offered by the Soviet reform policies introduced by the new general secretary, Mikhail Gorbachev. After several American- Soviet summits, in 1987 a breakthrough came on the disarmament question. Following an ❾ agreement on the worldwide reduction of landbased missiles—the Intermediate- Range Nuclear Forces (INF) Treaty—the ❿ nuclear weapons arsenal for the first time began to decrease. The sale of weapons to Iran and the diversion of the funds to the Contras in Nicaragua became public knowledge in November 1986 and became the Iran-Contra Affair, which weakened the Reagan government.

In 1988, ⓫ Vice President George H. W. Bush was elected as Reagan's successor. Under his presidency, the change in the global political situation—caused by the collapse of the Eastern bloc and the Soviet Union in 1989–1991—was completed.

10 Disarmament: Preparation for the destruction of the first Soviet medium-range rockets, August 10, 1988

11 The Republican President George H.W. Bush in October 1988

12 US Marines leave Beirut in armored vehicles, February 1984

1980 | Ronald Reagan's presidency
1986 | Iran-Contra Affair
28 Mar 1979 | "Three Mile Island" reactor accident
1981 | Economic sanctions against the USSR

Dawning of a New Age: The United States in the 1990s

In the early 1990s, the United States under President Bush was suddenly the only superpower within a "new world order." The Clinton presidency that began in 1993 was marked by increasing prosperity and a changing world role for the United States.

2 "Operation Desert Storm": Allied troops liberate Kuwait and invade Iraq with armored tanks during the first gulf war, February 25, 1991

The mainly peaceful process of change in Eastern Europe was supported ideologically, politically, and economically by the Bush administration. The East-West conflict that had defined the thoughts and actions of American politics since 1945 ended with the reunification of Germany and the collapse of the Soviet Union in 1991. The United States, as the only remaining superpower, took on the undisputed leading role in the new world order, which had been taking shape since 1991. In a military intervention in Panama in December 1989, US troops overthrew the country's dictator, ❹ Manuel Noriega. Following the invasion of Kuwait by Iraq in 1990, Bush forged an ❷ international coalition that, under a UN mandate, militarily expelled Iraqi troops from ❽ Kuwait between February and March 1991. He also tightened the trade embargo on Cuba in October 1992 with the openly declared goal of bringing down Fidel Castro's Communist regime. The United States reduced its military presence in Asia and Europe and initiated further moves toward disarmament with the Soviet Union and its core successor state, the Russian Federation. Meanwhile, the American economy fell into a recession and social tension increased. Serious ❺ racial unrest shook the country in 1992 following the release of a videotape showing police brutality against an innocent African-American.

Democrat ❸ Bill Clinton moved into the White House in 1992 with promises of social reform and a revival of the economy, bringing representatives of all major ethnic minorities into his government. An ❶ economic boom set in, triggered by the development of communication and media technology, and created millions of new jobs. The legal minimum wage was raised, but Clinton's health care reforms, which provided for health insurance for all US citizens, were blocked by the conservative majority in Congress.

3 William Jefferson (Bill) Clinton and his wife Hillary at an election rally in New Hampshire, January 1992

1 The technology stock market Nasdaq reaches a record high

Globally Clinton avoided asserting US dominance too strongly. In 1993, he negotiated the partial autonomy of the Palestinian territories in the Middle East. Russia was assured of economic aid. The United States was among the initiators of the Kyoto World Climate Protocol in 1997 to reduce harmful gas emissions. Clinton was also personally involved in the difficult peace negotiations in Northern Ireland. Beginning in 1998, however, Clinton's presidency fell under the shadow of a ❻, ❼ personal scandal, leading to an impeachment process that resulted in his acquittal.

4 General Manuel Antonio Noriega, July 14, 1987

5 Race riots in Los Angeles, arson and looting of buildings and shops

6 7 Bill Clinton and former intern Monica Lewinsky, with whom he had an affair

8 Kuwaiti people celebrate their liberation by flying US and national flags

1988 | George H.W. Bush's presidency
1992 | Trade embargo against Cuba
1992 | Bill Clinton's presidency
Jan 1999 | Impeachment proceedings against Clinton
12 Dec 2000 | George W. Bush named president

The War against Terror: The United States under Bush and Obama

Since the attacks of September 11, 2001, US foreign policy has been shaped by the international "War on Terror." Barack Obama pursues a less polarizing political course than the Bush administration.

9 Barack Obama, April 2011

The ⓫ presidential election of 2000, in which the Democratic candidate Al Gore ran against Republican George W. Bush, ended with an extremely narrow margin. On December 12, 2000, after weeks of legal disputes, the Supreme Court designated Bush as the 43rd president. With an agenda of conservative social and economic values, foreign policy was initially not a focus of his administration. However, the attacks carried out by the terrorist organization al-Qaida on September 11, 2001, on the New York World Trade Center and the Pentagon came as a shock to the entire country and shook ❿ society. Not since Pearl Harbor had there been a foreign attack on US soil. Bush proclaimed a "long war" against international terror and those supporting it, and since then foreign policy has dominated American politics. Domestically, immigration became more closely monitored and airport security was nationalized. In 2002, the ⓭ Department of Homeland Security was established, with a cabinet-level chief.

12 US Marines cover the head of a statue of Saddam Hussein with an American flag, Baghdad, April 9, 2003

13 Tom Ridge is sworn in as the first chief of Homeland Security, January 24, 2003

Supported by a broad, worldwide anti-terror alliance, US troops ousted the Taliban regime in Afghanistan in October 2001. The Taliban had granted refuge to ⓮ Osama bin Laden, the instigator of the September 11 attacks.

In 2002, Bush proclaimed Iraq, North Korea, and Iran to be part of an "Axis of Evil" and pursued a controversial national security strategy, allowing for preventive first strikes against nations that support terrorist factions or otherwise threaten the security of the United States. Citing the possible production of weapons of mass destruction, an international coalition of primarily American and British troops invaded Iraq without UN consent in March 2003. By April they had deposed the dictatorial regime of ⓬ Saddam Hussein.

14 Osama bin Laden was killed by US special forces on May 2, 2011

With great hopes, the Democrat ❾ Barack Obama was elected as the first African American president in 2008. In foreign policy he builds on diplomacy and avoids unilateral decision making. For his plans of nuclear disarmament, peace initiatives in the Middle East, and the gradual withdrawal of US troops from Iraq, he was awarded the Nobel Peace Prize in 2009. On the domestic front, Obama passed an extensive health care reform and has strengthened civil rights.

11 Bush (left) and Vice President Gore following a televised presidential debate, October 11, 2000

10 The slogan "God bless America" on a billboard, September 2001, New York

9/11

The Islamist suicide attacks on September 11, 2001, triggered a worldwide shock wave. At around 9:00 in the morning, two hijacked airliners smashed into the World Trade Center in New York City; both towers of the tallest building in the country collapsed. One and a half hours later, a third aircraft crashed into the Pentagon, the US Defense Department's headquarters near Washington, DC. A fourth plane, assumed also to be headed for Washington, crashed outside of Pittsburgh, Pennsylvania. A total of about 3,000 people lost their lives in the attacks.

A second plane approaches the south tower of the World Trade Center following the collision of the first airliner with the north tower

11 Sep 2001 | Attack on the World Trade Center and Pentagon

Oct 2001 | Military strike against the Taliban regime in Afghanistan

Mar–April 2003 | US-led invasion of Iraq

2008 | Barack Obama becomes president

LATIN AMERICA SINCE 1945

Rapidly changing authoritarian regimes, military dictatorships, and dependence on the United States were the realities of the political situation across most of Latin America until well into the 1970s. Since then, democratic regimes have emerged in most states, although they have sometimes been undermined by problems ranging from challenges to the state from the radical left and right, to poverty, corruption, and drug cartels. Enormous gaps between rich and ❶ poor continue to characterize South American societies. Attempts at political union and economic cooperation have often been undermined by the instability of the regimes in many countries.

1 Peruvians transport produce, March 2004

Problems and Development in Latin America

Stagnant economies and social conflict rooted in economic inequalities remain serious challenges to political stability and individual governments in Latin America.

Latin America has to contend with a spectrum of social and political problems. In order to promote regional economic collaboration, various unions were formed after 1945, such as the ❹ Latin American Free Trade Association in 1960 and the Latin American Integration Association in 1980. Led by Colombia, the smaller states founded the Andean Group in 1969.

The economic might of the United States has shaped the pan-American federations. The charter of the ❺ Organization of American States (OAS) was signed in 1948 with the intention of improving the relationship between South America and the United States. During the Cold War,

3 Archbishop Oscar Arnulfo Romero (center), December 1979

and especially after the revolution in Cuba, the United States used the OAS for the distribution of aid but also as an instrument in the fight against Communism. The US government supported authoritarian right-wing regimes and forced the expulsion of Cuba from the OAS in 1962. Under President Carter, the United States supported the democratization of the Latin American countries.

Internally, the ❷ gap between the rich minority and poor majority has altered little under either military or civilian rule. One of the key issues in most countries has been land reform, since the land has typically been in the hands of a small elite. The indigenous population almost always belongs to the poor and marginalized strata of society. Across the continent, ❻ urban populations have swelled with migrants from rural areas, and little provision is made for those living in shantytowns on the edge of huge cities. The wealthiest states, most notably Chile, have thriving export sectors and well-developed infrastructure, although the wealth is unequally distributed.

2 Businessmen pass a group of street children, June 2004

The Catholic Church has played an important role in Latin America. After supporting the dictatorships, the Church in South America became influenced by "liberation theology," which championed the cause of the poor and oppressed—a dangerous stance, as shown by the case of Archbishop ❸ Oscar Romero of San Salvador, who was murdered in 1980.

4 George W. Bush welcomes the members of the Latin American Free Trade Association, 2005

5 General Secretary of the OAS, Cesar Gaviria, speaks at the annual meeting, June 3, 2001

6 Social contrasts in São Paulo: luxurious high-rise buildings next to the slums

1948 | OAS founded
1948–58 | Civil war in Colombia
1960 | Latin American Free Trade Association founded
1969 | Formation of the Andean Group
1969–75 | "Peruvian Revolution"

Central and South America: Violence and Its Reaction

Since the 1980s, fighting between rebel guerrilla groups and government forces has inhibited the emergence of democratic structures in many states of South and Central America.

Nicaragua was ruled by dictator Anastasio Somoza from 1936 to 1947 with US support, and after his murder, his sons Luis and ⓬ Anastasio took over. After the Sandinista National Liberation Front came to power in 1979, its authority was undermined by right-wing Contra guerrillas, who were financed by the United States. The Liberal Constitutional party, which came to power in 1990, was defeated by the Sandinistas in elections in 2006.

In Guatemala after 1945, land reforms and a social welfare system were introduced. When the land reform threatened the interests of the American-based United Fruit Company in 1954, the government was overthrown by a US-sponsored military coup. Rebels resisted the military regime, and the nation descended into a ❽ civil war that finally ended with a peace deal in 1996.

The armed forces seized control of El Salvador in 1948. Power changed hands many times until the Party of National Conciliation formed an alliance with the military in 1961–1962. During the 1980s frequent guerrilla uprisings were countered with extreme violence when the government formed right-wing "death squads." Since a 1991 peace deal, ❾ democratic elections have taken place.

⓭ Colombia continues to be a turbulent country. Following the 1948 murder of a popular left-wing member of the Liberal Party, J. E. Gaitán, a civil war (known as La Violencia) broke out between liberals and conservatives and lasted for a decade. In 1958 a National Front coalition government was set up, staying in power until 1974. Beginning in the mid-1960s, left- and right-wing ❼ guerrilla groups formed to resist the government. The explosion of the drug trade has financed the private army and mini-state of the largest rebel group, the FARC (Revolutionary Armed Forces of Colombia). President Alvaro Uribe (2002–2010) and his successor Juan Manuel Santos have sought to weaken the factions with the support of the US.

Due to its large oil deposits, Venezuela is a potentially wealthy country, but revenues have been very unevenly distributed. A stable but corrupt party system was shaken by the election of left-wing populist ⓫ Hugo Chávez in 1998. He introduced some redistributive measures and has been critical of the US. Middle-class protesters failed to dislodge him in 2002, and since then he has moved to reinforce his power.

A civilian government in Peru was overthrown in 1968, and for the next six years General Juan Velasco Alvarado pursued land reform and the nationalization of sections of industry in a populist "Peruvian Revolution." After a coup by Francesco Bermúdez in 1975, a comprehensive privatization program was initiated. The Maoist ❿ Shining Path guerrilla movement started a campaign of violence in 1981. The authoritarian rule of Alberto Fujimori, which began in 1990, clamped down on the rebels. Since his fall from power in 2000, the economic and social situation of Peru has only gradually improved under his successors Alejandro Toledo and Alan García.

Colombian paramilitary troops of the FARC, 2004

The decades of civil war have cost the lives of thousands of people, Guatemala, December 1996

Government and left-wing guerrillas make peace on January 16, 1992, in Guatemala

Armed Maoist Shining Path guerrillas in Peru, April 1991

Venezuelan President Hugo Chavez, January 17, 2003

Nicaraguan President Anastasio Somoza with soldiers, 1979

Poverty and no prospects: children playing soccer in a street of the Colombian *barrio* El Jardin

1979 | "Sandinista National Liberation Front" government in Nicaragua

1980 | Oscar Romero murdered in San Salvador

since 1977 | Guerrilla rebellion in El Salvador

1990 | Alberto Fujimori ousted in Peru

Argentina, Brazil, and Chile

The popular postwar dictatorship of Juan Perón had a lasting effect on the political development of Argentina. In Chile the first freely elected Marxist president, Salvador Allende, was ousted from office in 1973 in a military coup.

Juan Perón became president of Argentina after elections in February 1946. With military support, he installed a dictatorship, which due to a booming economy was able to carry out social reforms benefitting the working class. All resistance to his government was suppressed. The most popular member of the regime was his wife, ❻ Eva Perón—known as Evita—who championed the interests of the poor. After her death in 1952, she attained an iconic status in the imagination of the Argentine public. As Juan Perón began to alienate employers and the Church, the military deposed him in 1955 and he was exiled. He returned after elections in 1973 to serve as president again but died one year later.

Chilean leader Salvador Allende

A repressive dictatorship under ❹ General Jorge Rafael Videla ruled from 1976. After the Argentine defeat in the Falklands (Malvinas) War against Great Britain, ❼ military rule collapsed in 1983. President ❺ Carlos Menem was elected in 1989 and consolidated democratic structures while liberalizing the economy. His successors up to Néstor Carlos Kirchner (2003–07) and his wife Cristina Fernández de Kirchner (since 2007) have had to face the consequences of the economic crash of 2001.

In Brazil in 1950, the authoritarian presidential government under Getúlio Dornelles Vargas launched an industrialization program; his successor opened up the country to foreign investment. After disturbances in 1964, a military coup deposed President João Goulart and backed a series of right-wing presidents over the next two decades. The Catholic Church, especially Archbishop Dom Helder Camara, spoke out against human rights abuses. General Ernesto Geisel introduced democratic reforms in 1974, and the first free elections took place under his successor in 1982. Since then, the democratic system has been successfully consolidated, although economic inequality and a large public debt have left the country vulnerable to crises.

"Angel of the poor": The popular first lady Eva Peron next to her husband,1952

In Chile, a country with a strong democratic tradition, the independent left-wing socialist ❸ Salvador Allende was voted head of state in free elections in 1970. His revolutionary social program, "the Chilean way to socialism," aimed to nationalize industrial businesses and divide up the large rural estates. It was resisted by the conservatives in parliament. On September 11, 1973, the army overthrew the president in a ❶ coup supported by the United States in which Allende was killed. The leader of the coup, ❷ General Augusto Pinochet, then ruled in Chile as a dictator until 1990. Thousands of his opponents were murdered. After losing a referendum in 1988, Pinochet was edged out of power, and the 1990 election of Patricio Aylwin as president heralded the return to democratic government. Pinochet remained commander of the armed forces until 1998, but was arrested in 2000. Since his death in 2006, the assessment of his regime has continued to polarize the public. President Sebastián Piñera came into office in March 2010.

Units of the military in revolt shoot at the president's palace, Chile, September 11, 1973

The Chilean dictator Augusto Pinochet, 1997

Seizing of power by the military junta: Jorge Videla (middle) is sworn in, March 30, 1976

President Carlos Menem, March 4, 1997

Naked prisoners bound to posts outdoors in an Argentine prison camp during dictatorial rule under Pinochet, 1986

1910–17 | Mexican Revolution
Feb 1946 | Juan Péron becomes president of Argentina
1952 | Eva Péron dies
1952 | Military putsch led by Fulgencio Batista in Cuba
since 1953 | Castro's and Che Guevara's guerrilla war against the Batista regime

The Special Cases of Mexico and Cuba

After World War II, both Mexico and Cuba followed independent courses vis-à-vis the United States, the political leadership of both resulting from left-wing revolutions. In 1962 Cuba was the scene of a showdown between the two Cold War superpowers.

The Mexican ⑩ revolution from 1910 to 1917 brought with it a social-liberal constitution that established national rights of access to mineral resources and the separation of church and state. The Institutional Revolutionary Party (PRI) held political power in a corrupt, semi-democratic system from its formation in 1946 until 2000. It pushed forward the ⑬ industrialization and nationalization of the economy, achieving high growth rates through the 1960s, and introduced social reforms. However, corruption and mismanagement of the economy led to virtual state bankruptcy in 1982, which was prevented only by US assistance. From 1988, under President Carlos Salinas de Gortari, the close connections and interlinkages between the state, the PRI, and the economy were slowly dissolved. Opposition forces gained popularity, and the candidate of the right-liberal National Action party, ⑪ Vicente Fox, won the presidential election of 2000. He was succeeded by Felipe Calderón in 2006.

Cuba, politically and economically dependent upon the United States, was ruled by the dictator ❽ Fulgencio Batista following a military coup in 1952. Marxist revolutionary Fidel Castro, together with Che Guevara, began a

Fulgencio Batista next to a statue of Abraham Lincoln, one of his favorite historical figures

Fidel Castro continued to hold the reins of power in Cuba, one of the last surviving Communist states, May 17, 2005

The Mexican leader of the revolution Eufemio Zapata, December 1914

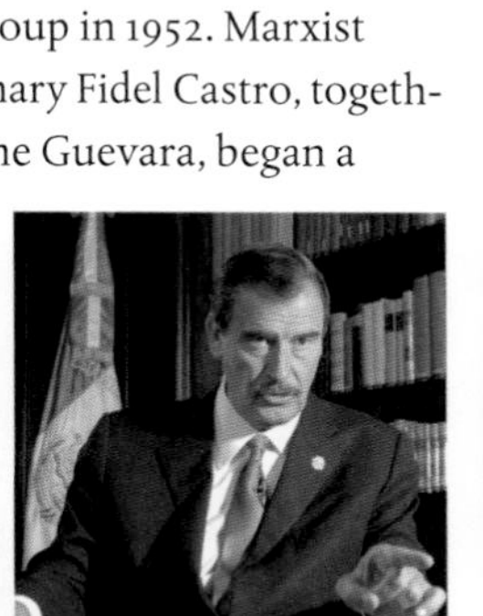

Mexican President Vicente Fox, February 2, 2004

Fidel Castro and his guerillas in the struggle against the Batista regime

Iron and steel factory in Mexico, ca. 1965

⑫ guerrilla war against Batista in 1953 and forced him to flee Havana on January 1, 1959. Castro proclaimed a socialist state and established Communist party rule. The seizure of American business assets and the close association of Cuba to the Soviet Union led to acute tensions with the United States and Cuba's expulsion from the OAS. A US-backed attempt to invade the island in 1961 proved a fiasco. The Soviet move to install missiles in Cuba in 1962 brought the world to the brink of nuclear war.

Despite its harsh repression of domestic political opposition, Castro's regime has long been an international symbol of resistance to US influence, and its social policies, such as free medical treatment, have helped keep it in power. The Cuban Communists ❾ survived the collapse of the Soviet Union in 1991, replacing Soviet subsidies with revenues from tourism. In recent years, the government has started to modestly liberalize the Cuban economy. After increasing health problems, Fidel Castro was succeeded by his brother Raúl in 2008.

Ernesto "Che" Guevara

Ernesto "Che" Guevara became an icon of international Marxist revolution and one of the heroes of student protest movements in the 1960s. A doctor, born into a wealthy family in Argentina, he joined the revolutionaries of Fidel Castro in 1954 and participated in the Cuban Revolution. As president of the Cuban national bank (1959) and minister of industry (1961), he was preoccupied with social justice in the economy. He left to continue the Communist revolution in other countries but was shot dead by government forces while training revolutionaries in Bolivia in 1966.

Che Guevara, who became a Communist icon after his death, 1965

1962 | Cuban Missile Crisis **1970** | Salvador Allende elected head of state of Chile **1973** | Pinochet's government in Chile begins

1 Jan 1959 | Batista flees **1966** | Che Guevara murdered **11 Sep 1973** | Allende deposed and murdered **1976** | Jorge Rafael Videla's dictatorship in Argentina

Globalization

Since the end of the East-West conflict in the early 1990s, the buzzword "globalization" has been used to refer to various processes affecting almost all areas of life. There really is no clear definition of this contentious phrase that does justice to all the interpretations of the term, but it generally means the homogenization of standards and procedures throughout the world. Through the ❷ fast-paced progress of information technology, which makes ❶ worldwide communication possible in real time, distances and national borders are increasingly losing significance in the financial, political, and cultural decision-making processes. Networks are created among national companies, and regional events now have increased economic and political effects on faraway parts of the world. In this respect, the acquisition of knowledge and media expertise are ever more important. Particularly in industrial countries, a "knowledge society" is replacing the "industrial society."

Thanks to modern technology, computer work can be done outside the traditional office

Economics and the Markets of the 21st Century

With the end of the competition between ideological systems in the 1990s and the consequent opening of additional markets, the internationalization of the economic world has taken on a completely different quality. Finance, product, and service markets throughout the world are increasingly interwoven. The most progressive sector in the process of globalization is the economic globalization of international financial markets, where huge amounts of capital are transferred from one country to another within seconds. However, economic crises immediately have global consequences. Transnational conglomerates coordinate their activities worldwide and choose the most advantageous production and delivery bases. Supply and demand are coordinated globally and ❹ price regulation is left to the market.

Faster and more productive: producing computer chips in Shanghai

Poster from the World Economic Forum in Davos, January 2005

Through this process, practically the whole world has become a ❸ market. Nations find themselves in harsh local competition for labor and the favors of mobile capital. Many states attempt to attract investors and "human capital" into the country through the lowering of taxes and the creation of advantages in the basic economic framework, by the deregulation of the labor market and the further liberalization of trade, for example. How far a state should strengthen—or balance with sociopolitical measures—the disparity between rich and poor resulting from the power of the mostly affluent businesses and investors is one of the politically contentious questions posed by the new economic world order.

Hustle and bustle at the stock exchange in Kuwait, March 6, 2005

Affluence and Poverty: The Consequences of a Globalized Economy

The global gross domestic product has multiplied by five since 1959. Since the mid- to late 1990s, global trade has been continually growing at a very fast pace; external investments are booming. A majority of direct investments still takes place between the industrial countries, but increasingly capital is flowing into the developing countries as well. Because ❻ labor is relatively cheap there, these nations are being integrated into the global production system of the transnational companies. Particularly in the newly industrializing nations, such as China or India, the opening of the markets has led to high growth rates and positive effects on the labor markets of the poorer countries.

On the other hand, this improvement is only relative. Sub-Saharan Africa, for example, remains cut off from the benefits of a global economy, and its popula-

Egyptian farmers on a donkey cart with cauliflowers, 2001

9 Nov 1989 | Fall of the Berlin Wall
1990 | USSR breaks apart
3 Jun 1991 | "African Economic Community" founded
1 Nov 1992 | Treaty of Maastricht comes into force
17 Dec 1992 | Founding of "North American Free Trade Zone" (NAFTA)

Chinese workers produce clothing for an international company

tion has ❺ little access to information technology and communication networks that are the positive consequences of globalization. Here, an increase in poverty is visible and economic output is in decline. Huge foreign debt burdens African state economies. Primary goods such as food and raw materials, which often constitute the wealth of the developing countries, are playing an ever smaller role compared to high-tech goods in the world market, and because the means for processing their own raw materials are underdeveloped in Africa, as well as in many of the countries of Latin America, these regions are increasingly reliant on imports from the developed industrial nations. Whether these developing countries will succeed in integrating themselves advantageously into the global world economy is very questionable, in view of the unstable conditions and the strong tribal and clan structures in these areas.

Two veiled Jordanian students surf the World Wide Web in an Internet cafe in 2001

"One World" versus "Coca-Cola Imperialism"

Globalization is reflected in other areas of life such as culture and lifestyle. ❽ Modern mass media and increased mobility favor a sort of cultural globalization. African cooking and Indian films have become as common in Europe as Western fast food has become in Asia or Hollywood films in Arabia. Optimists see this mingling of world society as a chance to integrate ❾ "the foreign" into one's own cultural value system and in this way to increase mutual tolerance. Growing commonalities in the sense of a recognized universal value system, such as human rights, can develop in this way. This perspective presupposes free access to information and knowledge.

In contrast, critics emphasize the economic dominance of the rich industrial nations in the media, through which they force their Western model of affluence on the weaker countries for their own economic advantage. This feeling of cultural hegemony is expressed in phrases such as "Coca-Cola imperialism" or "McDonaldization" of the world. The general commercialization and reshaping of national or regional cultures through foreign influences has in many parts of the world provoked movements seeking a return to their own traditions and values. One can trace the radical anti-Western or ❼ anti-American movements—up to and including terrorism—back to these perceived causes. The emphasis on regional, local, and new nationalist thinking can be seen as a reaction to globalization.

Arabic Coca-Cola advertising in the Tunisian capital Algiers, 2004

Global Domestic Policies

The challenges of globalization are diverse: concerns include the growing disparity between rich and poor, and the protection of the environment. The capacity of national governments to intervene directly in global economics is limited. Thus politics must essentially be globalized if humankind is to meet the worldwide problems effectively. In order to have a type of "world government" to guide the global economy, a strengthening of the system of the ❿ United Nations and a further concentration and linking up of international relations seems unavoidable. An example of this process in action is the development of the European Union into a supranational organization; the European national states have given up a part of their sovereign state rights to the union, while still protecting national and regional identities. Even the non-governmental organizations such as Amnesty International work through worldwide networks, in which democratic cooperation and the opportunity to influence the world outside state diplomacy develop. Examples of these non-governmental organizations (NGOs) are the worldwide action network "Attac,"which is critical of globalization and fights for social control of the financial markets, and Greenpeace, which operates internationally against the negative environmental effects of a globalized economy.

Iranian demonstrators burn an American flag, 1997

Vote in the UN Security Council in New York on an increase of peacekeeping troops in the former Yugoslavia, November 1992

1 Jan 1995 | WTO begins work
11 Jul 2000 | Founding of the African Union
18 Jun 2004 | Draft EU constitution is agreed upon
8 Feb 1994 | NATO's first military intervention in Serbia
1 Jan 1999 | European Economic and Monetary Union takes effect

Glossary

affluent Wealthy; flowing in abundance; having a sufficient and increasing supply of material possessions.

annihilation The destroying or nullifying of something; the ceasing of existence.

autonomy The quality or state of being self-governing; self-directing freedom and moral independence.

bloc A combination of persons, groups, or nations forming a unit with a common interest or purpose; a group of nations united by treaty or agreement for mutual support or joint action.

bureaucracy Government characterized by specialization of functions, adherence to fixed rules, and a hierarchy of authority.

coalition A temporary alliance of distinct parties, persons, or states for joint action.

commonwealth An association of self-governing, autonomous states loosely associated in a common allegiance.

cooperative An enterprise or organization owned by and operated for the benefit of those using its services.

decolonization The act of freeing a country from colonial status, gaining self-governing autonomy, and ending the authority and rule of a mother country.

détente The relaxation of strained relations or tensions, especially between nations.

disarmament To lay aside arms; to give up or reduce armed forces.

dissolution The dissolving of an assembly or organization; the breaking down, disrupting, or dispersing of something; the separating of something into its component parts.

dogma Something held as an established opinion; a doctrine or body of doctrines put forth as authoritative.

esoteric Requiring or exhibiting knowledge that is restricted to a small group; of special, rare, or unusual interest.

expropriation The action of the state in taking or modifying the property rights of an individual in the exercise of its sovereignty.

fundamentalist A movement or attitude stressing strict and literal adherence to a basic set of principles.

ideology A systematic body of concepts concerning human life or culture; the integrated assertions, theories, and aims that constitute a sociopolitical program.

nationalization The act of seizing control or ownership of private enterprises by the national government.

neutrality The quality or state of being neutral; the refusal to take part in a war between other powers.

nonaligned Not allied with other nations, especially with either the Communist or non-Communist blocs of the Cold War era.

partition The act of separating or dividing something into parts or sections.

perpetrator Someone who brings about, carries out, performs, or executes something, usually a crime.

proliferation To grow, spread, or increase in number by rapid production.

propaganda The spreading of ideas, information, or rumor for the purpose of helping or injuring an institution, a cause, or a person; ideas, facts, or allegations spread deliberately to further one's cause or to damage an opposing cause.

proxy Authority or power to act for another person or organization; a person authorized to act for another.

repression The state of being restrained, subdued, or silenced.

republic A government in which the head of state is not a monarch and in which supreme power resides in a body of citizens entitled to vote for representatives who will exercise that power.

secular Not overtly or specifically religious; relating to the worldly and temporal.

sovereignty Supreme power; freedom from external control and controlling influence.

xenophobia Fear and hatred of strangers and foreigners or of anything that is strange and foreign.

For More Information

Carnegie Endowment for International Peace
1779 Massachusetts Avenue NW
Washington, DC 20036-2103
(202) 483–7600
Web site: http://www.carnegieendowment.org
This non-profit organization is dedicated to fostering peace by promoting international cooperation.

Center for Arms Control and Non-Proliferation
322 Fourth Street NE
Washington, DC 20002
(202) 546-0795
Web site: http://www.armscontrolcenter.org
This non-profit, non-partisan organization works to increase global security.

Centre for Research on Globalisation
P.O. Box 55019
11 Notre-Dame Ouest
Montreal, PQ H2Y 4A7
Canada
Web site: http://www.globalresearch.ca
The Centre for Research on Globalisation is an independent research and media group of writers, scholars, journalists, and activists that is based in Montreal, Canada. The Centre is involved in book publishing, supporting humanitarian projects, and educational outreach activities, including the organization of public conferences and lectures. The Centre also acts as a think tank on crucial international and geopolitical issues.

Centre for Social Justice
489 College Street, Suite 303
Toronto, ON M6G 1A5
Canada
(416) 927-0777
(888) 803-8881
Web site: http://www.socialjustice.org
The Centre for Social Justice conducts research, education, and advocacy in a bid to narrow the gap in income, wealth, and power, and enhance peace and human security. It brings together people from universities and unions, faith groups, and community organizations in the pursuit of greater equality and democracy. The Centre supports social movements in the struggle for social justice and offers a non-partisan perspective on political, social, and economic issues. It also uses creative communications to educate Canadians about public policies.

Council on Foreign Relations (CFR)
The Harold Pratt House
58 East 68th Street
New York, NY 10065
(212) 434-9400

Web site: http://www.cfr.org
The CFR is an independent, nonpartisan membership organization, think tank, and publisher. It is dedicated to being a resource for its members, government officials, business executives, journalists, educators and students, civic and religious leaders, and other interested citizens in order to help them better understand the world and the foreign policy choices facing the United States and other countries. Founded in 1921, CFR takes no institutional positions on matters of policy.

International Atomic Energy Agency (IAEA)
IAEA Office at the United Nations
1 United Nations Plaza, Room DC-1-1155
New York, NY 10017
(212) 963-6010
Web site: http://www.iaea.org
The IAEA monitors nuclear materials around the world in the interest of promoting peaceful uses for nuclear energy.

International Forum on Globalization
1009 General Kennedy Avenue, #2
San Francisco, CA 94129
(415) 561-7650
Web site: http://www.ifg.org
The International Forum on Globalization is a research and educational institution composed of leading activists, economists, scholars, and researchers providing analyses and critiques on the cultural, social, political, and environmental impacts of economic globalization.

International Monetary Fund (IMF)
700 19th Street NW
Washington, DC 20431
(202) 623-7000
Web site: http://www.imf.org
The International Monetary Fund (IMF) is an organization of 187 countries, working to foster global monetary cooperation, secure financial stability, facilitate international trade, promote high employment and sustainable economic growth, and reduce poverty around the world.

The Library of Congress
101 Independence Avenue SE
Washington, DC 20540
(202) 707-5000
Web site: http://www.loc.gov/index.html
The Library of Congress is the nation's oldest federal cultural institution and serves as the research arm of Congress. It is also the largest library in the world, with millions of books, recordings, photographs, maps, and manuscripts in its collections. The Library's mission is to make its resources available and useful to the Congress and the American people and to sustain and preserve a universal collection of knowledge and creativity for future generations.

Nuclear Threat Initiative
1747 Pennsylvania Avenue, NW 7th Floor
Washington, DC 20006
(202) 296-4810

Web site: http://www.nti.org
The Nuclear Threat Initiative is dedicated to reducing the threat of weapons of mass destruction by strengthening global security.

Peace & Justice Studies Association (PJSA)
Prescott College
220 Grove Avenue
Prescott, AZ 86301
(928) 350-2008
Web site: http://www.peacejusticestudies.org
The Peace and Justice Studies Association (PJSA) is a non-profit organization that provides leadership in the broadly defined field of peace, conflict, and justice studies. It is dedicated to bringing together academics, K-12 teachers, and grassroots activists to explore alternatives to violence and share visions and strategies for peacebuilding, social justice, and social change. PJSA also serves as a professional association for scholars in the field of peace and conflict resolution studies.

Social Justice and Peace Studies Program
King's University College
The University of Western Ontario
266 Epworth Avenue
London, ON N6A 2M3
Canada
(519) 433-3491, ext. 4380
(800) 265-4406, ext. 4380
Web site: http://www.kingscollege.net/sjps/sjps_website/sjps_homepage.html
The Social Justice and Peace Studies program encourages critical reflection on structural injustices locally and globally and calls for social action to transform the world in the interests of equity and the pursuit of peace.

United Nations (UN)
Public Inquiries, Visitors Services
Department of Public Information
United Nations Headquarters, Room GA-1B-57
New York, NY 10017
(212) 963-4475
Web site: http://www.un.org
The UN is an international organization committed to maintaining international peace, developing friendly relations among nations, and promoting human welfare.

World Bank
1818 H Street NW
Washington, DC 20433
(202) 473-1000
Web site: http://www.worldbank.org
The World Bank provides financial and technical assistance to developing nations around the world.

The World Trade Organization (WTO)
Centre William Rappard
Rue de Lausanne 154
CH-1211 Geneva 21, Switzerland
(41-22) 739 51 11
Web site: http://www.wto.org

The WTO is the only global international organization dealing with the rules of trade between nations. The organization's goal is to help producers of goods and services, exporters, and importers conduct their business.

The Worldwatch Institute
1776 Massachusetts Avenue NW
Washington, DC 20036-1904
(202) 452-1999
Web site: http://www.worldwatch.org
The Worldwatch Institute is an independent research organization recognized by opinion leaders around the world for its accessible, fact-based analysis of critical global issues.

Web Sites

Due to the changing nature of Internet links, Rosen Publishing has developed an online list of Web sites related to the subject of this book. This site is updated regularly. Please use this link to access the list:

http://www.rosenlinks.com/wtoh/21

For Further Reading

Best, Antony, et al. *International History of the Twentieth Century and Beyond*. New York, NY: Routledge, 2008.

Blainey, Geoffrey. *A Short History of the 20th Century*. Chicago, IL: Ivan R. Dee, 2008.

Catherwood, Christopher. *A Brief History of the Middle East*. Philadelphia, PA: Running Press, 2011.

Chasteen, John Charles. *Born in Blood and Fire: A Concise History of Latin America*. New York, NY: W.W. Norton & Company, 2011.

Gelvin, James L. *The Modern Middle East: A History*. New York, NY: Oxford University Press, 2011.

Golden, Peter B. *Central Asia in World History*. New York, NY: Oxford University Press, 2011.

Harman, Chris. *A People's History of the World: From the Stone Age to the New Millennium*. Brooklyn, NY: Verso, 2008.

Hart-Davis, Adam. *History: The Definitive Visual Guide: From the Dawn of Civilization to the Present Day*. New York, NY: DK Adult, 2007.

Haugen, Peter. *World History for Dummies*. Hoboken, NJ: For Dummies, 2009.

Hoffman, David E. *The Dead Hand: The Untold Story of the Cold War Arms Race and Its Dangerous Legacy*. New York, NY: Anchor, 2010.

Holcombe, Charles. *A History of East Asia*. New York, NY: Cambridge University Press, 2010.

Keylor, William R. *The Twentieth Century and Beyond: An International History Since 1900*. New York, NY: Oxford University Press, 2011.

Lang, Sean. *Twentieth Century History for Dummies*. Hoboken, NJ: For Dummies, 2012.

Meredith, Martin. *The Fate of Africa: A History of the Continent Since Independence*. New York, NY: PublicAffairs, 2011.

Moya, Jose C. *The Oxford Handbook of Latin American History*. New York, NY: Oxford University Press, 2010.

Murphey, Rhoads. *A History of Asia*. White Plains, NY: Longman, 2008.

Paxton, Robert. *Europe in the Twentieth Century*. Boston, MA: Wadsworth, 2011.

Perry, Marvin, et al. *Sources of European History Since 1900*. Boston, MA: Wadsworth, 2010.

Reynolds, Jonathan T., and Erik Gilbert. *Africa in World History*. Upper Saddle River, NJ: Prentice Hall, 2011.

Roberts, J.M. *The New Penguin History of the World*. New York, NY: Penguin, 2007.

Smith, Bonnie G. *Europe in the Contemporary World: 1900 to the Present: A Narrative History with Documents*. New York, NY: Bedford/St. Martin's, 2007.

Westad, Odd Arne. *The Global Cold War: Third World Interventions and the Making of Our Times*. New York, NY: Cambridge University Press, 2007.

Zubok, Vladislav M. *A Failed Empire: The Soviet Union in the Cold War from Stalin to Gorbachev*. Chapel Hill, NC: University of North Carolina Press, 2008.

Index

All images from akg-images Berlin/London/Paris and from dpa Deutsche Presse Agentur, Hamburg.
Sämtliche Abbildungen akg-images Berlin/London/Paris mit Ausnahme der folgenden von dpa Deutsche Presse Agentur, Hamburg: 11/unten r., oben 2. v. l., oben r.; 12/1 l., 2 l.; 13/3 l.; 14/1 l., 2 l.; 15/4 l., r.; 224/4; 225/6, 9; 432/1; 456/2, 5; 496/4; 502 Kasten unten l.; 508/5; 509/6, 7, Kasten l.; 517/25; 528; 530/2; 531/6-9; 532/1; 533/11; 534/Kasten l.; 535/5–7, 10, 11; 537/9, Kasten; 542/Kasten; 543/8, 9; 545/7; 546/5, 7; 547/9–11, 13; 548/1–6; 549/7, 9, 11, Kasten; 551/Kasten; 552/2–5; 553/6–9, Kasten l. und r.; 554/1–4, 6; 555/8–10, 13; 557/Kasten; 559/8, 9, 11; 560/2–5; 561/9–11; 562/1–5; 563/8–10, Kasten; 564/4, Kasten; 565/6, 9, Kasten l.; 566/4–6, Kasten; 567/7–12, Kasten; 568/2–5; 569/6–10, Kasten; 570/1–7; 571/8, 10–12, Kasten; 572/1–3, 5, 6; 573/7–11; 574/1–3, 5; 575/6, 7, 9–12; 576/2; 577/7, 10–13; 578/2, 5, 6, Kasten; 579/7, 9–14; 580/1, 2, 4, 5; 581/7–11, Kasten; 582/1, 2, 4, 5; 583/6–11, Kasten; 584/1–5, Kasten; 585/6–11; 588/1–3, 7; 589/10, 14, Kasten; 590/3–5, Kasten l. und r.; 591/6–11; 592/1–8; 593/9–15; 594/1, 2, 4–6; 595/10, 12, 13, Kasten; 596/1; 597/8, 10–13, Kasten; 598/1, 4, 6; 599/8, 10–13, Kasten; 600/2, 6; 601/8–10, 12, 13; 602/1–4, 6, 7; 603/9, 10, 12–14, Kasten; 604/2–8; 605/9–13; 606/2–4; 607/8–10, 12, 13; 608/2, 4, 5; 609/9–13, Kasten; 610/1–5; 611/11, Kasten l.; 612/1–5; 613/6–11; 614/1–6, Kasten; 615/7, 8, 10, 11; 616/1, 2, 4, 5, Kasten; 618/3; 619/7, 9, 11, 12; 620/1–7; 621/9–13; 622/1, 4, 5, 7, Kasten; 623/8, 10–14; 624/2–6; 625/7–11, Kasten; 626/1, 3; 627/9, 11, Kasten; 628/2, 3, 5–7; 629/8–12, Kasten; 630/3–5, 7, 8; 631/9–13, Kasten; 632/1–8; 633/9, 11, 12, 14, Kasten; 634/1–7; 635/8–14; 639/8, 9, 13; 640/1, 2, 6, Kasten; 641/7, 9–12; 642/1–8; 643/9–14, Kasten; 644/1–6; 645/7–13; 646/1, 2, 4, 5, 7; 647/8, 9, 11; 648/1–5; 649/6–8.

The publishers would like to express their special gratitude to the team at akg-images Berlin/London/Paris who have made their incredible picture archive accessible and thus the extraordinary illustrations of this book possible.